# You Can Run,
# But You Can't Hide

# You Can Run, But You Can't Hide

DUANE 'DOG' CHAPMAN
WITH LAURA MORTON

## AUTHOR'S NOTE

Some of the dialogue in the book has been recreated, as my recollections are not always exact or complete, and may not reflect exact language exchanged at the time. My intent is to allow the reader to understand the circumstances and experience the moments in which those discussions took place. I have done my best to accurately portray my memory of the conversations.

First published in hardback in Great Britain in 2007 by
Orion Books
an imprint of the Orion Publishing Group Ltd
Orion House, 5 Upper St Martin's Lane,
London WC2H 9EA
An Hachette Livre UK Company
Published by arrangement with Hyperion

10 9 8 7 6 5 4 3 2 1

A CIP catalogue record for this book
is available from the British Library.

ISBN: 978 0 7528 9056 2

Printed in Great Britain by Mackays of Chatham plc, Chatham, Kent

The Orion Publishing Group's policy is to use papers that are natural, renewable and recyclable and made from wood grown in sustainable forests. The logging and manufacturing processes are expected to conform to the environmental regulations of the country of origin.

Every effort has been made to fulfil requirements with regard to reproducing copyright material. The author and publisher will be glad to rectify any omissions at the earliest opportunity.

www.orionbooks.co.uk

TO MY SOUL MATE, ALICE ELIZABETH CHAPMAN
& TO ANYBODY WITH A DREAM.
THEY DO COME TRUE.

# Contents

INTRODUCTION — 1

CHAPTER ONE   I Am Dog — 5

CHAPTER TWO   Seventh-Grade Beatdown — 9

CHAPTER THREE   Becoming the Dog — 13

CHAPTER FOUR   Prospecting for the Disciples — 20

CHAPTER FIVE   The Shoot-out on Mission Hill — 27

CHAPTER SIX   Leaving the Disciples — 33

CHAPTER SEVEN   Pampa, Texas — 36

CHAPTER EIGHT   One Night in Pampa — 42

CHAPTER NINE   Murder One — 48

CHAPTER TEN   Welcome to Huntsville — 57

CHAPTER ELEVEN   Light in the Darkness — 62

CHAPTER TWELVE   The Barber of Huntsville — 68

CHAPTER THIRTEEN   Free as a Bird — 73

CHAPTER FOURTEEN   Going Home — 77

CHAPTER FIFTEEN   Vengeance — 81

CHAPTER SIXTEEN   Shotgun Wedding — 84

CHAPTER SEVENTEEN   Selling Kirbys — 87

CHAPTER EIGHTEEN   Lucky — 92

CHAPTER NINETEEN   Zebadiah — 98

CHAPTER TWENTY   Salesman of the Year — 101

CHAPTER TWENTY-ONE   Getting My Boys Back — 105

CHAPTER TWENTY-TWO   Meeting My Soul Mate — 109

CHAPTER TWENTY-THREE   My College Education — 115

CHAPTER TWENTY-FOUR   Meeting Tony Robbins — 121

CHAPTER TWENTY-FIVE   Mistake — 127

CHAPTER TWENTY-SIX  Aloha From Hawaii                131
CHAPTER TWENTY-SEVEN  Mirror Image                   136
CHAPTER TWENTY-EIGHT  My Darkest Day                 141
CHAPTER TWENTY-NINE  Cracking Up                     147
CHAPTER THIRTY  Rock Bottom                          152
CHAPTER THIRTY-ONE  Getting Out of Hell              156
CHAPTER THIRTY-TWO  Kidney Stones Saved My Life      162
CHAPTER THIRTY-THREE  One Step Forward               168
CHAPTER THIRTY-FOUR  Going Hollywood                 176
CHAPTER THIRTY-FIVE  A Chase to the Grave            180
CHAPTER THIRTY-SIX  Ivan Van Thompson                185
CHAPTER THIRTY-SEVEN  Two Steps Back                 191
CHAPTER THIRTY-EIGHT  The Big One                    194
CHAPTER THIRTY-NINE  Entering the Hunt for Luster    198
CHAPTER FORTY  Carey, Shawna and Tonja Doe           203
CHAPTER FORTY-ONE  On a Mission from God             209
CHAPTER FORTY-TWO  Prey                              214
CHAPTER FORTY-THREE  Wheeling and Dealing            218
CHAPTER FORTY-FOUR  The Thai Trail                   221
CHAPTER FORTY-FIVE  One Last Warning                 224
CHAPTER FORTY-SIX  The Dog Cometh                    226
CHAPTER FORTY-SEVEN  You Can Run                     230
CHAPTER FORTY-EIGHT  You Can't Hide                  236
CHAPTER FORTY-NINE  Mexican Prison                   241
CHAPTER FIFTY  Posting Bail                          248
CHAPTER FIFTY-ONE  America the Beautiful             253
CHAPTER FIFTY-TWO  Justice Denied                    258
CHAPTER FIFTY-THREE  My Wedding Day                  265
CHAPTER FIFTY-FOUR  Room for Two More                271
CHAPTER FIFTY-FIVE  Second Chances                   273
CHAPTER FIFTY-SIX  Federal Marshals                  277
CHAPTER FIFTY-SEVEN  From Misdemeanour to Felony     283
CHAPTER FIFTY-EIGHT  A Final Thought                 287
ACKNOWLEDGMENTS                                      290

# Introduction

'Dad, pull over. He's stopping at a taco stand.' Andrew Luster, fugitive and convicted rapist, stood eating a taco. He had no idea I was on his ass. He turned to cross the street without a care in the world.

That was the first time I saw Luster with my own two eyes. Until that moment, he was a figment of my imagination. He was a photo, a sketch. And now he was alive – a living, breathing target. I saw his shoulders, his head, and his eyes. As I rose above the steering wheel, I could see what I had been eating, breathing, and looking for in my dreams.

I had Luster's picture taped up in my bathroom so I could see him at night before I went to bed and in the morning when I woke up. I kept a photo of him in my car. His Wanted poster was plastered all over my office.

My wife, Beth, taped up words of encouragement next to Luster's face – phrases like 'I will lead, not follow. I will create, not destroy. I will believe, not doubt. I will set new standards. I am the voice. I am a leader. I am going to proceed. I will succeed.' Every day I studied Luster's features as I filled my head with positive thoughts.

I recognised every inch of Luster. I knew his walk from footage I had studied, just as I knew his voice on the phone.

'Oh, my God. It's him.' I can never explain why I said that out loud. So many people had doubted my ability to catch this bum.

'Dog can't catch him.'

'Dog's a liar.'

'Dog's a felon.'

I heard all of those doubting voices in my head as I stood on the street staring at my prey. And then one voice came through loud and clear. It was the voice of my father. He said, 'Now is the time. This is it.' I don't know why I was thinking about my dad. He never understood why I do what I do. But now, in this moment, I think he would have approved.

There are times when you just know in your heart that your actions are the right thing to do and you can't imagine that there would be anyone who would object. And then it turns out to your great surprise that someone says it's wrong. But you're glad you did it anyway because you know it was the right thing to do. You do it to protect others who might be at risk. My dad would have called that a question of morality.

'Get him!' Every voice in my head was shouting. 'Get him!'

The entire time I searched for Andrew Luster, Eminem's song 'Lose Yourself' was like my theme.

That song came on the radio as I was about to pounce on Luster.

I was frozen, stuck in the moment. Fear and pure exhilaration flowed through my veins.

The guys were looking at me, waiting to see what I would do next.

This was the Super Bowl of bounties. It was my Indy 500, my turn at the Grand Ole Opry. I had worked so hard to reach this moment. I wanted to enjoy every second, every beat.

Luster looked around, as if to make sure the coast was clear, but didn't move. In that moment, I realised what the term 'bounty hunter' really meant. It wasn't about the six thousand other arrests I had made throughout my career. It was about right now. I thought about Big Lou throwing his cuffs at my feet the day I saved Bigfoot back in Huntsville. 'Cuff him, bounty hunter.' This was it.

'I'm going first. Tim, you come right behind me. Leland, when I attack, you go.' I looked over at Filiberto to get his signal that it was a 'go'. He nodded his head.

I crouched way down on the ground. I felt like a soldier manoeuvring across the desert as I shimmied my way closer to Luster. I wanted to scare him like a Samoan warrior. I got right in his face, spread my arms wide, and yelled, 'WHOOOOAAAA!' When I popped up, I scared the crap out of that boy. He tried to bolt, but Tim wrapped his arms around Luster's neck. I tackled him at the waist while Leland grabbed him in the leg. We all went down.

I heard a thunderous noise, like a stampede of wild horses. It was the sound of Luster's bodyguards trying to get close. It was too late. I cuffed him, stood up, and said, 'You are under arrest in the name of the United States government and Mexico!'

The bodyguards backed off.

Luster was mine.

When he looked at me, he said, 'I knew you were going to get me.'
'Damn right, Luster.'
'I knew it. I knew it, Dog. I've been set up.'
'You didn't get set up. You got hunted down.'

# CHAPTER ONE

# I Am Dog

*My name is Duane Lee Chapman.* My friends call me Dog – Dog the Bounty Hunter. For more than twenty-seven years, I have made a living hunting down more than seven thousand fugitives. I wear that honour as proudly as my shiny silver fugitive-recovery badge that hangs around my neck.

In the old days, there weren't enough lawmen for all the criminals on the loose, so sheriffs posted hefty rewards to capture crooks on the run. Legends of the Wild West, like Wild Bill Hickok, Wyatt Earp and Billy the Kid, all made their living hunting bounties. Now, I might not be as famous as some of those guys, but I am the greatest bounty hunter who ever lived.

A lot of people think of me as a vigilante. It's true, my recovery tactics are far from conventional, but I rarely fail at finding my man. For me, failure has never been an option. To get attention or be noticed in this world, and believed, loved, and trusted, you had better be extraordinary, especially nowadays. In my life, extraordinary stuff happens all the time.

Bounty hunting is not a game. It's definitely not for the meek or faint of heart. I don't do it to prove I'm a tough bastard or smarter than some other guy. I do it because I have been there. I have been the bad guy. I know first-hand how messed up the system can be. Despite it all, I still believe in truth and justice.

To be certain, bounty hunting isn't your average nine-to-five job. But then, I'm not your average guy. I have had guns pointed in my face so many times I've lost count. I've survived having the trigger pulled more than once or twice. I have been stabbed, scratched, beaten up, and hit with every imaginable (and unimaginable) weapon of choice – chains, boards, tyre irons, golf clubs and crowbars. I've been tossed through windows, pushed through walls and shoved through doors. Does that make me a tough guy? You bet your ass.

I was born in Denver on 2 February 1953. My parents were Wesley and Barbara Chapman. Mom was half Chiricahua Apache, which gave her beautiful thick, long, dark hair and a medium skin tone. Her eyes were an expressive chocolate brown that spoke from a stare without ever having to utter a single word. She had a way of looking *into* you, not just *at* you. Mom taught me to see people for who they are, not for the colour of their skin, their race, or religion. She was a devout Christian who lived her life according to God's word. She instilled those same beliefs in me from the day I was born.

I have always been proud of my Indian heritage. I never once gave a second thought to my mixed background or to how others might see me as being a little different. I've always had a pretty distinguishable look. Hell, it makes me easy to identify in a line-up.

My dad, Wesley, also known as 'Flash', had dirty-blond hair and piercing blue eyes. I am built just like him. He wasn't particularly large, though he was remarkably strong and fit. He had the most gigantic hands I ever saw. Dad was a navy welder, serving for many years. Flash earned his nickname boxing welterweight, because he moved with great speed and finesse. His boxing career was rather illustrious: he never lost a fight. Flash was a tough son of a gun – a real scrapper.

From the outside looking in, my childhood was pretty normal. Mom and Dad lived a decent middle-class life in Denver, Colorado. My two sisters, Jolene and Paula, and my younger brother, Mike, and I were not very close growing up. We all played together and probably watched too much of my favourite television programmes, like *The Lone Ranger*, *Sky King* and *The Green Hornet*.

Every summer, I looked forward to joining my mom on her annual trip from Denver to Farmington, New Mexico, down to Sister Jensen's Mission. Even though Sister Jensen's congregation was primarily made up of Navajo from the local reservation, they all loved to hear Mom spread the word of God. She wasn't an ordained preacher, but she was mighty and powerful in her love of the Lord and her unshakable faith. Until the age of twelve, I tagged along as her helper, passing out hymn sheets and collecting tithes.

One of the first life-lessons I remember Mom teaching me was that

God sees all of us as His children, which makes us all brothers and sisters. Listening to Mom preach gave me a will and inspiration to live the way God intended us to. I wanted to grow up to be just like her – to live a righteous, good, honourable, God-fearing life.

As a young boy, I never knew that other kids didn't get hit by their dads. I thought it was a rite of passage to have my father knock me around. I simply didn't know anything different. I can't recall any long stretch of time in my young life when my dad didn't hit me. He used a special paddle he'd made from some old flooring. Flash whacked me on the back of my legs and bare ass until I was black and blue and so sore I couldn't take another hit. To this day, if I get a sunburn anywhere on my body, it reminds me of my childhood and Flash's beatings. Just thinking of the abuse I endured can make me cry.

As a way to toughen me up, Flash began to teach me the basics of boxing. Although he never hit above the shoulders, I wasn't allowed to show any emotion after he threw a punch. A jab to the ribs, a left hook to the body – whatever came at me, I was expected to take it like a man. But I wasn't a man. I was a young boy looking for love and approval from my father. I was desperate for his affection, so I ignored the pain. Sometimes I even thanked him for it, as if I deserved what he doled out.

Because of my religious upbringing, I thought my dad was punishing me for being a terrible sinner. Until very recently, I never understood that none of his abuse was my fault. I just thought that was how all dads treated their sons, and yet I swore that I would never beat my kids. I wanted the Chapman family abuse cycle to die with Flash.

I was eleven years old when I first saw the movie *The Yearling*. I was very confused by the father's reaction to his son when he told him he'd done something bad. The young boy's father hugged his son and told him he loved him for being so honest. If I went to Flash to confess I'd messed up, all I got was the paddle or the back side of his very large hand against my cheek. I wanted the father from *The Yearling,* so the next time I screwed up, I told my dad. Instead of praising me, Flash hit me harder than ever. I was so upset I ran away from home. I rode my bicycle all the way to Fort Morgan, fifty-eight miles from our house in Denver. I would have gone further, but I was too hungry and tired. I called my mom's dad, Grandpa Mike, to come get me. I never told him why I ran away. If I ratted on Flash, Grandpa would have killed him.

On the weekends when I wasn't at church with Mom, Flash and Grandpa Mike taught me how to hunt and fish. Living in Colorado gave

7

them a lot of options to show me the ropes. I was pretty good in the woods. I loved to camp out, make meals over an open fire, and listen to their old hunting stories.

Flash made a sport out of finding new and undiscovered spots to hunt. He always made me feel like we were great explorers on a mission, going places, discovering secret locations no one else knew about. It was fun for a little kid. Flash was a survivalist. His navy training taught him how to make any situation work. His instincts in the great outdoors were the finest any son could ask for when learning to hunt. He showed me how to track everything from deer to fox, pheasants to ducks.

Flash and Grandpa Mike always made us hike to our locations. They were afraid we might get shot by some drunken hunters if we rode on horseback. We never took dogs. I was the dog. It was my job to figure our course.

I spent the first twenty-three years of my life on the wrong side of the law. For most of my childhood, I ran with gangs and bikers. The only thing I knew about the law was a thousand ways to break it. I got pretty good at that. It took a murder-one conviction to make me decide to change my life from committing crime to fighting it. It might seem strange that a man with my criminal past is so passionately concerned with what happens to the victims of crime. I have been misjudged, misinterpreted and misunderstood for most of my life. I have spent the last twenty-seven years trying to be one of the good guys. I love God, my wife, my children, and my career. In spite of those efforts to be seen as a moral man of virtue, I am still viewed as an ex-con, a criminal, a killer. I am many things, including those just mentioned. Put it all together and you will see: I am Dog.

# CHAPTER TWO

# Seventh-Grade Beatdown

I've always identified myself as being part Indian, but the truth is, I'm not really sure about my heritage. Whenever I pushed the issue, my mom and dad skirted it, as if to say they didn't really want me to know the truth about who my real father might be. I'm not saying Flash wasn't my biological dad; he might have been. I think a lot of kids fantasise that their dad is really someone else, especially kids who grow up in abusive homes, like I did.

Here's what I know for certain: I have a natural affinity for Indian culture, customs, music and designs. I can spot an Apache- or Chiricahua-woven rug a mile away. A few years back, I was in a shop in San Diego talking to four or five elderly Indian women. They asked if I had Native American in my blood.

'No. I've got Indian in my blood.' I was emphatic.

'Us too!' They all let out a laugh. We'd been talking for a few minutes, when one of the oldest women turned to me and said, 'If I believed in reincarnation, there's old stories about you, boy.'

I wanted to tell her what she already knew. Before I could say anything, she placed her forefinger up to her lips as if to say, 'Do not speak.'

When I played cowboys and Indians with the other kids in the neighbourhood, I never wanted to be a cowboy. My dad bought me a Western hat and six-guns to wear in a holster, but I only wanted a feather in my hair. I wasn't no damn cowboy. No way! I was an Indian. I used to tell my buddies, 'No bullet could ever hurt me, because I am on a mission.' They'd just laugh and pull the trigger on their toy pistols.

My great-grandmother's maiden name was Cochise. When I was a boy, she spent hours telling me stories of a courageous Indian leader named Cochise. He was born in Arizona and led the Chiricahua band of the Apache tribe during a very violent time in American history.

9

Cochise was five feet nine inches tall and weighed 170 pounds; a broad-shouldered, powerfully built man who carried himself with dignity. He was gentle in nature but was capable of extreme cruelty in warfare. He was a born survivor who was intelligent and sensitive. He was a peaceful man who believed in justice and the law.

His troubles began when the United States government was trying to take control of what we now know as Arizona and New Mexico, territory that at the time, 1861, belonged to his tribe. Cochise was falsely imprisoned on charges of kidnapping a white child. He beat the charges and settled on his reservation, where he died a peaceful death in 1874.

Now, I know what you're thinking. It sounds familiar, right?

I've always felt connected to Cochise in ways I cannot explain. I have visions of his life as if it were my own. To this day, when there is a full moon, I will walk outside and give praise to the Lord. Sometimes I begin to chant in an ancient tribal way. No one ever taught it to me. I just knew. Once an Indian chief told me I was giving praise to the Great Spirit. He kept saying, 'You're the one!' I felt like the guy from *The Matrix*, a man chosen to lead millions.

When I was a kid, I got picked on a lot because my mother was part Apache. Where I grew up, being a half-white boy who always carried a bible made me a minority, but being part Indian made me a target. From my first week in the seventh grade, I can't remember a single day I didn't hear other kids call me names like 'half-breed', 'dirty redskin boy', and 'Injun'. Listening to those kids made my skin crawl. A mighty rush of blood consumed every inch of my body each time those kids taunted or teased me. Sometimes I felt angry, other times ashamed. I knew I didn't have anything to feel bad about, but it wasn't easy to take.

By the seventh grade, I was fighting the Latinos for my pride on a pretty regular basis. I could always sense when they were behind me. There were five older kids who acted more like men than boys. There was no mistaking the sound of their leather boots clicking on the sidewalk. The gang leader was the toughest kid at school. That's a pretty big statement, because Rishel Junior High was filled with punks and bad-asses, each trying to prove he was the toughest.

One day, on my way to school, I found myself surrounded by him and his gang. I was walking through a deserted parking lot when the guys snuck up from behind. They were all carrying rubber hoses. I imagined I was in for a real beating, because it was five against one.

Flash had been teaching me how to fight. He and I practised boxing a couple of days a week. I was pretty good. I would have taken on any of these guys one at a time and probably beaten him. I knew I didn't have a prayer of surviving against all five. The only solution I could think of was God.

I pulled my bible from the inside pocket of my coat, held it up, and said, 'You are sinners. The Lord doesn't want you to do this. The Bible says to be kind to your fellow man!'

The boys started laughing their asses off. I thought I was off the hook until one of them took his hose and used it like a whip to send my bible flying across the parking lot. These boys weren't messing around. I crouched down, clutched my fingers together behind my neck, and waited for the brutal beating to end. When they stopped, I pulled my bloody, torn body across the parking lot towards my bible for whatever protection it might still offer.

My mother was a deeply religious woman who always told me the Lord would protect me. My attempt to move signalled the gang to start the whooping all over again, only this time they hit me harder.

My will was stronger than theirs. I kept crawling, scratching my nails against the pavement. One of the boys noticed that my bible was just outside my reach. He ran over, grabbed it, and ripped my precious book in half, tossing one part across the parking lot and the other at my feet.

I thought about God as I lay on the dirty asphalt that morning. The gang were through with me, but I wasn't done with them. I lost my will to love and forgive that day. I was mad as hell. Where was God? Why didn't He protect me?

I had taken plenty of beatings from Flash. I was used to taking his punches. Somehow this felt different. It made me angry and vengeful.

I wanted to run after those boys and clobber each one. I wanted to get up and hurt those bastards, but my body couldn't move. I watched them walk away, taking pleasure and pride in the damage they had done. My wounds were deep, far beyond the cuts and bruises I suffered at their hands. My heart hardened that day. I remember it well, because it took many years to learn to open it back up. I cried for hours. I was hurt in every way.

By mid-afternoon, I finally realised I could cry no more. I didn't want to shed another tear for the gang, for hatred, for my heritage, or my wounded pride. I could barely make it to my feet, let alone take the long walk to school. I tried to hold back my tears, but they kept coming, like a spout that couldn't be turned off.

When I got to school, I went straight to the see a teacher. I sat there, recounting the details of what happened in the parking lot. My nose was bleeding, my clothes were ripped, and I had deep cuts and bruises from head to toe. He listened silently. He didn't respond to anything I was saying.

He looked at me as if I were an alien who had just landed from another planet. He didn't believe a single word of my story. In fact, he was completely dismissive. My already growing anger was now a volcano on the verge of eruption. I may not have been a model student; I surely know I wasn't an angel. But his denial of my beating was as abusive as the event itself. My world was instantly turned upside down. For the first time in my life, an adult was accusing me of being a liar. The teacher excused me and sent me off to class.

A few weeks later, I found myself in the principal's office. This time, a teacher noticed bruises on my body during gym class and reported it. These bruises were from Flash's beatings. I barely noticed them any more. When he asked me what happened, I had no reason to be honest. What difference would it have made? He wouldn't believe me anyway. But he guessed the truth and asked my father to come in. When Flash got to his office, I thought, at the very least, the he would tell him to stop beating me. For a moment, I was relieved that someone finally saw what was happening to me at home.

Unfortunately, Flash thought I ratted him out, but I didn't. The next time he beat me, he hit me extra hard to make sure I knew he was still in control.

The school authority's refusal to protect me left a pretty sour taste in my mouth. I wasn't all that interested in school. I hated the kids and the system. So I dropped out of Rishel Junior High. The day I quit, I slammed my fist on one of the teacher's desk, shattering the glass that covered the top.

'Fuck you. You never stuck up for me when you knew I was getting beaten at home. You never believed a word I said. I quit!' I turned, walked out, and never went back.

# CHAPTER THREE

# Becoming the Dog

Once I dropped out of school, I had to find creative ways to fill my time. The first day I ditched, I went back to that empty parking lot where the gang beat me. There was an old abandoned car up on blocks, missing its doors and windows.

I walked up to the car, where I met a boy who looked to be about the same age as me. I asked him what he was up to, and he told me the Vatos were constantly kicking his ass. I knew just how he felt. The kid introduced himself as Paul. I gave a nod, letting him know I was cool if he was. He was a little guy, just like me.

I noticed he was holding a small plastic bag with the neck twisted at the top. 'What do you have in that bag?' I asked. Paul put it up to his mouth, took a deep breath, and held it in for what felt like an eternity before he let out a huge exhale. He sat motionless, staring into space for a minute or two before asking me if I wanted to give it a try. I was game. I did it just like he did. A feeling of complete and total relaxation consumed my body. After a few more huffs, I forgot about all of the pain and anger I felt for being abused by Flash, the teacher, and the gang.

'What was that?' I asked. I wanted to know everything I could because I never wanted that feeling to go away. He told me it was Testors aeroplane glue. He knew where to get some more. I stayed high from that day on.

I didn't have enough money to buy the glue, so Paul and I stole it. I was born with an innate knowledge of picking locks. It was a great skill to have at that age, especially when I needed to get high.

All of the goodness my mother had instilled in me was slowly fading away with every sniff. I was spiralling out of control into a world I had little understanding of. I was using dirty language around the house, which was especially upsetting to my parents, because they never cursed.

The worst words I ever heard my father say were 'dang' and 'darn'.

I was becoming unrecognisable to my family. Until I met Paul, I was a Bible-loving choirboy. After years of enjoyment, I stopped going with my mother to Sister Jensen's Mission and to her church on Sunday. It broke my mother's heart to see me turn my back on the Lord.

Flash was well aware of my newfound habit. The more I sniffed, the harder he hit. The more he beat me, the higher I got. It became an unbreakable cycle.

My parents tried everything to get me back on course. Flash even attempted to get me interested in martial arts. He thought karate might be a good way for me to work out my growing anger. The classes did teach me to control my emotions and helped me channel my rage into something more productive than getting high. I got pretty good at karate, earning belt after belt. I loved to fight in front of an audience. The sound of their cheering inspired me to push myself harder every time. Flash came to my matches now and then. He always encouraged me to show no pity. He told me that each opponent has a weakness. First I had to identify it and then mercilessly go after it. He said you never want to let up until your foe goes down. I knew that strategy far too well from years of having Flash beat on me.

Karate helped me develop into a muscular young man. By the time I was thirteen years old, I was probably as strong as most of the sixteen- and seventeen-year-olds. Because of my age, a lot of guys thought they could kick my ass. Every time someone tried, I took them out. I began building a reputation around town as the kid you didn't want to mess with.

In spite of my parents' best efforts to get me back to school, I was dead set on becoming a hood. I just didn't care any more. The only thing I was interested in was crime. I went from stealing aeroplane glue to breaking into houses. Paul and I wanted to take the excitement level up a couple notches, so we'd go in looking for jewellery, televisions, silverware, and anything else we could get our hands on to hock.

About this time, Flash was finding it harder and harder to dish out his constant beatings. I wasn't a little child he could catch off guard any more. I was too quick for him. I knew when he was about to throw a punch or try to grab me. Still, I wasn't quite at the point where I could completely throw down with him. As I got bigger, he eventually had to use all of his body weight to pin me to the floor or up against the wall.

And then one day, I realised I had another gift besides fighting. I could talk my way out of anything. I sharpened those skills every time Flash threatened to hit me.

'Let me just say something first.' I always looked him right in the eye to keep his attention on what I was saying. I used my hands a lot and bobbed my head like a fighter in the ring, trying to avoid a physical confrontation.

'I don't want to hear it, Duane Lee!' Flash wasn't really interested in talking.

'Wait a minute. What good is hitting me gonna do, Daddy? Calm down and let's talk this out.'

A lot of times he actually covered his eyes with his large hands, because he didn't like the way I was looking at him. He still came after me, though, even with his eyes covered. When I realised he couldn't see a thing, I led him right into a wall or the sofa. And if this tactic failed, I tried to talk Flash down by bringing up the Lord. He'd tell me to stop talking, but usually this would at the very least slow him down.

Dealing with Flash during those years taught me that talking things out is a lot better than fighting. You just have to be willing to put your own feelings aside and see things through someone else's eyes, even if they're covered.

By my fifteenth birthday, my parents had had enough. They could no longer control me, and they didn't like the influence I was having on my brother and sisters. So they sent me to live with Aunt Iris, who lived clear across town. She became my legal guardian. I loved living with her, because she never breathed down my neck and rarely checked up on me. I could go out whenever I wanted and didn't have to obey too many strict rules.

It was the late sixties. Hippies were popping up all over the place. I especially liked hippie chicks, who were always eager to get it on. I spent endless days and nights partying with them in the park. None of the hippies had jobs, so I wasn't really sure where they got their money. It seemed like most of them panhandled or sold drugs.

I wanted to help them make money legitimately, so I convinced some local businesses to hire them part time. I made my money by charging ten bucks for every job I arranged. I was the hippie headhunter. Eventually, I placed eighty-six of them with part-time employment, which meant I made 860 green American dollars. The local paper picked up the story and published a really nice article about how my entrepreneurial skills were helping the community. My mom was so proud of my efforts. I hadn't done anything in a long time to make her smile. It felt good to see her happy.

After a few months, I grew tired of hanging out with the hippies, so a couple of my buddies and I started our own gang. We called ourselves the Blue Demons. We seemed to share a lot of the same interests: robbing, stealing, and fighting.

One night, I was on my way up to a spot called Goat Hill, following Donny Miller and Richard Quintana in my old Chevy. I was dating Richard's sister Beverly, which made him nuts. Richard was in a gang called the Creek Rats. Since the rest of his gang wasn't around that night, I figured he wouldn't do anything crazy. We all hung out on the hill for a while, drinking and smoking.

Even though I wouldn't carry a gun today, back then I packed a .22 single-shot Luger. Richard asked if he could take a look at my piece. I should have said no right then, but I didn't think anything of it, so I handed it over. At first, he was completely nonchalant, looking at it as if he was just interested in my gun. Next thing I knew, he had it pointed straight at my head. Before anyone could stop him, he pulled the trigger. *Boom!*

I went down like a rag doll, with blood pouring from the top of my head. He started screaming as he threw the Luger to the ground. He was completely freaking out. I could hear him yelling, 'I didn't mean to! It just went off in my hand!' The bullet grazed the top of my skull but only penetrated my skin. Thank God I was blessed with a hard head! My hair suffered more than I did. For a moment there, I thought I was a goner, but the doctors just gave me a few stitches and sent me on my way.

Since Richard was my girlfriend's brother, I didn't rat him out. Instead, I told everyone that the Evans brothers had shot me, because all of the tough guys in West Denver were terrified of them. The gang even steered clear of those boys. Nobody did anything about the shooting, because I said it was all an accident. I figured it was a win-win situation for all of our reputations. I have to admit, I thought for a long time about what happened that night. I was so lucky Richard didn't blow my head off. That whole experience made me go back to the easy, free life with my hippie friends for a while.

I was smoking weed in the park one day when two big, mean-looking guys came through. I couldn't stop staring. They looked so cool. Someone told me those guys were in a gang called the Devil's Disciples. They were the baddest, meanest, toughest guys I ever saw. They were like gods. All the girls wanted to be with them, and every guy wanted to be them, including me.

As soon as I could get enough cash together, I bought a leather jacket and pants and a pair of motorcycle boots. Of course, there's the hair. You can't forget the hair. The mullet was born. I slicked my hair up into a pompadour and found a set of cool shades to wear. My hair was shorter than it is today, but my look hasn't really changed since.

The next time the Disciples came through the park, I wanted them to notice me. I watched their every move, trying to learn how they acted. They were always in complete control. There was no asking; these guys took what they wanted, and nobody dared mess with them. If a hippie had some weed, one of the bikers would just grab it from him. If a guy was hanging out with his girlfriend and the biker wanted her, she was his. If anyone tried to give them a hard time, the bikers would beat them with anything lying around – a chain belt, a tyre iron, whatever.

Eventually, one of them walked over to where I was hanging out. He whipped off his wraparound shades and looked me up and down. He was a giant with this long reddish beard that went down to the middle of his chest.

He said, 'Who the hell do you think you are?'

I shot right back with, 'Hey man, who the hell do you think *you* are?'

He couldn't help but smile, because I wasn't afraid to go nose-to-nose with him even though I was six inches shorter and fifty pounds lighter. One thing bikers admire more than anything is a guy who never backs down from a fight, no matter the odds. My ever-growing police record would vouch that I never backed off.

The biker dude introduced himself. 'Name's Tom. You can call me Tom Tom. I'm a Disciple. You a biker, boy?'

I blurted out, 'Yeah, I got a Harley,' doing my best to look mean. 'I got a couple of 'em actually.' It was such a big fat lie.

Tom Tom's smile grew even wider. 'Well, brother, I'd like to check your scooters out sometime. You ever thought about getting in with the Disciples?'

I didn't want to come across as being too excited, so I played it cool. 'Maybe. I'm not sure, brother. I've got a lot of things going on right now, so—'

'All right, I'll see you around, then,' Tom Tom said as he held his hand out for me to shake. 'Take it easy.'

Tom Tom and I began hanging out all the time. He showed me the way of the biker lifestyle – also known as getting really high and getting laid 24/7.

One cold Denver night, a few of us were trying to find the address of a party someone had told us about. When we finally got to the place, we found an abandoned house that looked like no one had lived there for years. It was a burned-out dump.

As we approached the house, I heard an awful noise coming from above the porch where we were standing. It sounded like a wounded animal crying for help. We looked up and saw a guy we called the 'Creature' hanging out of a window. He was one of the biggest, nastiest and ugliest mothers around. He was six four and weighed at least three hundred pounds. His face was all scarred up, and his teeth were as crooked as an old split-rail fence. I borrowed one of my best 'Dogisms' from the Creature, although I adapted it years later to fit my needs: 'I will crawl through hellfire, barbed wire, and brimstone to hunt you down.' That is the only good thing I can say I ever learned from him.

The Creature was hanging out the window, flipping God the bird, and saying, 'I fucking hate you, God! Go fuck yourself!' We could hear him yelling this over and over again.

'Forget that,' I said. 'I ain't going in there, man. That fucker is gonna get blown up by a lighting bolt in about two seconds for saying that kind of crap. You can't curse God like that.'

The rest of the guys, including Tom Tom, just laughed at me and walked up the front stairs into the house.

The place was supposedly the new clubhouse for a chapter of the Outlaws, which was a biker gang out of Chicago. The house was jammed with people partying and having sex everywhere. When a biker got trashed enough, he'd grab any chick and find a room or screw on the spot.

Tom Tom, the boys and I shouldered our way through the packed crowd in the hallway and finally found what used to be the kitchen. The Creature came barrelling into the room in a full rage. Something had got him all riled up. It was a crucifix hanging up on one of the walls.

'Hey!' he yelled. 'Who put that fucking hippie up on my wall? I'm turning that motherfucker upside down!'

Without any hesitation, I got right in his face. I may have been robbing, stealing, getting high and screwing everything in sight, but I still knew that turning that cross upside down would be the sign of the devil himself.

I looked straight up at the Creature as he towered over me. 'You ain't gonna do that,' I told him.

Everyone in the room stopped dead in their tracks.

The Creature inched closer. 'What did you just say to me, mother-fucker?'

I motioned to everyone else standing around us. They all looked terrified. 'God hears every word you say. If you curse Him, He will strike you down. If you invite the devil into your soul, he will surely come. God's wrath is real, brothers!' Of this, I was certain.

I could see that what I said stunned the Creature. He got really quiet. I thought he was going to shoot me dead. Instead, he took a step back with a look of fear in his eyes.

He stared down at the floor. 'Shit,' he said to himself. I let out a big sigh of relief as he walked away.

Tom Tom came running up and put me in a headlock.

'Chapman, you're a goddamned Bible-thumper. I've got a great idea for your nickname.' Seems all bikers had to have a nickname if they were going to be a part of the club.

'I think we're gonna call you Dog. That's God spelled backwards.'

'Hmmm. Dog, huh? I like it!' And I did. It fit me to a tee. I was mean like a dog and loyal, too. I could be your best friend or your worst enemy. It was perfect.

Tom Tom smiled at me and said, 'Now let's smoke some weed . . . *Dog*!'

I loved living the biker life in Denver, but Tom Tom and I were quickly wearing out our welcome. The city cops were trying to nail us on a few burglaries we pulled off. On top of that, I found out that one of the gang had been made vice president of a Mexican biker gang named the Hades Heads, which meant it was only a matter of time before we rumbled. It was like the old days of the Wild West: Denver just wasn't big enough for the both of us.

Tom said the time was right for us to go south and get in with the Disciples in Phoenix. I wanted to go, but I was pretty sure my parents and Aunt Iris would protest the decision. Somehow Tom convinced them that he could become my legal guardian. He said there were more job opportunities in Phoenix. In fact, he told them he had a few good ones already lined up. Somehow my dad had the impression we were going south to work manual labour. Naturally, Tom failed to mention that our prospective 'jobs' were actually heists.

So, in September 1968, Tom and I scraped together as much cash as we could to make the trip. I sold my 1959 Fairlane convertible, and Tom sold his Harley. We were still smiling as we walked on to Interstate 25 with only the leathers on our backs and a stack of cash in pillowcases. I adjusted my pillowcase on my shoulder, started walking, and stuck my thumb out.

# CHAPTER FOUR

# Prospecting for the Disciples

To make some extra money en route to Arizona, Tom Tom and I stopped along the way so I could box for cash. I knew I could whip just about anyone, so we rolled into towns, set up a match or two, wagered, and collected our winnings before splitting for our next fight. We did this for a couple of months.

I fought a lot of those fights at a bar in Grants, New Mexico. I was dancing in place, warming up in the centre of the ring at Salito's Bar, raised a glove in the air, but nobody could care less except for a group of Devil's Disciples hanging out at one table.

I went back to my corner, where my trainer for the night, a Disciple named Indian, peeled my robe off so I could step out. His real name was Dean Popovich, but sometimes the Disciples called him Dean Martin, because he looked just like him. I'm not sure where he got the name Indian from, because he said he was half Russian and half Italian. I didn't have the cash to get a real boxer's robe, so it was just something I scored for five bucks at the Salvation Army. Everyone loved giving me grief about it.

Indian slapped me on the shoulder and yelled in my ear, 'Here we go now!' trying to get me all charged up.

Indian was the most skilled fighter in the gang and the only Disciple I was truly afraid of. I tried messing with him once, which was a really bad idea. He beat the crap out of me. He'd always try to push my buttons by refusing to call me Dog. Instead he referred to me as Puppy.

Most of the crowd was made up of New Mexicans and Mexicans from Chihuahua. They were madmen around the fights – yelling, drinking, and putting down their bets. The Mexicans went especially wild when a gringo was set to fight, because most of the time he would get his ass kicked. So many gringos got busted up at Salito's that it was known as the 'Gringo Graveyard'.

I heard Indian yelling from behind me. 'Don't let that crap get to you, Puppy. Me and the brothers got over thirteen hundred dollars riding on you. You're gonna show this Red Lopez guy what's up tonight. It ain't gonna be like that shit with Titus.'

My only career loss had come at the hands of a young guy off the Navajo reservation. We called him Titus because he was a tough guy in the ring. The night I fought him, I fell for it. He connected with an uppercut to my jaw. Lights out. I took the eight count. I woke up at 'Nine . . .' I saw Porky Pig playing the banjo and heard the *Batman* theme in my head. I should have stayed down. The fight was over.

The Disciples lost over eleven hundred dollars on me that night. I was expected to pay back every last dollar for not coming through. A few weeks later, we had a rematch, and I ended up knocking Titus out in eight rounds. I beat his ass. I avenged my one loss and won back the Disciples' respect.

As tonight's opponent entered the bar, loud Indian war music blasted over the house speakers. The crowd erupted. Towards the back, I could see a boxer in a slick white robe making his way towards the ring. He was wearing a full Indian headdress. The announcer started saying something, but I wasn't listening. All I could see was this guy Lopez disrespecting Indians with his crazy costume and war-dance soundtrack. He was mocking my people. I could feel a kick of adrenaline rushing through my veins. My rage was building. Lopez was no Indian; he was Mexican. I glared across the ring at him, but he refused to lock eyes.

At the start of the first round, I came out firing. To my surprise, Lopez was ready. We traded a few jabs here and there, trying to find our respective ranges. I got careless at one point, and Lopez unleashed a right hook that dazed me. It felt like I had just got hit by a sledgehammer. Sensing I was hurt, he jumped all over me. Luckily, I was able to hold it together until the end of the round. When the bell rang, I said, 'Thank you, Jesus.'

I was still a little woozy as I stumbled back towards my corner. I fell down on to my stool and glanced across the ring at Lopez. He had cornermen and trainers buzzing all around him, wiping him down, rinsing out his mouthpiece, and massaging his shoulders. One guy was kneeling in front of him, giving him advice.

*My* cornerman's advice went something like this:

'What in the hell was that?! You gotta hit him, you pussy! Don't forget, we've got thirteen hundred dollars riding on you, Puppy.'

Over the next couple of rounds, I realised Lopez probably hit harder than any other fighter I had ever gone up against. His body shots bothered me more than anything, because my stamina was shot. My constant chain-smoking didn't help. I usually tried to keep my fights to no more than four or five rounds, because after that I was completely gassed. I had to get out before I faded and my opponent turned me into a human heavy bag.

By the end of the fifth round, I still hadn't landed anything on Lopez. The guy didn't even look like he was in the same fight. I was gasping for air trying to get back to my corner at the end of every round.

I thought back to when my dad first taught me to fight. He would say, 'Focus on one spot on your opponent and go after it. Do not stop until he goes to the canvas.' With Lopez, that was the area between his left ear and his chin. I had to go for it in the next round, or it was all over for me. Time was running out.

When the bell rang at the beginning of the sixth round, I jumped up and darted across the ring, only focusing on Lopez's weak spot. I tuned everything else out. It was just me and Lopez's jaw. He came after me with everything he had, but I didn't let that stop me. After he dipped down and threw a left uppercut, everything opened up for me. It was like a moment frozen in time. Everything in the bar stopped. I reared back and ripped a right cross to the left side of his jaw that buckled his legs and sent him down to the canvas.

The Disciples went crazy. The Mexicans weren't so happy. After all, this was the Gringo Graveyard.

When I finally zigzagged back to my corner, Indian grabbed me by the back of my neck in victory.

'You look like you could use a drink, Puppy,' he said, and handed me a bottle of whiskey.

I collapsed on to my stool. This would be my last fight for a while. I was beat in every way.

Two days later, Tom Tom and I hit Phoenix on a hot summer afternoon. In the worst part of town, we found the Devil's Disciples' clubhouse – a run-down motel with about a dozen rooms. As Tom and I made our way up the dirt driveway, we saw a ten-foot scarecrow dressed in full-on biker leathers and a real human skull for a head. Yup, this was definitely the place.

A few months back, while we were still in Denver, Tom had run into a Disciple from the Phoenix chapter, who gave him a courtesy card. All we had to do was show it to the Disciples' president when we got to the clubhouse. It was like having a temporary membership.

When we entered the clubhouse, we were met by a big, burly guy who came walking out of one of the back rooms. He was holding a half-gallon jug of cheap wine and smoking a cigarette. He stopped dead in his tracks to look Tom and me over. Tom handed him the courtesy card.

'Welcome to Phoenix, brother,' he said. 'Make yourself at home.' Then he looked over to where I was standing. 'Who's this?'

Before I said anything, Tom said, 'His name's Dog. I met him in Denver. I'm thinking about sponsoring him as my prospect. This brother's a cold-blooded mother, man.'

Some of the bikers who were looking at us from the other room started laughing. 'He don't even look like he's big enough to hold a Harley Hog up by himself.' Who the hell was this guy telling me I couldn't ride scooters? I'd been riding from the time I could walk. My whole family rode. My grandpa tried jumping a dirt bike when he was sixty-one and shattered his leg. But before we walked in, Tom had told me to keep my mouth shut, so I didn't say a word, but my blood was boiling. I could feel Tom's eyes on me. If I made a move on the president, every Disciple in the place would kick my teeth in.

When he asked me how old I was, I paused for a moment. I figured the Disciples didn't want to take any chances with some underage punk hanging around the clubhouse with all the boozing, drugging and fucking going on. If the place got raided, they'd go down for contributing to the delinquency of a minor. I used my deepest, most mature-sounding voice and said, 'Eighteen, brother.'

His eyes widened and he started laughing. 'OK then, big man. Come on in and grab yourself a drink.' He handed me his jug of Bali Hi wine. I grabbed it and took a huge swig. That was some bad wine.

Living at the Disciples' clubhouse was a zoo. The place was always crazy with people partying and loud music blaring. I got pretty tight with a lot of the Phoenix brothers, like Dago, Indian, Reverse, Pappy, and Little Pat. These guys would go out on their scooters and round up the hottest chicks in town. I'm not talking street whores, I'm talking about young, hot college chicks and bored housewives who wanted to party. Once the girls heard the thunder of the scooters rolling down the street and saw the boys in their leathers, it was a done deal. A college girl would come back to the house all shy, and before you knew it, she'd be up on the table dancing with her titties out.

When they weren't partying, the Disciples were robbing and stealing . . . or trying to, anyway. The cops kept showing up at all the jobs they were trying to pull off, because they kept tripping alarms, so they never got away with any loot. I thought it over and came up with a pretty good plan. I figured we could pretend to be the owner of a business and explain to the security company that we were having trouble with the alarm. That would make them think it went off because of a technical difficulty.

I finally got up enough nerve to tell The president some of my ideas. He was pretty impressed with what I had to say. For whatever reason, the guys never let me tag along, but it felt good to be able to contribute something. After that, most of the Disciples had a newfound respect for me, and even the ones who didn't, now knew I wasn't some dumbass.

My strength was devising a master plan, figuring out exactly how a job should go down. I wasn't all that keen on going out with the guys on their burglaries, anyway. A lot of them were loose cannons and way too careless. One thing Flash taught me was, you're only as strong as your weakest link – and, well, let's just say the Disciples had some very weak links.

When the Disciples were out pulling off jobs, they usually left me back at the clubhouse with their old ladies – just me and the girls. And man, did those honeys like the Dog. Before the guys made it out of the driveway, some chick would drag me into one of the back bedrooms and say, 'Don't tell nobody, because if my old man finds out, he'll kill me.' Sure, the Disciples had rules – like don't kill without a reason, don't steal from your brothers, and don't have sex with nobody's old lady unless he gives you permission. But I wasn't a Disciple yet, so I didn't think any of those rules applied to me.

I needed somewhere I could take a break from the chaos of the clubhouse, so I scraped together my money left over from boxing and got myself an apartment. It was a decent place on the north side of town.

Tom finally put me up as a prospect to the club a few months after we arrived in Phoenix. If you get taken in, you have to prospect – that is, be a prospect, or probationary member – for ninety days before you can become a full-fledged member. Three whole months before I could get my patch sounded like a lifetime. I was going to be nothing but a slave for the Disciples to fuck with. I've never liked being ordered around by anyone. Besides, I felt I had already proven myself to the gang.

On the inside, I was ready to burst. I needed to let out my aggression, so I began fighting again. Every time there was a chance to scrap, I would be right there in the middle, waiting to take my shot. I'd go to bars, pound whiskey until I was wasted, and then take it out back to throw down. Some guys brought chains, while others had baseball bats or clubs.

Tom Tom would look over at me and yell, 'Come on now, Dog!' I had to fight to win every time, because a prospect can never afford to lose. My probation with the Disciples went on for what felt like for ever. The guys gave me crap every day. It was only a matter of time before I cracked.

Somebody heard Jimi Hendrix was in concert nearby, so we rolled over to the show on our scooters. We were about to go in, when The president turned to me and a few of the other guys and said, 'All prospects hang out here and keep an eye on our bikes and our old ladies.'

I did everything I could not to lose my stuff. I kept thinking he was messing with us. There was no way I would sit outside in the parking lot with their old ladies while they went in and partied.

Tom wouldn't look at me, because he knew I was pissed. They went into the concert and left us with the scooters and the chicks. I really tried to keep my mind off of missing the show, but I couldn't. It was bullshit.

'Forget this, man. I ain't sitting out here like some idiot.' I got off my bike and went into the show.

When I got inside, I had no problem pushing right up to the front of the stage. Most people saw the nasty look on my face and just got out of the way. I needed something to take the edge off fast, so I walked right over to where this hippie was standing with a jug of wine.

'Give me a pull off that skin flask.' He handed it right over, no questions asked.

I took a long swig and then walked off in the other direction, still holding that flask. I could hear the guy swearing at me as I did, so I doubled back.

I lifted up my T-shirt so he could see the gun I had tucked in my waistband. 'What was that?' I asked.

His face went blank. 'Nothing, man. Nothing.'

Two Hell's Angels standing nearby must have been watching what I did. They walked over and said, 'What's your name, man?'

'I'm Dog.'

'Who you with?'

'I'm prospecting for the Devil's Disciples.'

The Angels were cool. They slapped a bunch of different-coloured pills into my hand before they split. I had no idea what any of them were, but I swallowed them down with a gulp of wine anyway. I wandered around the show like a zombie, taking people's weed and swigging their wine. I was trashed. When the music stopped, I stumbled back out to the parking lot. I could see all the Disciples down by the scooters, waiting.

The president was pissed. 'Damn, prospect, I could've sworn I told you to keep your ass put and watch the scooters.'

'Right,' I mumbled.

'And what were you doin' with those Angels? You think I didn't see you hangin' with them? Are you with us or are you with them, boy?'

'I'm a Disciple,' I said.

'Not no more,' he told me. 'Why don't you run off and find your other buddies.'

I was too wasted to calm myself down and think straight. My eyes started tearing up. 'Oh yeah? Well, as far as I'm concerned, all of you can go fuck yourselves!' I yelled.

He took a step back and looked over to where Tom was standing next to his bike. 'Your prospect's talking all this b.s. here, man. You better put a leash on that puppy.'

Without hesitation, Tom lunged over and ripped me down to the ground.

'Keep your mouth shut right now,' he told me.

I pushed Tom off and got up on my feet. My rage was out of control. For a second, I actually thought about swinging on him.

'Fuck you, Tom! And all you punks!'

I could have got the worst beating of my life for getting out of line like that, but I didn't. None of the Disciples would even look in my direction. I had completely embarrassed myself by disrespecting the entire gang. Without another word, they thundered out of the parking lot and left me behind.

In their eyes, the Dog no longer existed. I was crushed. I stood alone, wondering what I had just done. I'd come so far, just to throw it all away. I'd let my anger and frustration ruin everything I so desperately wanted. I got on my bike and headed home. I had to think of something to get back in.

# CHAPTER FIVE

# The Shoot-out on Mission Hill

When I heard the rumbling of motorcycles outside of my apartment a few days later, I knew it was the Disciples.

A dozen of them barged in and took over my place like it was their own. The president was walking around, tracking mud all over my carpet. He was just waiting for me to say something to him, but I kept my cool. He sat on my couch and put his boots up on the coffee table. He was trying hard to get me to react, but I wasn't budging.

'A real tough puppy, huh? That's what you are?' he asked.

A couple of the other guys were taking his lead, trying to provoke me, to get a response. I wasn't taking the bait. I tried my best to have no reaction, but the tears starting running down my face.

Little Pat, the club's sergeant-at-arms, saw me crying. 'Look at this, boys. Puppy's a little crybaby!'

Little Pat was a pretty tough guy. He was always riding me, probably even more than the rest of the guys. Tom Tom told me that sooner or later I'd have to take him on. I looked Little Pat dead in the eye, but I knew it wasn't the right time to make my move. I was confident I could destroy him if I had to. He got up from the couch. 'What if we ended up giving you your patch and then some motherfucker came along and tried to snatch it away from you?'

'I'd kill him dead,' I shot back at him.

The whole reason the Disciples came up to my apartment that day was so I could apologise to them. They wanted me to admit that I had screwed up. If I did, they'd reinstate me as a prospect, but I'd have to start all over again, which meant ninety more days of taking their bull. I wasn't interested. Either they made me a full-fledged Disciple or I was out.

'I ain't prospecting no more,' I said to him. 'I'm a Disciple.'

Little Pat started laughing and heading for the door.

I wasn't kidding. I stared him dead in the eyes. 'You want to see what I'm made of for real? Why don't you give me your patch and see what happens when you try to take it away from me?'

Everyone stood silent, waiting to see what happened next, because once again I was calling out the president of the Disciples. I had to take a stand and demand respect or I would always be a punk to these guys.

He looked around at the other guys in the room, and a grin came across his face. He suddenly broke out laughing.

'Somebody give this Dog his colours already,' he said, shaking his head.

Even though I was only sixteen, I wanted to be a presence in the club. I set a new standard for everyone else to be compared to. If the guys were drinking, then I drank them under the table. If the guys were smoking weed, then I smoked twice as much as they did. If a fight broke out, I hit harder than anyone else.

I took Little Pat's position as sergeant-at-arms about a year later, on 6 February 1970. It was a great honour. I was as proud as could be. Pat and I never ended up scrapping. When he backed down from me, he lost the Disciples' respect, and once that happened, he was finished.

The guys started calling me the comic-book biker because of my striking, over-the-top appearance in black leather and sparkling, polished chrome. I put a lot of thought and effort into my uniform. I made sure the straps on my boots were braided leather and my belt buckle was polished chrome master link.

My reputation was sealed because of my constant robbing and stealing. On a good day, I could scratch together as much as a grand before dinner. I made all of my money rolling hippies, because they were easy targets. They were always looking for drugs. Tom Tom and I rode our scooters down from Phoenix, along with a couple of the other guys, and cruised for a week, pretending to be drug dealers. Nearby towns, like Santa Fe, Albuquerque, Grants, Sedona, and Gallup, were packed with hippie communes and camps. I'd bring along a couple changes of clothes, and right before we'd bust into town, I'd exchange my oily leathers for a tie-dyed shirt and a pair of Levi's. I blended in perfectly with all the rest of the hippies. I'd start talking to everyone. We'd become fast friends. They never had any idea I was setting them up. It was too damn easy.

My job was to track down who wanted to score the most dope and who had access to the most cash. My story was always the same. I'd say a buddy had come across a large quantity of high-grade Mexican weed that we had to unload. I'd tell them we were willing to pass it on to them for a great deal because we were in a hurry to dump the dope. If they started getting cold feet, I'd whip out a joint and get them stoned.

You'd think most hippies were easygoing, but these guys were stingy when it came to drug deals. All I could do was stand and wait. I called it the silent close. I didn't want to break character and blow the deal. I quietly waited until they said yes. And they always said yes. It was amazing how a group of dirty hippies dressed in rags could suddenly scrape together twelve hundred bucks for drugs. The arrangement was always the same. I'd leave and come back later with my biker buddies.

We scared the high out of the hippies when we shoved our guns in their faces and took off with the cash and all their drugs, which we turned around and sold to other bikers. It was the perfect crime. They had nowhere to run. They couldn't tell the police. Not a chance. 'Excuse me, officer, some bikers took off with our dope money.'

As far as my parents were concerned, I was still working hard at a logging company. They might have suspected I was in with the Disciples, but they definitely didn't know where all my money was coming from. I was flush with cash. I spared no expense on my bike, and I even bought a couple of cars. Whenever I got the chance, I'd jump on my bike and head up to Denver to spend time with my girlfriend, Debbie.

During one such trip, I went over to the mall to waste some time one afternoon and spotted one of the most gorgeous girls I had ever seen. She had beautiful long brown hair and an unbelievable rack. I stared at her for a while, but she wouldn't look my way, so I walked over to where she was sitting.

'Hi, what's your name?'

'LaFonda.'

'Where you from?'

'I'm up from Texas, visiting my brother,' she said. Her accent was so thick I could barely understand what she was saying.

'Oh yeah, what's your brother do?'

'He's a policeman.'

'No shit,' I said slowly. I sure didn't want anything to do with any cops, but I couldn't keep my eyes off this girl.

She agreed to go out with me, so later on, that night, I thundered up her brother's driveway in my new Ford with a 390 engine. After our first date, I was crazy about LaFonda.

I made regular trips up to Denver a couple times a month. Even though I was now dating LaFonda, I continued to sleep with Debbie on the side. I was only seventeen and thought I could have it both ways.

In Denver, Washington Park was the place where most of the hippies hung out. I spent hours slinging drugs and finding out who the major players were. Mostly I was trying to get a feel for who would be the easiest score.

I got a tip on a house full of hippies and all sorts of drugs. It sounded like the perfect set-up for our latest scam. We were getting tired of pretending we were hippies. We had gotten to the point where we thought we could just barge in and take whatever they had. I asked a couple of my Disciple brothers to come up from Phoenix to help with the take-down. A couple of guys got word about what I was doing and wanted to tag along. Although they were members of the Hades Heads and not Disciples, we liked having them with us sometimes, because they were as cold-blooded as they come.

When we booted in the door, the house was filled with thick clouds of smoke from the hippies toking weed. We could barely see where we were going. They all just stared at us, glassy-eyed and stoned out of their minds, as we ordered them around. We found a mountain of speed on the kitchen table. One of the Disciples had taken along a .45-calibre Thompson submachine gun we named Woody Woodpecker. He stood in the middle of the living room and unleashed that fucker. *Rat-tat-tat-tat-tat!* The gun had such a strong kick, he had no control. When he was finished, most of the room was shredded to bits. There were chunks of furniture and shattered glass everywhere. The room was destroyed.

The guys hit an upstairs room where a hippie family was hiding. When they wouldn't hand over their stash, one of them grabbed the baby out of the mother's hands and dangled it Michael Jackson-style out the window. The other had one hand around the father's throat and the other clutching the mother's hair.

'Tell me where the fucking shit is!' he yelled at them.

Finally, the mother said, 'Check the cigar box.'

Jackpot. The box contained every drug known to man. There was coke, heroin, vials of liquid LSD, and pills of every colour and size. The other Disciples could barely carry all the bags of pot and speed they found all over the house. We had it all down like clockwork – from beginning to end, we were in and out in under three minutes.

On my way out, I saw one of the downstairs closet doors ajar, so I walked over and whipped it open. A stoned hippie was in there on his knees, completely freaked out. He looked up at me with crazy eyes and started laughing. He'd probably been in there the whole time tripping on LSD.

Rolling hippies was ridiculously easy, but there were a few occasions when we walked into some bad scenes. We figured that a house in Boulder would be just another group of stoner college kids who would hand over their stash and run for their lives. Man, were we wrong. It turned out they were seriously radical hippies, members of SDS – Students for a Democratic Society.

We were going to run the game like this: a few Disciples would hang back in their car just down the block to provide cover if we needed it. Me and my buddy were going to ride in the back of a camper that this chick would be driving. We planned to go to the house and explain to the main dealer that we had come across a couple of pounds of weed. We'd convince him to come out to the camper to take a look and talk business. Once he got out there, we'd shove a gun in his face and make him hand over all of his dope. If he was a hardass, we would hold him out there until the rest of the hippies gave it up.

When the front door swung open, however, there wasn't the scrawny, stoned-out hippie we were expecting. It was a big, ugly guy named Running Dog, who had a crazy-looking snake tattoo down the length of his face. When he saw us, he gave a mean scowl but never said a word. He just glared.

This was one scary-looking dude. After one look at him, I had doubts about the whole thing, but for some reason we stuck to our plan. We started making our way down towards our camper, when I heard gunshots zipping over my head. Holy crap! The hippies were shooting at us. This was an unforeseen turn of events. There were guys on the roof with rifles. They had spotted our lookout car down the street, and they knew it was a set-up.

There was instant chaos in all directions. Running Dog disappeared back into the house, while I was flat out on the dirt front lawn like a sitting duck. Our boys started shooting back. I decided to make a run for the camper, but before I had the chance, this long-haired freak came running down the front steps with a pistol. He aimed the gun right at my face.

'You're gonna lose your life, boy!' he shouted.

*Blam!* There was a bright flash, and I hit my knees. 'Ahhh!' I yelled out, but I could feel no pain. Was I already going numb from blood loss? I began patting my forehead, but there wasn't any blood. By some miracle, for the second time in my young life, the bullet missed me. I bolted across the street towards the camper. I could hear gunfire all around, so I stayed low. Since I didn't have a gun, I grabbed the curtains from the window of the camper and wrapped them around a tyre iron. I burst out of the camper on to the street and held it out like it was a machine gun. It was just dark enough so no one could tell the difference. All the guys on the front lawn ran for cover. Two of them sprinted towards the camper as we were driving off.

It wasn't long until the shooting picked up again. Just as he jumped in through the door, one guy got shot in his ribs. Bullets were ripping through the camper like a tin can. He was bleeding badly and used a curtain to apply pressure to his wound. The cops put up a roadblock at the end of the street. They had their guns drawn and made all of us climb slowly out of the shredded vehicle and lie face down in the middle of the road.

Since we'd all assumed it was going to be a breeze robbing the hippies, none of us had thought to bring a weapon along. That was an incredible stroke of luck. Since the four of us in the camper were all juveniles, we were released to our parents a few hours later. Some of the gang weren't as fortunate. They ended up doing some time in the joint. The SDS members were also arrested for their part in what the local paper called the 'Shoot-out on Mission Hill'.

The shoot-out probably should have caused me to take a few steps back and reconsider the path I was on, but it didn't. I was young and felt invincible. Nothing was going to stop me or even slow me down.

# CHAPTER SIX

# Leaving the Disciples

After the shoot-out at Mission Hill, I reached a point where I felt it was time for me to move on with my life. I was tired of Phoenix, and the constant travelling back and forth to Denver was burning me out. I lost interest in being the craziest badass biker in the Disciples. Mostly, it was my own fault, because, over time, I had created a monster. It was a role I had to live up to twenty-four hours a day.

The rest of the guys were always pressuring me into fights I didn't want to be involved in, and then they stood off to the side to hoot and holler. They'd be busy talking bull and laying down bets while I was taking punches, making them rich.

I had been getting angry with Tom Tom because, every time a few of us got into a fight with another gang, he finagled his way out. Finally, one night, I couldn't take it any more. I walked over and got right in his face. 'Man, you are chicken shit. I ain't sticking up for you no more!'

He seemed genuinely surprised. Without giving it much thought, I booted him right in the middle of the chest. When he got to his feet, he glared at me. 'You try that again and you are a dead man.'

The rest of the guys separated us before anything else could happen. From then on, everyone treated me differently, because I had lost my biggest ally. When my relationship with Tom Tom fell away, so did my interest in being in the club. When I went to the president to let him know I was moving back to Denver, he just nodded his head and went back to what he was doing. None of the Disciples really seemed to care. It was like I was already gone.

The night before I headed for Denver, we had a party at the clubhouse. I decided to take it easy, because I had a long day's ride the next day. The rest of the Disciples got completely wasted on pills and booze. When I woke up early the next morning to finish packing my things, there were guys passed out all over the house. I thought about all the fights they had pressured me into and the money they had made off of me. I was pissed off. I wanted revenge. Aside from a biker's patches, the most important things to him are his medals. Medals are badges of honour each club gives to members for various deeds. They're a little like merit badges. Some represent helping a brother in the club, while others might reflect doing hard time. I carefully made my way through the clubhouse, easing doors open and climbing over bodies. In all, I was able to steal eleven medals from different members. The medals weren't worth any cash, but they were priceless to me.

Before I could get the rest of my stuff completely packed, a few of the guys woke up and noticed their medals were missing. Indian came walking out with a few other guys. 'Wait just a minute, Dog,' he told me. 'Where's our stuff?'

'Huh? I don't know what you guys are talking about,' I told them.

They weren't buying it. He pushed me up against the wall and started patting me down. Indian said, 'Check his boots, boys.'

I had a sinking feeling. They ripped my boots off and shook them out. The medals rolled out on to the wood floor.

'Backstabbing motherfucker,' I said to Indian. What a rat. He knew me well enough to know I had those medals stuck in my boots.

I was in serious trouble. They had me boxed in from all sides. There was nowhere to run. I thought back to my days of battling with Flash. I thought back to all the ass-whoopings I had talked my way out of. *Keep talking. Keep them thinking and not acting.*

'Listen, I'm only a minor. I'm seventeen.'

Nobody made a move. He looked over at me. 'I knew you'd use that on us one day,' he said.

Indian stepped in and held a few guys back. 'Listen, if we mess him up, they'll come after us and we'll be up shit's creek,' he told everyone. He looked back over at me and said, 'You better get the hell out of here before we change our minds.'

I wasn't going to wait around while they thought it over. Juvenile or not, all it would take would be one guy to make the decision to take a swing at me, and the rest would join in.

I tore out on my bike and didn't look back. As I made my way up the ramp on to the Interstate, a crap-eating grin came over my face. I still had four of their medals.

My time with the Disciples may have been over, but that didn't stop me from being a criminal. When I went back to Denver, I married LaFonda and picked up right where I left off – robbing and stealing.

When I found myself in a courtroom once again, my lawyer, Gary Lozow, who had known and represented me since I was fifteen, pulled me aside. I liked Gary and respected him very much. In fact, he's still my lawyer today. He told me I had to get straight, because I was on a path of destruction. He asked if I had ever considered joining the army.

The war in Vietnam was in full swing at the time, and shooting machine guns and blowing stuff up sounded like fun. At the recruiting office, they had me fill out a long application. When I got to the section where they wanted me to list all of my arrests, I ended up running out of space on the paper. I wrote all over it. Then I flipped the paper over and started writing even more. I sat in the waiting room until they called me back into the office. The recruiter explained that, between my involvement in the Devil's Disciples and my lengthy police record, it didn't look like the United States Army wanted a guy like me. The recruiter told me, 'We'd rather take women and children before we take you. You're classified 1-F. You're done, Chapman.' Ouch!

LaFonda and I needed a change of scenery. To be honest, I wasn't being a very faithful husband. My mom sat me down and told me to leave town before everything caught up with me.

I took her advice and moved with LaFonda to Plainview, Illinois, just outside of Chicago. I immediately got work operating a backhoe, digging graves and holes for septic tanks. I should have been satisfied with LaFonda, but I just couldn't stay loyal to my wife. Women have always been my biggest weakness.

One night, I hooked up with a sexy older chick I met in a bar. We decided to head back to her place. On the way, I had my head in between her legs while she was driving. When she had an orgasm, she jerked the wheel, sending the car skidding across the road into a tree. We both managed to escape without any serious injuries – that is, until LaFonda showed up and one of the cops told her what happened. LaFonda had had enough. She left for her mother's house in Pampa, Texas, the next day.

I tried to convince myself that I was better off without her, but I wasn't. I missed her like crazy. I was really in love with LaFonda, and I needed her. I was stupid to let her walk out of my life. I had to go down to Texas and prove my love. To my surprise, when I called her to tell her to expect me, she begged me to come. So, of course, I did.

# CHAPTER SEVEN

# Pampa, Texas

I arrived in Pampa in September 1972. LaFonda was living with her mother. She was five months pregnant with our first child, Duane Lee. Our marriage had been on the rocks since before we moved to Illinois, but catching me with that other woman was the last straw. It took me two months to follow after her. But once I realised how much I loved her, I had to go win her back.

LaFonda and I had to sleep in a tiny bedroom on the top floor of her parents' house. We couldn't make any noise when we had sex, because her mother's room was directly beneath us. Her family had never met anyone like me. I was a long-haired biker who looked meaner than I really was.

I began searching for a home so we could have our own place before the baby was born. I scoured the paper for available houses to rent. Everything I looked at was either too expensive or unlivable in. Finally, LaFonda's mother told me about a friend of hers whose husband had recently died and who was leaving her place vacant. I didn't care that the old man had died in the house, so I went down to Roberta Street to see it.

It was beautiful, with plush carpeting and wood panelling in every room. It was perfect for us. The homes in the neighbourhood were all well-kept cottages. I thought the house was worth sixty to seventy thousand dollars. The dead man's wife told me she wanted to sell the house in a package deal with the one next door, which they also owned. I couldn't afford to buy one house, let alone two. But then she said, 'I'll sell both to you for five thousand dollars!' It was too good to be true.

Even though the asking price was extremely reasonable, I didn't have that kind of money. LaFonda wanted the house as much as I did, but how would we ever qualify for a loan? Up to that point, I had been a career criminal. I was only nineteen years old. I didn't have enough credit to get a loan even if I did have a steady job. I thought, what the hell, I'll go to the bank, anyway. It can't hurt to ask, right?

We thought LaFonda's mom, Elwanda, might be able to help secure a loan, because she owned a bunch of real estate in the area. We went to the bank and sat outside while she talked to the loan officer. I could see him shaking his head no through the glass window. My mother-in-law came out and told us he wouldn't give her any more loans.

I couldn't let that stop me. I walked in and asked to see the head loan officer. I went into his office and shut the door.

'You see that woman out there?' I turned and pointed to my very pregnant wife.

'I love her. I just got married and I'm trying to change my life.'

The banker looked half-scared and half-shocked as I spoke.

'I've been a criminal most of my life, but I'm not any more. Where do I start if I need to get a loan?'

The banker said, 'Right here.'

'I have no record or convictions. I'm trying to live right. Can you help me?'

'Yes I can.' After he calculated my monthly payments, he gave me a chance few others would have dared to offer. We made a deal on the spot. I was so grateful for his generosity and understanding.

LaFonda and I were homeowners. It was incredible. I made the monthly payment by renting out the cottage next door. I never charged a dime more than our total mortgage, which meant that the tenant paid for both houses. It was a bargain for everyone.

At the time, LaFonda was working at a local bra factory, because I couldn't get a job anywhere. I tried to get work, but no one wanted to hire me. I went to the oil fields, but I was afraid of heights, so working on the derricks was out of the question.

Next, I went to the local slaughterhouse. When they brought in the first cow for me to kill, I couldn't do it. The steer looked me straight in the eyes. It was like he knew he was going to die and that I was the guy who was going to kill him. I didn't have the heart to pull the trigger. I walked out the door before I broke down in tears.

A local tree-trimming company had some jobs available. My job was to feed the cut branches into the wood chipper. One afternoon, the boss called me over and told me to get into the bucket they hoisted with a crane to the tops of the trees.

I didn't want to admit to the boss I was afraid of heights. I had finally found a job I was good at. I didn't want to say no, but there was no way I was going up in that bucket. I just said, 'No, sir. I can't do that.'

'Chapman, you get into that bucket or you can go home.'

My job was on the line. LaFonda was pregnant. We needed the money. By now, the boss and other workers had figured out I was scared. I reluctantly agreed to get in. They hoisted me up sixty feet and began shaking the damn thing. It felt like an earthquake. I got so mad I threw the tools over the edge and screamed, 'Get me down!'

They were all laughing at me. When I got down, I bitch-slapped the boss. One of the workers called the cops. The sheriff came down. This was the second time he and I met in the few weeks I'd been in Pampa. He warned me that the next time we crossed paths, he was taking me in.

Then, next morning, LaFonda found a Help Wanted ad in the paper. The Bison Vacuum Company was looking for employees. The ad read, 'Will train. Make $300 a week!'

LaFonda was nine months pregnant. I needed to find a job fast, because she couldn't work after she gave birth. With a baby on the way, we really needed the money.

I went for an interview that same day. They gave a demonstration and explained that all I had to do was to show the vacuum thirty times a week and I'd get paid three hundred bucks. It sounded easy.

A couple of weeks went by. I showed the product dozens of times, but I hadn't made a single sale. During the third week, I got called in by my manager, Dale Hunt. He said, 'Listen, Duane, if you don't sell any vacuums, you can't get another pay cheque.' That wasn't the deal. They had said all I had to do was to show the damn machines.

I was born with a gift. My gift of the gab saved me many times from Flash's wrath. It was easy to talk my way into a customer's house. What I needed to learn was how to sell those damn things. Dale Hunt suggested he and I go out on the road so he could teach me the ropes.

If a sale is what they wanted, I could do that. I went on the road for a week by myself. I made two sales. The best salesman in our region was a guy by the name of Bobby Walker. Next time I went out, he wanted to go on the road with me. He and I had a wonderful rapport. We drove all over Texas in my blue 1963 Chevy.

It wasn't long before I developed my own brand of selling. I found out this ol' boy had talent. I was personable and likable to everyone I met. A customer once told me I could sell God the gates of hell. I flirted with the women as much as I shot the bull with the men. I began telling customers how I'd just sold their neighbour Mrs Jones two vacuums, so Mrs Smith would buy three. I loved selling to farmers' wives. They bought anything, especially a product one of their neighbours had just bought. They're a very competitive bunch of women.

Now, the farmers are a different sort. They don't like to part with their money. I usually got their attention by demonstrating the Bison.

I'd say, 'Is that an impressive machine?'

They'd always respond with one word, 'Yup.'

This is where I hooked the poor bastards. I'd say, 'I know you love your wife.'

That wasn't what they were expecting. Their wives were always standing right there in the room. How could they respond, other than to say, 'Yup, I love my wife.'

'Now, the day you married her and said you loved her for better or for worse, I am certain you would have agreed she needs one vacuum for upstairs and one for downstairs, am I right?'

With the farmer's wife sitting right there in the room, there was only one answer – 'Yup.' Blam. Another sale.

Eventually word got out about my technique. Several farmers got to talking, and whenever I showed up, they'd slam the door in my face, saying something about my marriage mumbo jumbo not working there. I had to laugh. It tickled me to think these good ol' boys talked about me, vacuums, and their wives all in one sentence.

Every now and then, I'd pull the old price switch. After proving how well the Bison could pick up dirt, the final question always boiled down to price.

The customer always asked, 'Well, how much is that there vacuum gonna cost me?'

'I'm glad you asked that, sir.' I'd jot a few numbers down on a piece of paper, like this:
Original Price: $650.00
Discount: $100.00
Final Price: $450.00

Every single time, I could see the customer's eyes widen, not wanting to let me know I'd made a hundred-dollar error.

They always said, 'Is this your bottom line?' thinking they were going to pull a fast one. A man's handshake is as good as his word. When we shook hands, we had a deal.

We'd get the paperwork signed, I'd collect the cheque, and then I would hear something like this: 'I really got you, Dog. You made a big mistake. You should have collected $550 from me! Ha! Ha! Ha!'

'Oh. Well. Guess the joke's on me, huh?' I was coy for a moment. Then I'd always say, 'No, there was no mistake. The machine sells for $450.00. Gotcha!!'

I was proud of how I sold the Bisons. I was good at it. I've never been the kind of guy who could take no for an answer. I stayed until I closed the sale. I'd ask the customers if I could try my pitch again, until they said yes. I realised that when customers immediately tell you no, what they're really saying is, 'You haven't showed me enough yet.' So I kept on trying until I either made the sale or was told to beat it.

I remember meeting a salesman on the road who was trying to sell safes. Now, that was a hard product to move door-to-door! He was fifty-six years old and drove a brand-new Cadillac. He must have sold a lot of safes to get a car like that. He told me a story about a young man who took his girlfriend out to the drive-in movie one night. He asked her if they could do the wild thing. She said, 'I would if this was a convertible.' So the guy gets out of his car and saws the top right off. A good salesman will do whatever it takes to make his sale. For all of you guys out there, think of it like this: how many times does it take to get the girl of your dreams to finally say she'll go out with you? If you're like me, you'll keep asking until she finally gives in. That's what makes a good salesman.

Many of my best life experiences were garnered during the years I sold vacuums. Selling door-to-door taught me how to deal with rejection, how to overcome obstacles, and how to talk my way in or out of every situation.

I learned the value of relationships and camaraderie. I considered all of my customers my friends. I gave them free vacuum belts and bags. Whenever they saw me in a restaurant, they'd tell their friends, 'There's Duane. Don't be frightened by how he looks. He's really a nice guy.'

My record was selling sixty-two vacuums in a single month. I began making some pretty good money, too. I was able to pay off the house and buy LaFonda a new Subaru.

Duane Lee was born in January 1973. Things were going pretty well.

I held that little baby in my arms and couldn't believe I'd helped make this precious thing. I was instantly in love with that boy. My mother-in-law forced me to hold him right away. I was so scared, thinking I wouldn't know what to do. I thought I might break him or hurt him. When I got him home, I called the sheriff to register Duane Lee.

'This is Duane Dog Chapman and I'm calling to register my son.' The sheriff must have thought it was a crank call. He said, 'You don't need to do that, Chapman. Are you crazy, boy?'

'I just wanted you to know that I have my son here at the house. He's my child and I promise I will take care of him.'

Again, the sheriff said, 'You don't have to tell me this.' I put my hand over the receiver and whispered to LaFonda, 'He's saying I don't have to tell people I have a kid!' LaFonda rolled her eyes in total disbelief that I was making this call at all. I had no idea I would be trusted with another human life without telling the authorities. I was so young and naïve.

I made a deal with God right there and then; I promised Him I would never join another motorcycle club again. I swore I wouldn't commit another felony as long as I lived. The love I felt for my son was on a different level to any love I had ever known. I wanted to promise the Lord I would be good so He would continue to bless my life with lots and lots of children.

One day, when Duane Lee was three months old, my mother-in-law came to visit. She picked up the baby and held him in her arms. Duane Lee held his head up, focused his little eyes, and reached out for me – his daddy. I have never felt so needed or wanted as I did that moment. My dad was always so abusive. I never felt love from him like Duane Lee or the rest of my children would feel from me.

I loved my life. I thought I had found my calling. But I was still living like a biker, even if I wasn't affiliated with a gang. When I wasn't out on the road selling, I was hanging with other bikers. I kept my promise to God. I never joined the club. But I still hung around those guys. I couldn't give up the lifestyle. I stayed out at night, screwing around and drinking – but no more crime.

# CHAPTER EIGHT

# One Night in Pampa

By 1976, LaFonda had given birth to my two oldest sons, Duane Lee and Leland. I'd given up trying to make a living doing manual labour. Even though I was married, I was still enjoying the biker life, whoring around, smoking pot, and drinking whiskey until I was completely out of control. Since the vacuum job didn't work out, I needed to find a way to make money, so I could take care of my family. A buddy of mine from the Disciples helped me get a part-time job with a local trucking company.

I thought life was really good. I had everything a man could want. But I pushed the envelope until, one day, things went a little too far. After 16 September 1976, my life would never be the same.

LaFonda warned me not to go out with the boys that night. She had a great ability to foresee things. I wish I had listened to her.

Donny Kurkendall, Ruben Garza, Cheryl Fisher and I all decided to go out and raise some hell. Ruben was a short, fat biker. He hung around us all the time, but no one wanted him in the gang. Cheryl was a typical young and pretty Texas teenager who had a thing for hanging out with bad boys. Kurkendall was a true Disciple, willing to do whatever he had to do to pull off a score. He was a creepy-looking guy, the type you might see on the evening news for a mass murder. I called him Handsome Manson. He was unpredictable and known to fly off the handle for no reason at all. *I* wasn't scared of him, but most people were – especially those who knew the crazy shit he was capable of.

We had been partying pretty hard that night, although I wasn't drinking as much as the others. I recall Donny was drinking Wild Turkey and chasing it with Mad Dog 20/20. He was bombed. We were looking to buy some pot, but the town was pretty much dry. We couldn't even score a joint. We tried all the usual suspects. There was a hippie in the car who started talking crap about robbing some black guy. I asked who he was talking about. He said my old friend Jerry Lee Oliver.

I thought no way. I didn't want no part of robbing Jerry Lee. I just thought we should get some pot and go hunting in the woods. We stopped to buy some beer and fill the car up with gas. That's when the hippie got out.

Donny was on a mission, though, one I knew wouldn't go away until we got what he was looking for.

I was pretty sure Jerry Lee would have a secret stash, especially when no one else was holding. It was worth a shot. Donny gunned his old Thunderbird towards Jerry's house.

When we got there, Donny and Ruben got out of the car. Donny went inside the house. I knew Jerry would recognise me. I tried to hide my face by putting the paper bag from the beer over my head, but I purposely ripped it so I wouldn't have to participate in the plan.

I knew Jerry Lee had about as bad a temper as Donny did. I didn't want him to be an asshole. We all thought that he had been jumping Donny's wife. We hoped Donny didn't know. By his determination, though, I could tell he probably did.

I liked Jerry. He and I were cool. I'd helped him out once, and I considered him my friend. He was a cool brother. I loved him, and he loved me.

'Be cool, brother,' I said. 'Don't mess with that guy.'

I didn't see anything happen, but I heard a sound like a muffled gun ring out.

'Fuck! I've been shot.' Donny came running back to the car, screaming and bleeding. For a moment, I actually thought that Jerry shot Donny. But the truth is, the shotgun blew up in Donny's hand.

Blood was gushing everywhere. We had to get Donny to the hospital. On the way, I asked him, 'What the hell happened?'

'I only hit him in the shoulder!'

'What?!' I couldn't believe what I was hearing. 'You're so stupid! Is he dead?' I could feel my heart beating through my thick leather biker jacket.

'I only hit him in the shoulder.' Donny was absolutely certain about that.

I pulled Donny by his hair. 'What'd you do?' I was mad. I didn't want any part of a shooting. This was just plain stupid drunken b.s.

Cheryl got behind the wheel and punched the gas. I didn't want to be in that car. It was a hot, late summer night. What if Donny had killed Jerry Lee?

I had to check on Jerry Lee.

They dropped me at my house and I called an ambulance. I gave the operator all the information I had, then got off the phone. I didn't want her to know who was making the call.

I began pacing the kitchen, running my hands through my hair.

'Duane, what the hell is going on?' LaFonda was pissed and confused.

I told LaFonda I hadn't done anything wrong. Jerry had no idea I was there. I had nothing to hide. I was completely innocent. I didn't even know Donny had a gun. It was a drug buy gone wrong. Shit.

I discovered later that the phone was slightly off the hook. Pampa was a small town. Back in those days, the operator could come back on the line if the phone wasn't hung up. She heard every word of my confession that I was there – even if I didn't pull the trigger.

By the time I got to Jerry Lee's, the medics were bringing him out on a stretcher. I walked alongside him and we spoke – he was awake and alert while the Pampa police tried to get his statement.

'It was the Devil's Disciples. They were the ones who did this to me.'

I knew the officer who was interviewing Jerry Lee – good old Officer Love. And he knew me. Don't be confused by the cop's name. He was a down home country boy.

'Do you know who did this? Who was it? What was his name?' Love kept pushing for a name.

'Yeah . . .' Jerry could barely speak. 'It was a Disciple . . .'

Suddenly, Love noticed me. He glared into my eyes like he was about to settle some score between us.

Love looked back down at Jerry Lee and asked, 'Was it Dog Chapman? Did Dog shoot you?'

'No man . . . it wasn't Dog . . .'

I helplessly watched the medics lift Jerry into the ambulance. I knew everything was gonna be all right. Love blocked me. He didn't want me anywhere near Jerry Lee.

Since I knew Love heard I wasn't the shooter, I left Jerry Lee's house certain that I wouldn't be charged with pulling the trigger. And I truly believed Jerry Lee would survive. All I had to do was convince Donny and the gang to just lay low for a little while. A month or two would go by, and I thought this whole thing would blow over. I felt like I had dodged a bullet – big time.

The next morning, LaFonda and I woke up to the sound of the morning news blaring from the clock radio next to our bed. We were still half-asleep until I heard something like, '. . . local police are searching for Duane Chapman in connection with the murder of Jerry Lee Oliver late last night . . .'

Murder? Did he say murder? That meant Jerry Lee was dead. And they think I did it.

'LaFonda. Get up. Get up. We gotta go. Get the kids, honey. We have to get outta here.'

There was no time to talk. I got dressed as fast as I could. I told LaFonda to grab whatever was essential and drive our camper out to Skellytown.

'Honey, you gotta hurry. Wait for me by the highway. I will meet you there as soon as I can.'

I wanted to get over the Texas state line and into Colorado. With God's help, we'd be eating dinner at my momma's house in Denver within twenty-four hours.

I moved quickly and cautiously. The cops were already outside the house. I told LaFonda to answer the door like she didn't know a thing.

'Tell them I'm at work. Tell them I already left.'

She answered the door cool as could be.

'Yes? May I help you?'

*That's it. Stay calm.* LaFonda was cool.

I could hear the officers asking if I was home.

'No, sir. Duane has already gone off to work.'

They bought the story. The cops left, though I knew it wouldn't be long before they'd discover I wasn't at work. I had little time to make a run for my freedom.

We lived on a quiet street, but on this particular morning, it seemed like you could hear every little thing. Just as I was about to leave, I heard the sound of the toggle switch revving up. It was getting louder. One turned into two. Two turned into a symphony of sirens. The cops were coming for me.

I fully expected a couple of cops to be drawing down on me as I blasted through my back door. I never stopped to open it. The door came right off the hinges. No one. I couldn't believe it. I stood motionless for a second before I realised I still had a chance. I made my move. I sprinted across the backyard, hopped the neighbour's fence, and began my Olympic run down the alley. I kept thinking I had to run as fast as I could. I was sure the cops were just seconds behind me.

Wrong.

They were right in front of me.

I got to the end of the alley, where I was met by a parked police cruiser. I recognised the cop right away. It was Officer Bailey. I'd had a few run-ins with this old man a couple of times. He wasn't the sharpest tool in the shed, but needless to say, I thought I was done. My foot chase lasted less than three minutes. Some fugitive I turned out to be.

Bailey was sitting in his patrol car, watching what was going down in front of my house. I thought about turning back the other way. Bailey hadn't seen me yet. I could've made another run for it. But I kept asking myself why I was running in the first place. I didn't kill Jerry Lee. All I was guilty of was being in the wrong place at the wrong time. My mistake was allowing a drunken asshole like Donny Kurkendall to hold my fate in his hands.

Just then Bailey turned around. He nodded his head hello, not realising it was me. It suddenly sunk in who was standing on the other side of his car. He turned back around. I could see his eyes widen with fear.

He was so scared he could hardly speak. He asked me not to do anything stupid or get crazy on him.

The thought never even crossed my mind. I had been arrested many times before, but I never felt like this. This time was different. In my gut I knew I was going to do hard time. I had a wife and two babies. Who was going to watch over them? My heart ached for what I'd done to them and to my good friend Jerry Lee. Killing wasn't my crime of choice. I was a thief. I was a con man. Hell, I was even a drug dealer. But I was no killer.

Another officer came running towards the car. It was J.J. Rizman, a cop I knew well from my youth in Denver who happened to move to Pampa. He had his gun drawn.

'You're finally going down, Dog Chapman.' Rizman smirked while Bailey gingerly cuffed me.

I was placed in the backseat of the patrol car while they waited for backup.

I tried to explain what happened, but Rizman didn't care about what I had to say. He wasn't the type of cop who was interested in hearing the facts. Over the years, I haven't met many who were, but Rizman seemed to be downright happy about my taking the fall.

He told me I was under arrest for the big one. I told him I wanted to exercise my rights and we sat silent for the ride to jail.

Later that day, the police picked up Donny, Cheryl, and Ruben in Amarillo. By nightfall, we were all sitting in small holding cells on the top floor of the Pampa courthouse. We were charged the next morning. The DA went for first-degree murder. Each of us would be charged the same. Under Texas law at the time, anyone who was with someone and aided them in the commission of a crime was equally guilty of the crime. As far as the DA was concerned, we were all guilty of murdering Jerry Lee Oliver.

# CHAPTER NINE

# Murder One

The judge set bail at fifty thousand dollars each. There was no way I was getting out of jail. As it was, my job barely paid me enough to cover my bills. I tried to make extra money by renting a room to women, but I always ended up sleeping with them before I could collect the rent. They'd leave, or I'd kick them out so LaFonda wouldn't know the truth. Whenever I had an extra few bucks, I squandered it on weed, whores, or my bike.

I sat in my cell with nothing to do but think. I had really messed things up. I didn't realise how much I loved LaFonda and our boys until I sat alone in my cell that first night in jail. I'd taken so much for granted – my family, my freedom, my entire life. Suddenly it was all gone. I hated Donny for screwing it up. My anger grew with every painful passing second. It wasn't fair. It wasn't right.

Yeah, I know. A guy died. Someone had to pay for taking his life. Someone had to own up to the crime – to take the responsibility for what he'd done. Why did Donny do it? Why'd he shoot Jerry Lee? Why didn't I stop him? Why didn't I know he had the gun?

There were many times I wondered if Jerry Lee would've been killed if I hadn't been there that night. He was my friend. I don't believe Donny would have gone to his house if I hadn't been in the car. Did that make me responsible? Did that make me accountable? The more I thought about this, the angrier I got. My rage was becoming unmanageable. If I was going to rot in jail for killing a man, I might as well kill one. I wanted to rip someone's head off. I didn't care who it was.

My rage was out of control. The sheriff would put all the drunks in with me and 'encourage them' to help settle me down. I beat the crap out of every guy they put in there with me. I was unstoppable.

I would've beaten up a minister if they'd put one in the cell with me.

Reverend Gerald Middaugh from Pampa's Assembly of God church wasn't your typical preacher man. He looked eighteen years old, even though he was in his early thirties. It didn't seem like he was old enough to be a reverend. I wasn't sure why he came to visit me in jail, but I was certain I wanted nothing to do with whatever he had to say. I was still angry about the whole situation. I didn't do anything wrong. I wasn't supposed to be in jail.

The reverend stood outside my cell and began to talk.

'Dog, do you mind if I call you Dog?' He looked scared as hell.

'LaFonda tells me you were once a spiritual man. She said you have a strong belief in the Lord. I'm here today to talk to you about that.'

I stared him down. I could feel the blood rush to my face.

'Move along, reverend. I ain't got nothing to say to you.' I spoke in a soft, low growl.

'Now listen, Dog. I know you're angry. God knows you're a good man. A decent man. You're in a bad situation here.'

I slowly moved my face towards his.

'What do you know about my situation, reverend? You don't know nothing.' I held on to the cell bars as tight as I could. My knuckles turned white from the strength of my grip.

'Dog. You of all people should know that God will show you the way. He will lead you from this dark place into the light. You have to trust the Lord. Put your life in His hands.'

I was pissed. I didn't want to hear about God or His almighty plan. All I wanted to hear was that I made bail and was a free man.

'Unless you're here to post bail, reverend, I suggest you get out of here. I ain't interested in anything you have to say. I'll use your bible for rolling papers.'

The preacher stood motionless, unfazed by my anger. Hell, I was locked up behind bars. What was I going to do? I couldn't touch the guy, and he knew it. Still, his willingness to take my mouth was surprising.

'If you want the Lord's help, Duane, you have to ask for it. If you want your bail reduced, then ask God for a reduction in bail. Ask and ye shall receive.'

He spoke with such confidence and assurance. I didn't care. I walked to the back of my tiny cell and never turned around until I heard the reverend slowly walk away.

*Fuck him*, I thought. *Who does he think he is, coming in here, telling me about the ways of the Lord?* I walked in small circles, thinking about what he had said. He didn't know me. He didn't know dick about my life. If he did, he surely wouldn't be wasting his time on a guy like me.

Life in jail wasn't as bad as I thought it would be. I had been arrested many times before, so I kind of knew what to expect. I was able to sneak in some drugs, mostly pot, which helped calm me down and pass the time. It was easy to smuggle in the drugs. I lowered a string from the window of my third-floor cell, and one of my Disciple brothers always hooked me up. Usually it was Little Earl, who tied a bag of weed or Fiorenal to the string so I could pull it back up.

To be perfectly honest, I could have gone down to get the stuff myself. I discovered that previous inmates had tried to saw through the bars on the window. It took me a few days, but I finished the job using a sharpened metal lid from a jar. I'd sneak out at night by shimmying down a drainpipe. Little Earl was always there. We'd head over to the local bowling alley to grill up a couple of cheeseburgers. It never once occurred to me to run. Where would I go? Besides, if I ran, I would have to give up LaFonda and the boys. I wasn't willing to sacrifice my family for my freedom. Those kids meant the world to me. They needed their dad. I wanted to be around to see them do all that kid stuff. I wasn't going to do anything stupid, like bust out of jail.

Sheriff Rufe Jordan didn't see it quite the same way as I did.

'What the hell are you doing, Dog?' the sheriff asked, as I swung my legs through the window leading back into my cell.

I was speechless.

The sheriff looked completely shocked. I'm guessing it was a first for him to actually have an inmate break *in* to jail! He never said another word about it.

Despite my consistent dismissals, the reverend kept coming to visit, trying to lead me back to the Lord. LaFonda even brought my bible, in the hope that I would find God's love and light. It had been years since I'd read my bible. It took me a few days before I cracked it open. But as I began to read, I kept denying the reasons why.

I read it because I was bored. Alone. Sad. Angry. Frustrated. That's what I kept telling myself. But looking back, it was because of so much more. Reading the Bible brought back happy memories from years ago. It reminded me of when I was a boy, going with Mom to Sister Jensen's mission and to church with her on Sundays. Slowly I began to realise the words were uplifting and healing. I began reflecting on my life. I knew I had made some bad choices along the way, but reading the Bible in jail helped me see that I had probably done more damage than good in my first nineteen years. That wasn't how I wanted people to think of me.

I am a proud man. I had a set of values that guided me. I thought of myself as a moral criminal. Yes, I stole, but that didn't make me a killer. I fought, but I was not a violent man by nature. I sold drugs and partied. I could chalk that up to being young and stupid. But deep down, I wasn't an asshole. That I was sure of. I hoped it wasn't too late to change my life. In my heart, I wanted to be good. I wanted to be on the straight and narrow. I didn't want to waste my life, spending the rest of my days and nights as a hoodlum biker.

So, for the first time since I was a young boy, I began to pray. I asked the Lord for help. I begged for His forgiveness and guidance. I took the reverend's advice and asked God to reduce my bail. I pleaded with God to show me the righteous path. I promised I wouldn't run around with the Disciples or cheat on my wife. I told the Lord I would go straight, get a job, and make money on the up and up. I even told the Lord that if He helped me, I would sell my beloved bike. That might be the hardest promise I ever made.

The proof would be at the hearing, which was set forty-eight hours after I began to pray. There was no way I could come up with fifty grand.

'All right, God. If You're really out there, show me you have heard my prayers. I am being sincere, Lord. Please, God. Help me. Let Thy will be done.'

Two days later I appeared in front of Judge McIllheney.

'Bail is set at five thousand dollars.'

I threw my head back in utter shock.

'Shit.' That was all I could say.

Damn, I was gonna miss that bike.

When you make a promise to the Lord, you'd best keep it.

As soon as I could, I began to fulfil all the promises I made to God in jail. He showed me He is a man of His word. Now I had to be a man of mine. First chance I had, I paid a visit to my old friend Dale from Bison, who was now selling Kirby vacuums.

'Dale, I need a job. You gotta help me.' I was practically begging.

He said, 'OK, Dog, I'll put you back on . . . but you can't bring your troubles here, friend.'

Next, I went to see Reverend Middaugh. I wanted to thank him for his guidance and tell him that he was right. I asked, and God provided. I wanted to share my rediscovered belief in God. The reverend offered me a job as the church janitor. He even trusted me with a key to the church. That man was my friend.

He said, '. . . and, on Sundays, you can help with collections.' I smiled, knowing no one would let Dog pass by without putting money down. The reverend told me tithing went up significantly in the weeks I passed the collection plate. He was a smart dude. I had to give him credit for seeing that opportunity.

Finally, I sold my Harley to a friend for three thousand dollars. It almost paid for my fast-growing legal fees. I loved that Harley Panhead. It was by far the fastest and best-looking motorcycle in Texas, if not the world. For years, my entire identity had been being a biker. Without a bike, who would I be?

I spent most of the year waiting to go to trial. I was trying to make up for all the years I'd wasted breaking the law and ignoring God. I committed myself to seeing the error of my ways. I went to church as often as I could. LaFonda and I went every Sunday. Duane Lee sat on my lap as we raised our spirit to God. In addition, I often found myself alone in church, praying for hope and guidance. I wasn't sure what the future held, but I was confident the Lord had a plan.

I was selling a lot of vacuums, making more money than ever. After one especially good day, I decided to go out and buy Reverend Middaugh a new suit to show my appreciation for all he had done. He thanked me, though his mood quickly shifted from grateful to serious.

'Duane, you've made wonderful strides in your life. I am so proud of you, son. Have you given any thought about what you want to do with your life when all of this is behind you?'

I wasn't sure how long a sentence I would receive. I was told I could serve anywhere from five to ninety-nine years in prison. The trial was nearing. I had spent the past year and a half doing nothing but thinking about my future. The Sunday before I gave the reverend his suit, I went to Brother Love of the First Assembly of God in Lubbock to preach to his congregation and tell them my story of redemption. I stood in the back, still feeling like a sinner in my leather biker clothes and long hippie hair. I noticed a guy who looked a lot like me go forward during the altar call. Eight people, including a grandmotherly woman with silvery white hair, were praying over this man. He was on his knees, begging Jesus to forgive him. He wept as he asked for God's love. I had never seen anything like it. A tough biker just like me, brought to his knees!

I was next in line. I got a little nervous, wondering if I would have the same reaction. The old lady placed her hand on top of my head. She leaped back as if the contact had caused some type of electric shock.

'This young man will lead millions of children to the Lord. People are going to love you.' The old woman made her proclamation for several minutes, looking at me with such conviction. She stood firm in her prediction that I was blessed by the touch of the Lord.

Finally she asked, 'What's your name, son?'

'You can call me Dog. I am here to tell my life story tonight.' I rose to my feet.

'I'm right! Praise Jesus. More confirmation that He truly walks with each of us!'

The preacher came forward, handed me the microphone, and said, 'Speak now.'

I spoke of my jaded history, my upcoming murder trial, and how the Lord showed me the way. I was filled with God's love. I told the story of Jonah and the whale. I said I felt like I had been in the belly of that whale.

'If anyone here has lost a loved one or you need me, come forward.' The words spilled from my mouth, but they came from God's love in my heart. This was the first time I had ever done something like this, and I thought it would be a short altar call, but the entire congregation came up. I had no idea how talking about my life and mistakes could help others. Afterwards, I was physically exhausted. My clothes were drenched in sweat from my energetic testifying.

So, when Reverend Middaugh asked me about my future, I turned to him and said, 'I think God wants me to preach His word.'

The reverend looked as surprised to hear my proclamation as I was to make it. Previously, if someone had told me I would want to become one of God's great messengers, I would have lit another joint, taken a big long drag, and laughed in his face. But I truly believed this was my calling.

Unfortunately, I was the only one who heard God's call. When I pursued my dream, the elders at the Assembly of God church turned me down. After all, I was still an accused murderer. I was destroyed by their rejection. I thought they were all a bunch of hypocrites, because I believed sinners belonged in church. They didn't see it that way.

My trial began a few weeks later. Despite the certainty that I was going to prison, I was determined to stay on my path. I thought I had a good chance of beating the rap. My lawyer, Bill Kolius, called several witnesses, including Reverend Middaugh, Ruben, and Cheryl. Donny's lawyer wouldn't let him testify for me, saying it would hurt his own case.

My lawyer also called a famous lawyer by the name of Richard 'Racehorse' Haynes, who testified on my behalf. He made a name for himself by orchestrating dramatic courtroom scenes where he created doubt in an otherwise certain jury. In one famous case, he told the jury that the dead wife of the man he was representing was about to walk through the door. The jury heard a woman walking towards the court-room. When the door opened, it wasn't her. But, he told the jury, if they believed for one second it might have been, they had to acquit his client for murder. Racehorse Haynes told me I had nothing to worry about, but I was still scared.

A friend was supplying me with a steady flow of Valium to keep me calm throughout the trial. To be honest, I was completely spaced out the entire four days. The hippie I threw out of the car the night of the mur-der showed up to testify against me. He told the jury I told him to get out because I didn't want him to be in on the plan, because he wasn't a Disciple brother. I was the only outsider on trial. The rest were local Pampa kids. I didn't stand a chance.

In his closing statement, the DA advised the jury that Texas law was very clear on one point, which would be my downfall. He said, 'Ladies and gentlemen, the law states that if the defendant was present during the crime, then he is guilty.'

It didn't take the jury very long to make their decision. Within a few hours of adjourning to deliberate, they returned with their verdict: Guilty of first-degree murder.

Judge McIllheney was the personification of what a Southern judge should look and act like. He was larger than life. He spoke in a deep, serious Southern drawl. He took his oath and his responsibility to uphold the laws of Texas very seriously. He wasn't the type of judge to show mercy.

On 10 August 1977, Judge McIllheney sentenced me to five years under supervision of the Texas Department of Corrections. I had until the end of the month before I would be taken into custody and shipped off to the Huntsville Penitentiary.

When the others got their day in court, the verdicts were pretty much the same. All of us were found guilty of first-degree murder. Cheryl was given five years probation, and Ruben was sentenced to ten years pro-bation. Because he pulled the trigger, Donny was sentenced to do ten years of hard time.

While waiting to go to prison, I spent the bulk of my time high, try-ing to avoid the inevitable. Reverend Middaugh did his best to convince me not to give up hope. He attempted to help me find the courage to stay strong in my faith and to trust in the Lord, but I was filled with doubt. I was now a convicted killer. The courts branded me an outlaw. In my mind, I was condemned to hell. I told the reverend to get out of my house. I didn't want to face him or all the good he stood for. I didn't feel worthy of his kindness or support. He genuinely appeared hurt by my words. I'll never forget the look on his face as he turned to walk away. At the time, I didn't much care what he thought. I was reckless and was once again spinning completely out of control.

I wanted revenge. I wanted to say things to God one shouldn't say.

'Murder one, God?' I screamed and shook my fists in the air.

'Well, screw you. Who cares about You, God? What else can You do to me? Lord, if you can hear me, I don't care what You do any more. I hate you!'

Before they took me into custody, I wanted to show the Pampa Police Department they had messed with the wrong guy. My life was ruined. Of course, it was *their* fault, not mine. I'd show them who was boss. After a few drinks and a couple of joints, I got an idea to seek my revenge by convincing two of my Disciple brothers to follow me to the city maintenance grounds where I used to work. We proceeded to dump gasoline all over the tool shed and a bunch of city maintenance trucks, and then lit a match. We destroyed $380,000 worth of equipment. I didn't feel it was enough to cover the damage that had been done to my life. I needed more revenge. I craved further redemption.

I was concerned that LaFonda would be strapped for money when I went to prison, so I got an idea to report my Subaru stolen after I torched it in a nearby vacant lot. That way, LaFonda could collect the insurance money, and I could cover my ass from the fire I had set earlier that same night.

I walked away from the vacant lot without ever looking back. My car was gone. My life was over. I wanted to die. How the hell did I get here? I walked three and a half miles asking myself that question over and over and over again, until I finally got home and passed out.

I awoke the next morning to the sound of loud banging on my front door. It was the cops. I was blurry-eyed and hungover.

I cracked open the door, half-dressed and half-awake.

'Good morning. Mr Chapman?'

'Who's asking?' I could see it was a cop, but it wasn't anyone that I recognised.

'Uh. Yes, sir. I see here that you reported your car stolen last night. Is that correct, sir?'

'Yeah. So?'

'Well, sir, it's still smouldering in a nearby lot. Seems someone lit your car on fire.'

'Aww. Man. Damn. I loved that little car.' I was one syllable short of sarcastic. I didn't want to appear too smug.

'Well, you see, Mr Chapman, it ain't that simple. We have witnesses who saw you light the match at the dump last night. We have reason to believe you torched your own car and reported it stolen to collect on insurance.'

I took one step closer to the arrogant son of bitch and said, 'Oh, yeah? Prove it!' I didn't care. I was already going down for murder one. What was a little arson charge on top of that?

'Fuck off.' I slammed the door and went back to bed. As I tried to go back to sleep, I thought about what I had said to God the night before. It probably wasn't a good idea to say bad things to the Lord. The next day, they threw me in jail without bail.

My lawyer, Bill Kolius, came to see me in jail and informed me that the Pampa police had enough evidence to prove I burned the dump. My only alternative was to accept a plea bargain from the DA to do five years in jail with no chance to appeal the murder case. Bill told me I could possibly win an appeal, but it might take as long as three years. If I accepted the plea bargain, with good behaviour, I'd be out of prison in less than two. He actually thought a couple of years behind bars would do me some good. As he described it, it would be like going to boot camp. Some tough boundaries and discipline might help get me on track to lead a more productive, honest life. Despite my ambivalence, I took the deal.

When the judge sentenced me he said, 'I hereby sentence you to five years of hard labour to the Texas Department of Corrections. You are hereby remanded to the custody of the Sheriff's Department herewith, to be extradited very soon to Huntsville State Penitentiary.'

I grabbed LaFonda like the day we got married and walked arm in arm with her. I turned to the judge and said, 'Your Honour, I can hold a snuff can over a bear's ass for five years.'

The judge took one look at me and said, 'Good luck!'

# CHAPTER TEN

# Welcome to Huntsville

Sheriffs from the Pampa Police Department put me on a bus with a load of other prisoners to Amarillo before going on to Huntsville. The windows on the bus didn't open, so the lack of air, combined with the intense heat, made me really sick. Once I got to the Amarillo facility, I was thrown into a holding room and ordered to put on prison whites. This was my introduction to hell.

'I ain't gonna wear that,' I barked at them.

The guards exchanged a look. 'Oh, you ain't, huh?'

Two guards took hold of my Levi's and literally tore my jeans right off of my body. Before I knew it, they'd almost raped me. I told them the only thing they were going to get from me was a dying quiver.

Afterwards, one of the guards smiled wide. 'You think you can take off your shirt, or would you like us to do that for you too?' I got their message loud and clear.

I was taken from the holding cell in Amarillo to another facility in Dallas before boarding the final bus. The sweltering trip to Huntsville gave me a migraine headache that made my head spin. I gritted my teeth and puked my guts out the whole way. I have had terrible migraines my whole life.

When we arrived at the prison gate, I saw the razor wire, the barking dogs, and all the guards up in the towers with their rifles. It scared me to death. This wasn't the Pampa county jail. Huntsville was the real deal. I was rehabilitated right then – scared absolutely straight.

As soon I arrived, I was issued my prisoner number. From that day on, I was simply known as prisoner Chapman, 271097.

From a raised platform, the warden looked down over me and all of the rest of the new inmates. We were all now citizens of the Texas Department of Corrections. No rights, no liberties, no justice at all. The warden was a tall, thin Texan in an oversize white felt cowboy hat and mirrored aviator sunglasses. This particular warden ran the evaluation centre, which we called the Fish Tank, the first stop for all new inmates.

'Now listen up! The word prison is derived from the word punishment. And that's what we're here for. We don't give a shit about trying to rehabilitate y'all. We are in the punishment business, not the rehabilitation business. You will not make a move unless we say. You will not breathe unless we say. You want to be some tough guy and try and make trouble? My men and I will open your eyes to a new level of suffering and pain. Now, any of you who thinks he's a badass or is a fuckin' faggot, step up.'

During the two-day bus trip from Pampa, I'd already been labelled a troublemaker, so a wave of fear hit me when I noticed the bus driver whispering into the warden's ear. A scowl came over the warden's face. I had a terrible a sinking feeling in my gut. The warden yelled, 'Where's prisoner Chapman?'

I didn't want the other prisoners to think I was queer, so I raised my voice to everyone within earshot and said, 'I'm stepping forward because I am one hundred per cent badass.'

'There you are, Chapman,' the warden said, staring me down. 'You've already earned the privilege of spending your first night at Huntsville in the shitter.'

Uh oh. I knew all about the shitter, also known as the hole or solitary confinement. It was a dark and dingy eight-by-eight cell with a hole in the ground for a toilet. The unbearable stench in the summer heat was the best thing I could say about being in there. The immediate isolation was horrible. Instantly, I knew my life was no longer my own. I made my way through that first night by crying and praying. I didn't sleep a wink.

The next morning, I was allowed to rejoin the other inmates. Then we were given a series of tests and interviews to determine which farm we were sent to. The cold-blooded killers and psychos were sent to a facility called Burning Ham. It had a reputation as the most terrible farm at Huntsville, where prisoners rumbled to the death practically on a daily basis. The younger, less threatening inmates were placed in a farm called Clemmons – also known as the Grab Ass Farm, because everyone was constantly grabbing ass and fighting. The old and handicapped inmates got put out at Wynn Farm, and there was a prerelease camp for the short-timers called Jester One. After Jester One, there was Jester Two, also known as Kindness, because it wasn't as harsh as the other Huntsville farms.

On my first day at the Fish Tank, I met a stocky guy from Pampa named Bobby White who had been in and out of the joint before, so he knew the ropes.

'Hey, kid, you're gonna learn the hard way that the tough-guy routine doesn't mean shit here. One thing in your favour is that you're in for murder one.'

I didn't understand why he said that, so I asked Bobby, 'How's that good for me?'

'Killers are the most feared and respected inmates in prison, because everyone already knows you're a killer. They ain't gonna mess with you.' Good to know. Bobby also warned me that the wardens were going be asking me lots of questions and testing me to determine which farm I'd get sent to. He said, 'When you answer, make them think you're Jesus Christ.'

'What do you mean?' I asked.

'You want to get shipped out to the Burning Ham? You heard the stories about that place? It's stacked with cold-blooded killers. They'd eat you alive out there. Jester Two is where you want to be. So, how do you reply when they ask you, "You walk in on your woman fucking your best friend. What would you do?"'

'I'd slaughter both of them right there.'

'See, now, that's not the right answer. Remember, you're Jesus. He would forgive both of them right away. No killing.'

I totally understood what Bobby was saying. His advice saved my ass. It got me shipped out to Jester Two, just like I had hoped.

Make no mistake about it – hard labour meant hard labour in Texas. All the farms at Huntsville expected their inmates to be self-supporting, and Jester Two was no exception. Inmates who didn't work didn't eat.

As soon as I arrived at Jester Two, I got sent to my dormitory, where I was given a hoe-squad number and a bunk assignment. They stuck all of the complete screwups in Squad Number One and then sorted the rest of us out to the other nine squads. I got put in Hoe Squad Three.

Early in the morning, the lieutenant would bust in shouting, 'Three Hoe . . . in the hall!' When the squad was lined up, they would march us out.

One of the other Hoe Squad Three inmates turned to me and said, 'You might think you know hard work, boy. But I know you ain't never seen nothing like this.'

I just laughed at him. The next two hours of gruelling fieldwork quickly changed my attitude. I found hell on earth chain-ganged in the fields of Texas. Each given a long hoe, we were lined up side by side. Then we cut grass. We called it 'hoe and go'.

If you stopped working for a second, there were inmates called strikers who beat the hell out of you. When we were allowed our first water break, a Mexican guy ran up and kicked me right in the face while I was resting. The guards sat back and ignored what was going down. He caught me off guard, and I was too damn tired to hit him.

Later, a black guy pulled me aside and asked, 'Are you gay?'

'What the . . . ? No.'

'You're gonna be tonight unless you fight back.'

I didn't want to lose my good time, so I told him that's why I didn't want to retaliate.

He said, 'It's either that or your asshole.'

The Mexican guy continued messing with me all through dinner. At one point, he walked up and said, 'You just wait, gringo. Tomorrow in the fields, I'm gonna fuck you up.'

I knew I had to get him before he got me, so the next day during our water break, as he put the metal cup up to his mouth to drink, I kicked him *hard* in the face. I tried to take his head off. Each corner of his mouth split back into his cheeks about two inches. Everyone was standing there watching what I'd done. Nobody said a thing.

A big son of a bitch named Espinosa happened to be our field boss that day. Boss Espinosa was a rugged man who could have kicked the crap out of any inmate around, so everyone gave him plenty of respect.

He gathered all us inmates together and said, 'All right, boys. Now who's the one who went and cut the Mexican in the face?' For some stupid reason, I stepped forward.

'Congratulations, Chapman. You'll be at the front of the line tomorrow.'

The troublemakers got sent to the front of the line. They were there to set the pace for everyone in the field. Any falling behind or slacking off and the strikers would step in and bust them up. Afterwards, they would toss what was left of the guy into an old wagon and take him directly to the shitter. There was no stopping at the infirmary for medical attention.

After only two days, I began physically breaking down. On the first day, my hands were already horribly bleeding from gripping the hoe. I tried wrapping them with rags, but it didn't make much of a difference.

They bled straight through.

My survival instinct told me I'd best make friends with one of the strikers. If I didn't, it would only be a matter of time before I was going to be on the receiving end of a nasty beating.

I was able to use a combination of my talking skills and faith in God to win them over. Right before lights out, I called one of the strikers over and said, 'Listen, I'm gonna work as hard as I possibly can tomorrow out in that field. But there ain't no way I'm gonna be as fast as every-body else.'

After thinking for a moment, he said, 'We're gonna give you some slack, just a day or two, though. Don't forget that Boss Espinosa is going to be eyeballin' you out there, so you better set a pace or it ain't gonna turn out so good.'

The next morning in the fields, I was a man on a mission. I knew my ass was on the line, so I worked as hard as I could. At the end of the day I could barely stand. As we came back into the yard, Boss Espinosa pulled me aside, 'You're back with your regular hoe squad tomorrow, Chapman.'

What a relief. Gradually, I was learning how to get on the good side of the guards, but fitting in with the other inmates was still a challenge.

# CHAPTER ELEVEN

# Light in the Darkness

When I got to Huntsville in 1977, it was still a segregated prison. The two-storey cellblock had white inmates on one side and blacks on the other. They painted the white section a pale lime-green. It was the kind of colour you found at the hospital. It wasn't a feel-good green.

At night, you could hear the guards off in the darkness patrolling along the tier. I had to angle a little mirror through the bars of my cell to keep an eye on them. I didn't want a guard sneaking up on me if I was doing something I shouldn't be doing, like reading or jacking off.

There was no shortage of opportunities to fight. I felt like I had to keep proving myself to the others, so I fought all the time. The fights usually ended in a draw, which was good because then neither of us was considered a punk.

I'd heard terrible stories about rape in prison. I was only approached one time in the joint. As far as I'm concerned, it was one time too many. One evening while I was cleaning my cell after work, four homies suddenly appeared. They were looking at me like I was fresh meat.

The fattest, oldest one of the bunch said, 'Now, you know what we want, boy. We won't beat ya too bad if you cooperate.'

I should've been freaked out by the fact that these guys were cornering me, but I wasn't. I knew something like this was going to happen at Huntsville sooner or later. I'd been preparing myself for it since the day I arrived.

These ugly brothers didn't scare me. I'd whooped the toughest bikers around.

I yelled, 'What makes any of you ugly motherfuckers think I'm anyone's bitch? I sure as shit ain't! The only thing you're going to be fucking is my lifeless corpse, because I'll fight you all to the death. You might get me, but I'm going to kill at least one or two of you before you do! So, who wants to die today?'

They didn't make a move. They didn't know what they were getting themselves into. I stood with my fists clenched, waiting for them to step up. But they never did.

I was a cocky twenty-four-year-old biker who thought he had all the answers. Everything I did, I did the hard way. I had no idea what the easy way meant. I was now six months into my sentence, and I still hadn't learned to pick my battles.

One day in the cafeteria, I heard a Muslim prisoner talking about how he didn't eat pork because it wasn't clean.

I told him. 'Listen, man, anything that is blessed can be eaten. And it isn't worse than any other kinds of food.'

To prove me wrong, he took a piece of bacon and sealed it in a jar. A couple days later, the Muslims shoved the jar in my face. One of them said, 'What's this look like to you. You see the worms?'

I pushed it away. I was unimpressed by their demonstration. 'That don't mean crap,' I told him. 'You put any kind of meat in a jar and it's gonna do the same thing.'

I didn't know it at the time, but I was seriously pushing my luck. What seemed like minor disagreements were of major importance in the joint, because that was all you had on the inside – right and wrong. Everything else was stripped away from you.

A few days passed, and the same Muslim came walking back up to me with another little jar. It had a piece of beef in it, and there weren't any worms.

'Looks like I proved you wrong,' he said, smiling.

I should've been smart and told him he was right, but I couldn't help myself. I said, 'Well, could be, but your Allah ain't nothin' compared to my almighty God, so go fuck yourself.'

By the look on his face, I don't think it was the answer he expected to hear.

Later that day, the Muslims sent a guy named Whitaker after me. I felt confident going up against him, because we were about the same size. We stared each other down. I always talked all kinds of bull before my fights to try to psych out my opponent.

I'd yell, 'I'm gonna throw a stiff left cross into your nose and a straight jab to your right eye.' As they thought about what I was telling 'em, I'd connect with a flurry of four or five quick punches. Most of my fights stopped right there. Before I made my move, Whitaker started doing the same thing to me. He told me, 'Your jaw's gonna get smashed with an uppercut, then a left to your nose, a big right to your eye.' All of a sudden *blam, blam, blam,* he landed a few on me, but I never went down. I've taken a lot of punches, but I've never felt anything like Whitaker's when he connected. He was the strongest man to ever hit me.

The few punches I landed had no effect on the guy. It was a one-sided fight.

The typical scrap in the joint would go for a minute or two, but the ass-whooping Whitaker put on me seemed to take for ever. If any of the guards saw you fighting, you got thrown into the shitter. But this time the lieutenant of our cellblock stood off to the side smiling as he watched it all go down.

Whitaker was kicking my ass, but I had to hang in for as long as I could, because all the convicts considered him to be the best fighter in the joint.

Because I didn't back down, I earned the respect of the other inmates. Whitaker and I emerged as friends. I was so impressed by his technique that I asked him to teach me how to be a better fighter. Whenever inmates saw us walking together, they'd shout out, 'There goes Salt and Pepper.'

I had finally adjusted to prison life, when my world was turned upside down yet again. A process server showed up at Huntsville to serve me divorce papers. LaFonda had fallen in love with Jim Darnell, one of my best friends.

I was heartbroken. How could that bitch do this to me? After everything we'd been through, I didn't expect her to abandon me, especially for my friend. It was a good thing I was locked up, because I wanted to hurt both of them. And I would have, too. I was filled with rage.

The long days out in the fields were taking whatever strength I had left. I was already an emotionally broken man, and my body was physically breaking down from the stress. It got so bad I bit my tongue so I could spit the blood in a cup and tell the boss I was pissing blood, so I could be sent to the prison hospital. I met a guy there who ate poison mushrooms and had a gut that looked like he was about to give birth. He was slowly killing himself. I was disgusted by the grotesque size of his belly. One day, he asked me to sit with him by his bed. He was almost too sick to speak. He had iodine all over his bed, sheets and clothes. I didn't want to go near the guy, but the Lord told me to go over to him. He said the guy needed me.

'Man, you think there's really anyone out there? You think God is real?' he asked me.

His question made me reconsider my own faith, something I had all but given up on before coming to Huntsville. I had drifted so far away that I wasn't sure if I would ever come back. Before I answered the poor bastard, I asked myself, 'How would the Lord answer?' After a long pause, I said, 'As long as you have faith that He is up there, brother, He will forgive you for your sins.' I must have given him the right answer because he told me he was talking to God. He told Him he was on his way to see Him.

As I got up to go back to my bed, the thin guy in the next bed over started yelling, 'What you sayin' that bullshit to him for? You two stupid pricks! There ain't no God up there! There ain't nothing up there!'

I told him, 'Don't say that. What else is there to believe in in a place like this, the devil? If you believe in the devil, boy, he'll surely get you.'

At the moment, I feared that poor bastard. Yet, I felt God's hand upon my heart. I had opened myself up to Him and He was there. I knew I never wanted to be without Him or my faith ever again. His strength, his love, and his guidance would help me cope with losing LaFonda and being trapped in prison.

The next morning, I went to the prison chapel to pray. I prayed for redemption, I prayed for the Lord to ease my pain, and I prayed for the nonbeliever I met the night before. I wanted to commit suicide. I knew the Lord would understand. I felt he would let me into Heaven. 'Please, Lord, bless me with Your presence, Your wisdom, and Your almighty light.' In the chapel, a black man started singing the most beautiful version of 'Amazing Grace' I'd ever heard. It brought tears to my eyes.

On my way back up to the hospital, I caught a glimpse of the man who ate the bad mushrooms, lying dead on a gurney.

When I got back to my bed, the man who challenged me about God was gone too. I asked the orderly what happened. He said, 'Kinda weird. One died right after the other.'

That night, God came into my dreams. He was sitting on a throne and was letting the mushroom guy pass though the gates into heaven. The other guy, who'd been arguing against the Bible with me, was standing there as well, pleading with God. 'Please, Lord,' he said. 'Just give me a chance.' An angel then came over with a movie screen that was playing a movie of him and me arguing about the Bible. The Lord told him, 'I did give you a chance.' A voice came out of somewhere and said, 'I will never turn against you, Dog. Everyone else has, but I will not.'

The officials at the prison couldn't have cared less about inmates' personal issues. There was no sympathy. An inmate was supposed to be in pain, but to the other prisoners it was different when it came to a man losing his family. No one deserved to suffer through that. To help me get through my heartache, the others reached out and offered their support – food, smokes, whatever they could.

It was the darkest time in my life, but I looked to the Lord for guidance and strength. Every night, while other men cried out in pain, I talked to the Lord. I closed my eyes and told him, 'Please show me the way out of this darkness, Lord.'

It was about this time that the Jester Two warden, Curly Horton, began to take an interest in me. He was a short man with a thick head of wavy hair.

He found out I was helping some of the other inmates write letters. One day, he walked up and said, 'Listen Chapman, I want you to tell me the spelling of the word "criminal".' After I spelled it correctly, Horton asked, 'You know anything about numbers, Chapman?'

'Yes sir, Boss.'

'Can you spell names?'

'Yes, sir, Boss.'

'All right, boy. I'm promotin' you to new laundry bookkeeper.'

It was one of the better prison jobs. It sure beat grinding it out all day out in the fields with Hoe Squad Three. My basic duty was to keep everybody's clothes in order.

I needed an assistant, so I convinced the guards to let me take on Whitaker. He helped me interview the incoming cons. If one of them thought he was a tough guy, the bus driver signalled us. While we took down his sizes, the guard on duty would wander away for a while so Whitaker and I could make our move.

When I had enough of their smartass bull, I'd give Whitaker the signal and he'd come up on him like a bad dream.

Kapow! He'd go down with a single punch. Once he pulled himself back up to his feet, I'd start the interview over again. He'd always get it right the second time around.

The new guys didn't understand that *acting* tough and *being* tough were two different things. The smartasses ruin it for everyone. The last thing you need is for some mother to piss off a guard. It was important to let the badasses know the deal as soon as they stepped out of the bus.

I'm glad someone like Whitaker wasn't around the day I arrived at Huntsville.

Even though Warden Horton acted like he hated me, deep down I think he really liked me. The same went for Boss Espinosa and Boss Brunson. Boss Ironhorn, on the other hand, was a different story. Every time I saw him, he'd just glare at me.

One day, Ironhorn came into my cell with another guard and told me to get up against the wall. I did as I was told and he stepped up and looked me over for a moment.

'Boy, you need to shave,' he said.

'Yes, sir, Boss.'

'You got a razor in here, Chapman?'

'No, sir, Boss.'

To tell the truth, I never had to learn to shave. Even though I was twenty-four, I'd never had facial hair. I always had a light peach fuzz moustache that didn't amount to much.

Boss Ironhorn eyed me like I was some kind of redneck moron. 'You don't know how to shave, boy? Your daddy never taught you?'

'No, sir, Boss.'

'All right, Chapman,' he said, letting out a sigh. 'You ain't going into laundry today.'

I couldn't understand why he wanted me to stay in my cell and not go right out to work. I saw him walk over and say something to one of the guards, who immediately took off down the hallway. He returned a minute later and handed something to Ironhorn.

'You're going to learn how to shave, boy,' he said. I could see he had a towel and a razor in his hands. He laid them out on the sink.

My own daddy never taught me how to shave. I don't know why Ironhorn cared so much. For a moment, I thought it might have been a trick so he could cut my throat. I couldn't let him know I was suspicious. I had to go along, or I'd end up in the shitter. But it wasn't a trick.

The way Boss Ironhorn taught me to shave that morning is the exact same way that I shave today. This was the first act of kindness a guard showed me in prison. It meant the world to me. It was a vulnerable moment for both of us. We became friends. After that day, I got anything I needed from Boss Ironhorn.

# CHAPTER TWELVE

# The Barber of Huntsville

One afternoon, a guy came strutting down the hallway in the cleanest set of prison whites I'd ever seen. He looked slick. I noticed all the inmates talking to him with great respect. Even the guards were treating him differently. I stared at him in awe. When he walked past my cell, I realised he was even wearing cologne. I figured he had to be connected to the mob.

I immediately found Boss Bronson. 'Hey, Boss, who is that guy?'

'He's Warden Horton's barber,' he answered. 'He's getting out in two weeks. I heard his job is going to be open.'

'How do I get the barber's job?'

'If you were a barber in the real world, you can put your name in and wait your turn.'

'That's great,' I told Boss Bronson. 'I'm the best barber in Texas.'

He narrowed his eyes a bit. He knew I was bullshitting him, but he nodded anyway. 'Is that right, Dog? Just to be safe, why don't you grab a few books from the library and brush up on your technique.'

The only book I could find in the library that had anything to do with being a barber was from around 1937. I only read it at night. I had to burn toilet paper so I could see. Everyone already knew that I was gunning for the job, and 'the best barber in Texas' didn't want to be discovered with some instructional book.

Finally, a few weeks later, they gave me a chance for the job. All I had to do was pass one test – give Warden Curly Horton a haircut.

A couple of the guards brought me down to the barbershop. It looked like a set from *Gunsmoke*. There were three barber chairs and a coffee table covered with some magazines. The first guy I met was Ronnie Coleman, the shoeshine boy. He showed me where everything was.

As soon as I had put my white smock on, Warden Horton strolled in, flanked by a couple of guards. I hadn't even got a chance to look through the combs or anything. I straightened up immediately and flashed them a smile.

'Come right in and have a seat, Boss,' I said, welcoming him.

I couldn't let the warden see I was nervous. I acted like I had been cutting hair for years. I cut a little here and there and smoothed it all out with gel cream and hairspray. I'd spray and then pat the hair down. When I was finished, the warden looked at himself in the mirror and smiled. 'I'll tell you, boy. Looks like you've done a real good job,' he said.

I'd made it through the test. Or so I thought.

The following morning, I went to the barbershop to start my first full day of work. I'd made sure that my whites were clean and starched, and I even threw on a splash of Aqua Velva for good measure. I was in the middle of checking myself out in the mirror when Warden Horton came in. He looked pissed.

He sat down in the barber chair and glared at me without saying a word.

Finally, he said, 'Last night, I went home and took a shower. When I got out, my wife looked at my wet hair and said that every single hair on my head was uneven. This has to be the worst haircut in the history of haircuts! What in the hell did you do, boy?'

I scrambled. 'Ah, Warden, I figured you were in a big rush, so I thought I would complete the other half of your haircut today.'

He fell silent, probably out of utter amazement that an inmate would tell him such a ridiculous lie. Warden Horton sat in the chair shaking his head.

'Well, Chapman, I'd advise you to fix it, or you'll be spending the rest of your time in the shitter.'

Ah, he said 'wet hair'. So, I wet his hair to even it all out, so I could see what I was doing. If I didn't, I'd find myself back in the fields 'hoeing and going.'

When I was done, he walked over to the mirror and carefully checked my work. I held up another mirror so he could see the back of his neck line. After a long silence, he nodded his head and said, 'Everything looks OK now, but I don't know how you were a barber out in the world.'

I didn't respond.

Later that day, Boss Ironhorn got ahold of me in the hallway.

'Wait up a minute there, Chapman,' he said. 'Somebody told me you're Warden Horton's new barber.'

'That's right, Boss.'

'I want to know about something, though, Chapman. You say you're a barber out in the world, huh? A barber that don't know how to shave?'

I didn't answer. Ironhorn smiled and walked away. I hoped he wouldn't rat me out.

One morning as I was cutting Warden Horton's hair, he said, 'Chapman, I think it might be a good idea if you sign up for A.A. It would certainly help your case with the parole board.'

I'd never heard of A.A. before, but if going to those meetings would help get me out of Huntsville sooner, I was all for it.

I was trying to do the right thing by going to the meetings and listening to the warden, but I nearly blew it all on Mother's Day in 1978. All the mothers were allowed to visit. My momma didn't, because Denver was too far away.

Since I had a knowledge of religion, Warden Horton selected me to recite the invocation prayer. When all the inmates had got seated with their mothers in the auditorium, the warden pulled me aside. He held out a piece of paper with the prayer written on it and looked me dead in the eye. 'Now, boy, I want you to read precisely what I've put down on this paper here. Repeat after thee.'

'Of course, Warden. No problem at all,' I answered.

As soon as he walked away, I looked at the paper. It was all bull. All fake. I knew right away I wouldn't utter a word of it.

The warden stepped up to the microphone and flashed the audience one of his phony grins. 'I want to welcome all of you here today. Please bow your heads as Dog Chapman leads us in prayer.'

I stepped up to the microphone and looked out over the crowd.

'Dear Lord, please forgive us for the sins which we have committed against you. For when we commit a sin against you, we are committing a sin against our families. We know that we've hurt our loved ones, especially our mommas, whom we love desperately despite our sins. Lord, in our hearts You know we are good men, because we come from good women. Please bless our mommas who are here with us today and those who could not be, whom we love just the same. Lord, sometimes we have disagreements with the guards, but they know they can never talk about our mommas. In your name, oh Lord. Amen.'

When I finished, there wasn't a dry eye in the auditorium. Well, except for Warden Horton's, of course. He had a crazy look on his face.

When I got back to my cell, I began gathering my things. I was pretty sure my defiance had just bought me a one-way ticket to the shitter. It wasn't long before the lieutenant showed up at my cell.

'Consider it your lucky day, Chapman. Looks like the warden's gonna cut you some slack. You can start unpackin'.'

A minute later, Warden Horton showed up. He stood in the doorway to my cell and told me, 'Somewhere along the line, Chapman, we've had a failure to communicate. You just rocked this rock we live on. I provided you with the prayer that's supposed to be read and you say some other crap you just make up. I've got mommas that are still bawling out there. I even got lieutenants that were crying out there, Dog. I just can't have that.'

I was worried the Mother's Day massacre would ruin any chance I had for my upcoming parole hearing. Ten months after getting to Huntsville, I met with the parole board for the first time. I was nervous as hell. The other inmates said it didn't really mean shit. All you had to do was sit there and try not to say anything stupid. The hearing went even quicker than I expected. The board glanced at my paperwork, then closed the file and said they were giving me a 'setoff' for ten months. This meant I would be given another hearing at that time. Later, all the jail administrators said what the board had done was the weirdest thing, because typically they gave you a setoff for at least a year. It didn't add up. They also said they had never seen parole for first-degree murder raps in Texas.

Ten months was a long time for me to be without a woman. I was completely desperate – and desperate times call for desperate measures. It's no secret that inmates masturbate all the time.

One day I got an idea. First, I went down to Supply and grabbed an extra mattress, which I sliced an opening in. Next, I took some calf liver from the guards' kitchen and stuffed it into the hole in the mattress. I strategically placed a poster of Raquel Welch next to the hole. After me and Willie had our go-round, I charged the brothers to take a turn on it.

It wasn't just about the sexual desire. It was much more than that. It was a longing for a woman's affection. In prison, just a letter from a woman could get you hard.

One day I met a guy named Lightning Eddie. His sister's friend started sending me letters, and she'd put a little spray of perfume in the envelope. I couldn't get enough of that scent. I taped the letter to the grate of the fan I had and let the smell fill my cell. I'd sit back on my bunk and take deep breaths. It immediately took me to another place, and a warm feeling washed over me. I cried for what I was missing. The perfume was like a powerful drug I couldn't get enough of.

Once Huntsville became desegregated, I was moved to what was once the black cellblock. I shared my perfumed letters with the brothers. They stopped by my cell and asked me, 'Damn, boy! What is that?'

I'd say, 'Have a seat, stay a minute, and have a whiff. No jerking off in here though!' On occasion, there could be four or five of us packed into my cell, sitting in complete silence, lost in our own fantasies.

When Christmas came, Boss Espinosa came down to my cell and handed me a brown bag.

'Merry Christmas, Chapman,' he told me. He kept a hard look on his face to let me know he was still the boss even though it was a nice gesture. When he walked away, I opened the bag and found a white handkerchief full of the scent of a woman's perfume. That hanky became my most valued possession. It offered me an escape in my otherwise cold, lonely world of prison.

# CHAPTER THIRTEEN

# Free as a Bird

One of the biggest inmates in Huntsville was a black guy everybody called Bigfoot. He was so big, he wore a size sixteen shoe! When Whitaker and I checked him into Huntsville, there weren't any shoes big enough to fit his feet. That's why we started calling him Bigfoot.

One morning, Ronnie Coleman and I were on our way to the prison barber shop when we spotted him in line with some other inmates from Jester Two waiting for mail call.

It was standard procedure for the guards to screen everyone's mail before they delivered it to inmates. If someone was getting bad news, the guards would tell him to step out of line. They'd surround him just in case he tried to run away. Inmates ran all the time when they'd read their momma or daddy died or their wives were leaving them. They always tried to make a break for the nearby creek to try to escape.

Today was Bigfoot's day for some bad news. They said, 'All inmates with mothers still alive, take one step forward. Not so fast, Bigfoot.' His mother had died. The guards told him to step out of line, but they couldn't get themselves into place before Bigfoot went berserk. The guards were unnecessarily cruel. Boss Espinosa tried to get him by the arm and drag him away, but Bigfoot tossed him to the ground like he was a little kid. Before the other guards could get him to the ground, Bigfoot was already in a full sprint. He was making a break for the creek. Lieutenant Hillegeist, whom we called Big Lou, drew his .38 and took aim at Bigfoot as he ran. We all knew he had the right to shoot the escaping convict.

'Don't, Big Lou!' I yelled, without even considering what I was saying as I turned my back to him to make a run after Bigfoot. I swear I heard the click his of gun being cocked and felt the bullet pierce my body, but Big Lou never pulled the trigger.

Ronnie and I took off down the road. I was no track star, but Ronnie was fast. I called his sprint the African strut. There was no doubt in my mind that Big Lou would have shot to kill. Bigfoot had already made it to the creek by the time Ronnie caught up to him. Ronnie tackled Bigfoot from behind, but Bigfoot just popped right back up. Before he could make another break for it though, I was right on top of him. Ronnie pushed Bigfoot on to his stomach, while I got Bigfoot's arms behind his back. By that time, Big Lou had found us.

He tossed his handcuffs down to me and said, 'Hook him up, bounty hunter.'

I slapped the cuffs on Bigfoot's wrists. Ronnie and I tried to walk him back towards the prison with dignity. After we handed Bigfoot off to the guards, I looked over and saw Ronnie had a scared look on his face.

'Man, I think we messed up,' he said. 'They're going to kill us back in the yard for what we did.'

Warden Horton must have felt the same way, because he told us he had no choice but to transfer us to another farm right away. He knew what was going to happen to us once we were put back in the population. I pleaded for him to give us one night to straighten everything out with the other inmates.

It took a lot of fast talking, but Horton agreed. I told Ronnie we needed to make sure all the inmates understood that Big Lou had a gun pointed at Bigfoot. We weren't rats, we saved his life.

That night in the yard, all the inmates were staring us down. Ronnie and I knew we had to act fast before anyone had the chance to make a move on us. We approached a group of Muslims. As we got closer, one of them said, 'You two are as good as dead.'

Ronnie sat down at the far end of the table. 'Fuck that, nigga. Me and Dog saved Bigfoot's ass. Big Lou could have put a bullet in his head, but Dog stopped him. And Big Lou could have killed Dog right there. Bigfoot tried to make a run for it. That nigga should be happy he ain't dead right now.'

Another one of the guys looked over at me. 'Is that how it all went down, Dog?'

'They told Bigfoot that his momma was dead,' I said. 'He went crazy and took off running for the creek. I didn't want to see Big Lou have to shoot him because his momma died.'

The Muslims seemed satisfied by our explanation. It was a great relief, because we knew they'd spread the word.

I found all sorts of gifts outside my cell the next morning. The inmates

74

left me lighters, cigarettes, coffee, and sandwiches as tokens of gratitude. I hid it all in my cell as quick as I could, because I was worried Big Lou would write me up for contraband. He pulled me aside but didn't come down on me. He told me, 'Well, bounty hunter, looks like your bread is buttered.'

By leaving the gifts, the inmates let me know I had done the right thing, and they also lifted my spirits at a time when I desperately needed it. After that, all the inmates looked at me different than before. They appreciated what Ronnie and I did in saving Bigfoot. My nickname became 'Dog the Bounty Hunter'.

A year into my sentence, I had the privilege of cutting Head Warden Jaka's hair. During the haircut, he asked me about my parole hearing. I told him about the setoff the board gave me. I also told him the story of what happened the night of the shooting that landed me in Huntsville.

I could tell Warden Jaka was paying extra-close attention as I spoke.

The following day at count time, the guard yelled, 'Ain't no barber today! Everyone else on the line!'

Everyone started out for work. I remained in my cell. I didn't know why, but I had a feeling something bad was about to go down.

'Is there a problem, Boss?' I asked.

The guard didn't say a word.

Once everyone else filed out, the goon squad came into my cell wearing full body armour and holding shotguns. 'The warden don't like being lied to. We're taking you to the shitter.'

I kept my head down and quickly gathered my things.

As I was leaving my cell, I looked over to where Boss Ironhorn was standing and asked, 'Do you think when I get out, Boss, I can get my old job back?

'I can't promise you anything. I'll see what I can do, Chapman.'

Luckily, the guards came for me the next morning.

After hearing the story I told him that day, Warden Jaka thought I had to be lying. He didn't understand why I would be given five years for murder when I was half a block away from the crime, waiting in a car. Later on, I was told that the warden eventually made a call to Sheriff Rufe Jordan, who explained what really went down on that terrible night of the shooting.

Where mercy is shown, mercy is given.

Not long after, Big Lou got me out of my cell and told me, 'Chapman, your bread is buttered.' That's it. Nothing else. One day in December,

Lieutenant Elliot came to me and said my parole papers had come through. I was scheduled to be released on 6 February 1979.

I was stunned. I was overcome with emotion. I only served eighteen months of my five-year sentence. It was nothing short of a miracle.

The board required that I present a parole plan to them before setting me free. They wouldn't release me until I had a permanent address so they knew where to find me on the outside. I told the parole board I was all set to go to my mom and dad's, even though I hadn't secured those plans with my folks. I left home when I was fifteen years old, and I've never looked back. But now I was a grown man with nowhere else to go. Much to my surprise, Flash said to come home.

The men I met inside those prison walls of Huntsville were the strongest, most loyal men I have come across in my entire life. They were my brothers. Of course, there were parts of life in jail that were a complete living hell. But all the time I spent with the other inmates, the stories they told and the lessons they taught me, were more important than anything I had learned before going in.

I got the education of a lifetime in Huntsville. It prepared me to confront any situation without having to go look up some answer in a textbook. All I had to do was think back to the times with Boss Ironhorn, Bigfoot, Warden Curly Horton, and Whitaker. It was a time when every choice had a sudden and often horrible end result. Accepting the consequences of my actions taught me the true meaning of responsibility. The Texas Department of Corrections broke me down and built me back up again. They taught me what it means to truly be a man. To this day, when I am overwhelmed or confused by all of the things going on in my life, I look back on my time in Huntsville for answers and guidance.

I wore an ear-to-ear grin on my last day. I was getting my things ready when I spotted Boss Ironhorn walking by. I probably should have gone about my business, but I was too excited.

'How ya doin' there, Boss?' I asked him.

He immediately stopped and whipped his head around. 'What in the fuck did you just say to me, boy?' he shouted. 'Are you being a smartass? Up on the wall now! I don't want to hear another word out of you, Chapman! There's a difference between going home and being home, boy. And for the moment, you are still mine.'

At first, I couldn't understand why Ironhorn was so pissed off at me that day. It took me a long time to figure out that he didn't want me to have any fond memories of Huntsville. He hoped I would never be back.

# CHAPTER FOURTEEN

# Going Home

The day I got out of Huntsville, I was handed a cheque for two hundred dollars, along with the personal belongings I had when I went in. I didn't have much – just an old pair of Levi's, a pair of boots, and my old, tattered chain wallet. I was told it is a Huntsville tradition to kneel down in front of the large clock we inmates called Big Ben and flip it the bird, so when I got out, I followed suit.

My next order of business was to get my cheque cashed. The prison preacher had a small trailer set up right next to the clock where he'd cash inmates' cheques – for a 20 per cent surcharge. That rotten son of a bitch knew most of those guys were leaving helpless and homeless. Some of them had been in for fifteen or twenty years. Two hundred bucks is all they had to their name. I thought it was a scumbag move, so I wouldn't let him cash my cheque.

I needed cash to get far away from Huntsville as fast as I could. I went into town to buy a cheap suit. I showed the clerk my discharge papers saying I was on parole for murder and then handed her my cheque. Her hands were shaking when she gave me back my change.

Once I had money, I decided to get myself a thirty-dollar whore. Then I was able to find a .25 automatic for twenty bucks. I was going home to shoot Jim Darnell, the bastard who stole LaFonda. Before I left Huntsville, I told the warden to save my cell. I was sure I'd be back soon. I wanted to shoot the son of a bitch dead. I was a man on fire, obsessed with vengeance. The only information I had was that they were still living in Pampa. My plan was to go back to Denver, get a car, and drive down to Texas to hurt them both.

I hopped a bus from Huntsville to Dallas, where I bought a one-way plane ticket to Denver for ninety dollars. I was almost bone-dry out of money. Mom and Dad were picking me up at the airport. Somehow, I got through security with my gun stuffed down the backside of my pants. I figured I could distract the head of security if I walked up to him and flashed my parole sheet that said I was out on murder one, so he would motion me on through without a pat-down. I was cocky, arrogant, and stupid. If I had been caught with a concealed weapon, I could have gone right back to prison. I wasn't thinking right. I was still in my convict frame of mind. Living inside the prison taught me many things, but one of the most important was how to survive in a world of criminals. You have to think like one, live like one, and eat, sleep, and breathe like one if you want to stay alive. The transition to being a free man would take time and nothing short of a miracle.

I hadn't had a drink in almost two years. The moment I got on the plane I ordered up a couple of tiny plane-size bottles of vodka and slammed them, blam, blam. Then, I ordered a couple more. Fifteen minutes into the flight, I was drunk off my ass. I noticed a tall, red-haired man seated next to me at the window. Now, as long as I can remember, I never got along with redheaded guys. They were the whitest kids in school. For whatever reason, they used to pick on me the most, calling me 'half-breed' and Injun. So, when I noticed the guy sitting to my left, my defences went straight up, thinking we were going to rumble.

I was about to slam my fifth vodka when I felt the redheaded man put his hand on my arm.

'Where you going?'

I looked straight at him and said, 'You ever hear that song, "Hey Joe, where you going with that gun in your hand?"' He nodded his head yes. 'Well, I'm going to shoot the man that stole my wife.'

I began to tell him my whole life story. I found myself talking openly and freely. I hadn't felt that comfortable in years. He seemed genuinely concerned for my well-being. He tried to comfort me with his kind words and warm way of talking. 'God's got a plan for you,' he said. He seemed to know something I couldn't begin to understand.

'I'm not sure I'm following you, friend.' I was too drunk to put a lot of thought into what he was saying.

'God has huge plans for your life. Hang in there.'

Whatever. God wasn't even on my radar screen. I had given up hope and faith when I was in jail. I was so consumed with revenge and hate, I didn't have the desire to think about God's great eternal plan.

By the time we landed in Denver, though, I began to think about trying to do something better with my life. I turned to say goodbye to the redheaded gentleman, but he was gone. As I disembarked, I asked the stewardess if she had seen the guy sitting next to me.

'Sir, the seat was empty. There was no one sitting next to you.'

I thought she was crazy. 'No. I was seated on the aisle, and he was sitting in the window seat. Tall guy. Red hair. We talked the entire flight.'

The stewardess looked at me as blank as a sheet of paper. 'No, sir. There was no one there. You spent most of the flight talking to yourself.'

Mom and Dad were waiting for me right outside the gate in Denver. Mom and I hugged first. I didn't want to let go. It felt so good to hold my mom. Dad wasn't a hugger. He put his arm around my shoulders, pulled me close with his huge hand, and patted me a few times. Dad had enormous hands. When he grabbed something, it was gone. His hip brushed against the gun I had shoved in my front pocket.

'No, Duane. Not like this.' Dad reached down to pull the gun from my waist.

'I know, Dad, I know that now. Wait, I want you to meet a friend I made on the plane.' Once again, I looked around for the redheaded man, but he was gone.

My mother could see I was confused. 'Duane, what happened?'

I told her about the man on the plane. I was sure he was there, but the stewardess said no one was sitting next to me. I didn't understand why I was so mixed up.

'Son, I believe you were sitting with an angel.' Mom put her arm around me as we walked to the car.

A lot of the guys I met in prison often talked about how they could see angels. I wondered why they could and I never could. I met a preacher in prison who told me the only way to see one of God's angels was to pray – pray as hard as I could. Later that night, I went back to my cell to see if I could summon one up.

'Lord, right now. I want to see an angel. Please, Lord.' Eyes closed, fists clenched, I prayed those words over and over.

All of a sudden, I was overcome by fear. Something terrified the hell out of me.

The next day, I went to see the preacher. I told him what happened.

'Whew. You were summoning up an angel all right, but probably the angel of death. God will show you what you want to see in His own time. What God needs from you right now is faith.'

I never forgot what the preacher said. Faith is what God needed from *me*. I've spent most of my life asking for what I needed from *Him*.

Up until that plane ride home, I didn't think I'd ever see an angel. But I sure as hell have met the devil – more than once. But maybe Mom was right. Maybe the red-haired man was truly a messenger sent by God. Prison stripped me of everything, including my faith. I wasn't sure I'd ever find it again.

On the ride home from the airport, I had to lie down on the backseat. The oncoming headlights were so bright that my eyes couldn't take the light. I kept ducking my head down in the backseat to avoid them.

'Duane, what the hell is wrong with you?' Flash was practically yelling.

'Damn, those lights are bright, Dad.' Other than my time hoeing in the fields, I hadn't seen the sun, moon, stars or headlights in almost two years. The occasional glimpse of the moon I did get on the inside made it look like a dull flashlight.

Anything above a sixty-watt fluorescent bulb was excruciating to my eyes. I was convinced the cars coming the other way were going to crash into us. I was paranoid and scared. I wasn't big, bad Dog Chapman, that's for sure. I began to sweat from nerves and stress.

'Duane, get a hold of yourself, son!' Flash tried to look back from the front seat to see if I was all right.

I just wanted to die.

# CHAPTER FIFTEEN

# Vengeance

My parents fixed up their basement for me to live in when I got back from prison. I spent the first week drunk and high. I hardly ever got out of bed except to pee and eat. I found it really hard to adjust to life outside of prison. I actually thought it was easier to be inside. The strict regimen had been easy to get used to. Total freedom was a challenge. Though I had only served eighteen months, I could barely remember what life on the outside felt like. I had become used to someone else telling me what to do all the time. In fact, I kind of missed it.

When I finally did get out of bed, I was in search of whatever drugs I could find to keep me numb. I got our family doctor to prescribe fifty Valium, which I told him I lost so I could get fifty more.

My mother tried to get me up so I could start looking for a job. At the very least, she wanted me to eat. I was losing weight from not eating. I developed a cyst on my neck from dehydration and too much Valium. I was a pathetic sight. I didn't want to live without my family. I was filled with burning rage towards LaFonda for leaving me while I was in prison. She had my two babies and was shacked up with my former buddy, Jim Darnell. I wanted to kill the son of a bitch. He took my wife and my family. And like a coward, he did it while I was locked up, unable to defend what was mine.

My mom kept telling me I was in love with a memory. She knew my marriage to LaFonda was far from perfect. Still, I couldn't help missing her. One day, my mom came to me and said, 'Son, God will give you everything you desire. His son, His house, His heaven, every blessing, the angels – but He won't give you one thing.'

Curious, I asked, 'What's that?'

'God will not give you His vengeance. God says, "Vengeance is mine.

I shall repay." If you go shoot Jim Darnell, son, you're robbing God of His vengeance.'

I was blown away. How could my sweet, gentle, kindhearted mother possibly understand what I was thinking?

'Duane, if you stick a gun at Jim's head, you're sticking one at God's head.'

Mom understood how I felt, and yet in her heart she had faith that God would take care of business for me. But it would have to happen in His own time. Meanwhile, Mom wanted me to pull myself together. She insisted it was time for me to get out of bed. But I wouldn't budge.

Unbeknownst to me, Mom called up a man she knew named Herman Cadillo, a Kirby vacuum salesman who lived in Denver. He came to the house to see if he could encourage me to go out on the road and sell some vacuums.

I liked him. He was a big, stocky Latino with a crooked smile. Despite his valiant attempts, I wasn't interested. I had no interest in leaving my parents' basement. Not now. Not ever.

Being the salesman he was, however, Herman refused to take no for an answer. He literally picked me up and carried me to his car. Whether I liked it or not, I was going on the road. Our first stop was Fort Morgan, Colorado. He checked me into a cheap motel room and gave me twenty-four hours to come down from the drugs and clean up my act. I guess he didn't know how far gone I was, because it took closer to five days for me to be completely sober. I spent most of the time praying to God to make the pain go away. My heart was shattered and my mind was filled with fog. I needed the Lord to help me get off the drugs and past my hurt.

It took a week, but I emerged drug-free. I was back to my old self. The cyst had subsided, my depression had lifted, and I began to look healthy again. Herman got me back on my feet. I didn't know it at the time, but when Mom called Herman, she gave me one of the best gifts ever. She literally handed me back my life. I found faith, regained self-esteem, and found the courage to forgive Jim Darnell for what he had done.

I no longer wanted to run with the Disciples, but I had to earn a living. Finding a job after prison was hard. No one wanted to hire an ex-con – especially one who looked like me. I was a mean-looking, long-haired biker who wanted to change my life, *not* my looks. Selling vacuums was an easy way to satisfy my need to remain myself. I was my own boss.

Back in my biker days, I'd ride my Harley through town, and grandmas would roll up their car windows. But I was always polite.

I'd pull up and ask, 'Is the bike too loud?'

They'd respond by saying I looked scary.

'Ah, ma'am, it's just the way I look. I'm really a nice guy.'

I'd always smile a big toothy grin before pulling away.

It just goes to show you can't always judge a book by its cover. When it came to selling vacuums, no one seemed bothered by how I looked. It was great. I was emerging from a darkness that had shrouded my life for close to two years. I was rediscovering who I really am. I felt reborn.

# CHAPTER SIXTEEN

# Shotgun Wedding

When I got back to Colorado, I wasn't sure I'd ever find another girl I loved as much as LaFonda. After my self-induced pity party, I wanted to go out and meet some girls. I'm the kind of guy who always has to have a woman in his life. I had a pattern of picking women who are very volatile and high-strung. This time around, I wanted someone different, someone easier to get along with.

I went to a party at a local motel with some biker buddies. I walked into the room and saw Ann sitting by herself. I fell for her on the spot. They ought to teach prisoners to ignore all women for a certain period of time after being released, because, as I can now admit, at that moment, any woman would have looked good.

Ann and I hit it off right away. I asked if she wanted to leave the party and take a ride to the mountains in my truck. I hadn't been with a good girl since I got out. I paid the whore in Texas and called up a few old girlfriends when I got home, but I was looking for a nice girl. Ann appeared innocent, sweet, and very inviting. We drove up I-70 for two hours until we got close to Vail. The sexual tension built as we talked and drove. I couldn't take it any more. I pulled over and we did the wild thing. It was intense. I hadn't felt like this in over two years. I wasn't sure this would be a long-term thing, but Ann was right for the moment.

I smiled all the way back to Denver. I turned up the car radio while Ann sang along to 'Bad Girls' by Donna Summer. She had a sweet, child-like voice.

When I asked where she wanted to be dropped off, Ann said, 'You know I can't go back home now.'

I couldn't imagine why she said something like that. 'Why not, honey?'

Ann wouldn't make eye contact at all. She mumbled something that sounded like she said, 'I'm only seventeen.'

Oh, my God. I hadn't been out of jail more than a month, I was on parole for murder, and I'd just screwed an underage girl.

As the saying goes, 'Seventeen gets you thirty.'

As far as I could tell, the only way out of this was to marry Ann that day. When I asked her about her family, she told me her mom was a Mormon who had been married and divorced five times. I could tell she was a professional divorce artist. Ann explained that she lived with her grandmother, who was her legal guardian.

We could get married that day if I got permission from her grandmother. So I called her to ask permission to marry Ann.

'Well, I don't know.' The old woman didn't have a clue who I was. She'd never heard Ann speak of me. We had only met the night before. Why would she let me marry her granddaughter? I begged and pleaded until she gave me permission. We got our blood tests, filled out some paperwork, and then the judge married us in his chambers.

I called my mom to tell her the excellent news. I don't think she thought it was very good. She was quiet as I pretended I was thrilled to be married again. I didn't love Ann. I married her out of desperation, to keep my freedom.

The hardest call I had to make that day was to my parole officer, Charlie Moss. In the short time I knew him, Charlie had become like a big brother. When he took me on, Charlie told me Colorado only had two murderers on parole. That made me a high profile parolee in the eyes of the state. Charlie worried he might lose his job if I screwed him around. My mother talked him into taking me, so I didn't want to do anything to let either of them down. Every mistake I made, large or small, my first phone call was always to Charlie. I told him everything – probably to a fault. I thought his job was to be there for me, to listen when I needed someone to talk to, and to give me advice. Charlie was quick to remind me that his job was to revoke my parole if I messed up. I thought of him as a friend. He was, but he was also my parole officer. I was praying he would be happy for the good news. Let's just say it didn't go over as well as I had hoped.

He completely freaked out. First, he yelled at me for leaving the county. We had driven to Limon, just over the Denver county line, to tie the knot. I wasn't allowed to freely go anywhere I wanted. I had to check in and get permission to leave the county. My bad.

Second, one of the conditions of my parole was that I couldn't get married. I didn't know that.

Charlie said no one ever asks about that condition until the day they get married. I could tell he was unhappy about my careless execution, but he sincerely wished us well. I was so relieved.

What was done was done. There was no turning back. Turned out Ann got pregnant the first night we met. She moved in, and we tried to make things work. We didn't know each other at all. We were both so young and probably wouldn't have got married if she hadn't been under-age the night we met. When Ann began showing her pregnancy, everything sort of changed. There's something quite magical about a woman carrying your baby, but although I tried to love her and make it work, that magic just wasn't there.

Note to self: don't marry the first woman you sleep with after prison. In fact, you probably shouldn't marry the second, third, or fourth one, either.

It was only later that I found out: seventeen was legal in Colorado!

# CHAPTER SEVENTEEN

# Selling Kirbys

A year after Herman got me started selling Kirby vacuum cleaners, business was so good, I decided to break off on my own. It didn't take me long to really start kicking ass. I got up at five in the morning and didn't come home until eight or nine at night. I set goals for myself, and when I reached those goals, I set the bar even higher. I'm competitive by nature, but selling vacuums brought out the animal in me. If the other guys were selling one a day, I had to sell two. While the other guys were aiming to win the free trips to Mexico, I set my sights on becoming the head of the company. Every couple of months, there was a contest in which you could win a car, a boat, a trip, or whatever. I'd ask how many Kirbys I needed to sell to get the prize.

They'd say twenty-five.

Blam. Done. The boat was mine.

I went on free trips every couple of months. I started taking Zig Ziglar seminars, learning how a millionaire puts his pants on in the morning, so I could imitate every move. I began studying *The Power of Positive Thinking* and reading other inspirational books to help me excel and sharpen my sales skills. Despite my unorthodox appearance and aggressive sales pitch, I rapidly worked my way up the company ladder.

Within a year of leaving Huntsville, I had completely turned my life around. I had money, a new car, a happy parole officer, and a job that made me happy to get out of bed each and every morning.

For the first time in my adult life, I no longer felt like a criminal. I was a legitimate and respected businessman. I liked the way that made me feel. People saw me as Duane, the salesman, not Dog, the killer. I had new-found confidence in everything I did. I fully believed I had paid my debt to society and that my past was in the past. Huntsville would always be a part of my history, but it didn't have to dictate my future. I wanted to get as far away from being #271097 as I could.

When LaFonda found out I was making a pretty good living, she decided to take me to court for back child support that I couldn't pay from before I went to prison until the day I got out. She took my boys away from me and never let me see them. She never asked for money until she discovered how well I was doing. I didn't even know where my boys lived. So why would I give her a penny? I didn't think she deserved the sweat off my brow. The courts disagreed.

I had been fighting LaFonda's request for child support for several months with zero success. When the time came to see Judge Levi again, I asked my mom to drive me to court. If that dumb bastard ordered me to pay up, I was prepared to flat-out refuse. I was pretty sure my decision would land me back in jail. I went to court holding a pair of faded jeans, a black T-shirt, and some rolled-up tube socks, all tied together with my three-inch-wide, worn-out black leather belt.

Judge Levi addressed me firmly and directly.

'Tell me, Mr Chapman, are you here with that payment I asked you to provide the last time I saw you in my courtroom?' He doubted that I had complied with his last request.

'No, sir, I do not have the money,' I stubbornly answered as firmly and directly as he had asked.

The judge took a deep breath as he closely examined my file. I could see him crunch his eyebrows trying to absorb all of the information. I had a long history, which meant we stood silent in the courtroom for what felt like an insanely uncomfortable amount of time. I could hear the second hand on the courtroom clock ticking. It was making me nuts. My future was at stake.

'Mr Chapman, I see here that you were responsible for the recovery of an escaped convict while incarcerated in Texas. Warden Horton praises your efforts for helping with the capture. That's rather unusual for a man with your history. Would you say you're good at tracking down criminals?'

I didn't know what to say. I thought about Judge Levi's question for a minute. 'Well, I've hunted practically my entire life, your Honour. I guess I could hunt anything if I had to.'

I had no idea where this was going. I was in court to talk about child support payments. Why was Judge Levi asking me about tracking down criminals?

'Have you ever heard of a bounty hunter, Mr Chapman?'

Mom and me, 1953

Mom and Dad, 1952

Hiding under the bed

Dad, Mom, Jolene, Paula, and me on Easter, 1959

With my cousin

Aged one with my dog Cookie

**DUANE CHAPMAN, LEFT; MASON SMITH, CENTER, AND DEAN MARTIN SEEK WORK**
About 2,000 hippies are looking for permanent, full-time jobs in Denver area.

# Hippies Eager to Work, But Won't Get Haircuts

**By RICHARD O'REILLY**
Denver Post Staff Writer

"Hippies Wanted." That's the notice a collection of Denver youths want to see in your help-wanted advertisements, Mr. Employer.

A three-member delegation of hippies came to The Denver Post Tuesday with a petition bearing about 70 signatures of their fellows who want jobs—believe it or not.

The trio complained that they are discriminated against because of their long hair.

They said they are quite willing to put on a shirt, tie and clean blue jeans and go to work —but the hair stays.

They already bathe, contrary to popular notions, once a week at least and more often if they're girls, the hippie delegation explained.

"Do we smell?" asked Dean Martin, 19, of Albuquerque, N.M. "You don't see people running around here holding their noses do you?"

For the record, no odor was detectable and nobody was holding his nose.

**WHY JOBS?**

"If we get jobs we can get out of the hole at Barnum Park (a reference to the temporary camp site the city is providing this week for persons who came in for the Denver Pop Festival last weekend and are staying over for a peace march July 4) and rent places to sleep," said Duane Chapman, 16, of 6950 Olive St., Commerce City.

The trio said they are tired of listening to the "straights" complain about how lazy the hippies are.

They said they've been to the Colorado State Employment Service and the day labor outfits seeking jobs, but all they get is "told to get a haircut."

Why don't we get haircuts?

**'WE LIKE IT'**

"Because we like it. If we didn't have long hair, nobody'd know us," Chapman said.

"It feels good," said Mason Smith, 18, of 5620 E. Alameda Ave.

"It's our symbol of peace," Martin said. "Besides, if we clean up then they'll just draft us.

But they do want jobs. They seemed quite serious about that. And they made it clear they feel very discriminated against because of their long hair. They will work full time and permanently, they said.

**WAGE EXPECTATION**

But they do expect the minimum wage. "We don't want nothing for 50 cents an hour or nothing like that," Chapman said.

So, Mr. Employer, just how do you go about hiring the hippies?

You merely insert the phrase "Hippies Wanted" in your classified ad, they said.

"We'll all be looking in the paper," Chapman said. And, he noted, "we" is a potential work force of about 2,000 hippies.

Helping the Hippies (*Article and photo courtesy of* The Denver Post)

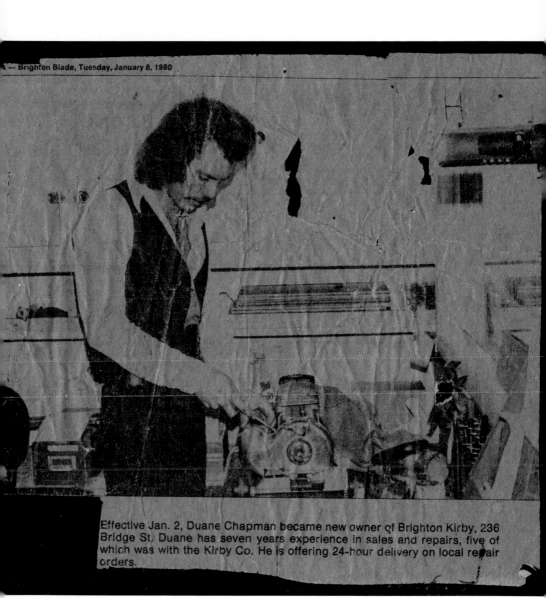

Effective Jan. 2, Duane Chapman became new owner of Brighton Kirby, 236 Bridge St. Duane has seven years experience in sales and repairs, five of which was with the Kirby Co. He is offering 24-hour delivery on local repair orders.

Original newspaper article *(Photo courtesy of* The Brighton (CO) Standard Blade)

Original Kirby card

Mike Chapman
and me at church
just before I go to
prison. I am out on
bail for murder.

With Ken Tweet, 1972

Original Lucero's ID card

AAA Bail Bonds ID card, first bounty hunting company

I had. I knew that a bounty hunter is someone who seeks escaped fugitives in return for money. Unlike traditional law enforcement, a bounty hunter can enter a private home without a warrant. Where I come from, that was called breaking and entering.

I had to laugh because this was the third time I'd heard that term. The first time I heard it was from the man I once met in Pampa who'd left a hundred dollars on my kitchen table after I let him stay the night. Turns out he was a bounty hunter looking for a fugitive. I heard it for the second time at Huntsville after I helped run down Bigfoot. And now, here was Judge Levi bringing it up again in his courtroom.

I was trying to figure out where this was all going before I finally answered the judge. 'Yes, sir. I have some idea of what a bounty hunter does. If you don't mind me asking, what does this have to do with child support?'

The judge laughed and said, 'I've got an idea, Mr Chapman.' He showed me a mug shot of the guy he was looking for.

'You think you can find this guy?'

I looked at the photo. I didn't recognise the punk, but I thought it couldn't be that hard to find him. He didn't look smarter than me.

'Yeah, sure. What the hell.' I knew the surest way to create a belief that you can do something, anything, is to do it. Just once. If you succeed that first time, it's far easier to form the belief that you'll succeed again. You can choose beliefs that limit you, or you can choose beliefs that empower you. One thing I knew for sure: I wasn't paying no damn child support if I didn't have to.

Judge Levi said, 'I'll tell you what, Mr Chapman. You go out and get this guy, and I'll pay the first two hundred dollars towards your child support.'

It sounded too damn good to be true.

'What's the catch?' Why was Judge Levi giving me this break? What was his motivation to help a guy like me? In his eyes, I was a deadbeat dad. It made me very suspicious that it might be a set-up.

'No catch, Mr Chapman. It's pretty simple. You get this guy, and I will put the bounty fee towards your first payment. Have we got ourselves a deal?'

'Yes, sir. I believe we do.'

I went to court expecting the sheriff to treat me like a common criminal. Much to my surprise, I left the courtroom as a man out to *get* a common criminal. Who would have believed it? The sheriff took me across the street to his office, where he handed me a copy of the warrant and mug shots of the wanted man.

I didn't know what to say. I sure as hell didn't know where to begin. This was all new to me. Here I was, in a police station, but this time was different. Now I was on the same side as the law.

The sheriff looked as confused as I felt. He was clearly trying to figure out why Judge Levi did what he did. To be honest, so was I. I didn't know anything about tracking a criminal, but, after years of experience, I did know how a criminal thinks.

When you believe something is true, you can make it real. I was empowered to do something good. I knew I could find the guy. I had already done it once in prison. How hard could it be?

The fugitive Judge Levi asked me to find was a young black guy named Gerald, who was wanted on outstanding warrants and had missed his court date. It was minor stuff. In my book, this guy wasn't even a real criminal. I didn't know any special tricks to bring this guy in, but instinctively I knew what to do.

First I called his momma and said I was from one of the local black radio stations. I imitated the voice of a jive-sounding DJ and spun a little white lie: 'I'm trying to reach your boy because Gerald won our radio contest. All he has to do is come down right now to Stereo City, where we are broadcasting live, and claim his prize: a thousand-dollar stereo of his choice.'

Sure enough, Gerald showed up around three o'clock to claim his prize. I grabbed him getting out of his car. He never saw me coming. It was so easy – except . . .

'What am I supposed to do now?' I turned to my friend David Bautista, who came along to help. I was hoping he knew the answer, because I didn't have a clue.

'I don't know, Dog. Maybe you oughta handcuff him?'

I didn't bring any cuffs – it never even occurred to me – so I removed my belt and wrapped it tight around his wrists. I wedged Gerald in the front seat of my truck, making him sit in between David and me.

I didn't know where to take him, so I drove over to the courthouse, hoping Judge Levi was there. I grabbed Gerald by his shirt collar and dragged him through the hallways up to Judge Levi's chambers. He wasn't there, so I walked across the hall to his courtroom.

I cracked open the door and gave the judge a little wave. I tried to get his attention as he was presiding over another case.

'Pssst. Judge. It's me – Dog.'

He gave me a hard look that basically said, 'Shut the fuck up, you asshole.'

I guessed he didn't recognise me, so I grabbed Gerald and shoved him through the door. Judge Levi's eyes almost popped out of his head. I'll never forget the look of complete and utter shock on his face.

'Jesus Christ, Dog. You got him!'

The judge turned his attention to Gerald, berating the poor bastard for ten minutes. He ordered the bailiff to take him to the sheriff for booking.

'Mr Chapman, I'm not sure what impresses me more – how quickly you caught this guy or the fact you got him at all. Do you know what a bail bondsman is?'

I smiled and said, 'Uh, yes, sir. I've had a little experience with them.' I had. Probably too much! A bail bondsman provides a money guarantee that an individual released from jail will be present in court at an appointed time. If the individual doesn't show up – that is, 'jumps bail' – the monetary value of the bond is forfeited to the court.

'Well, there is a bondsman I'd like you to meet named Lucky. With the way you brought Gerald in, I can safely say he'll give you enough work chasing fugitives to get you current in your back child support.'

It sounded pretty good to me, especially since the job meant I wouldn't have to do time for my back payments.

From ages sixteen to twenty-two, I broke the law. From the moment I caught Gerald, I no longer wanted to. I had to try both ways to know which one was a better fit. I was completely convinced defending the law was a better choice.

# CHAPTER EIGHTEEN

# Lucky

Want to know what makes a bounty hunter? Well, he's a lot like a biker, but to be a really good one, it also helps to be a convict, a rebel and a preacher – all those things rolled into one. And like a good salesman, he never takes no for an answer. He keeps hunting until he finds his man. As ironic as it seemed, my new-found dual careers actually complemented each other.

I did a little research on Lucky before I met him. Word on the street was that Lucky's business was booming, which made him a very unpopular man with criminals in and around Denver. Every now and then, a pissed-off fugitive would put a bounty on *him*. A full-fledged contract. In fact, I had heard there were more than a few times when bullets whistled right past his head. I'm not sure whether they were warning shots or the work of second-rate hit men. It appeared Lucky always lived life on the edge and took too many chances. Somehow, I knew we would really hit it off.

The very first time I strolled into his office, Lucky was screaming at someone on the phone, so he just waved me over towards his desk and pointed to the tattered old leather club chair. He looked like a Mexican hippie who hadn't bathed or shaved for days. He had spent some time in Vietnam, and it looked as if he had seen some hard times in battle. He didn't smell bad; he just had a rough appearance.

When Lucky got off his call, he abruptly shook my hand and said, 'Good to meet you, Dog. Let's get started right away.'

My first target was a familiar face. She was the old lady of one of my Disciple brothers. I hadn't seen her for years, but I knew her man. I figured this would be an easy hunt. I called an old friend, D.B., to see if he knew where the Disciples usually gathered at night. It had been a few years since I ran with these guys. I wasn't sure they still hung out in the same spots. D.B. knew exactly where to go. He drove me in his old Buick LeSabre and parked right up front at a diner just off of 170. I held the photo of the chick in my hand, looking for her before we walked through the door. I wanted to be absolutely sure she was there before we made a move. After all, I didn't want to be careless while dealing with a coffee shop full of Disciples. One false move and my brother status wouldn't mean a thing.

I told D.B. to get the car and bring it around to the back of the place. I wanted him to pull it up real close and keep the engine running.

When I walked through the door, the guys recognised me right away. They only knew me as a fellow Disciple, so I fell right back into that role. They had heard about the ex-sergeant-at-arms on parole for first-degree murder, so I instantly had their attention and respect.

I spotted her old man passed out in one of the booths and made my way over to the chick I was chasing, cool and smooth. I chatted her up real nice.

'Hey, baby. How'd you get to be so pretty? You look familiar. Have we ever met?' I did everything I could to make her believe I was hitting on her. She fell for it hook, line and sinker. I knew if I could get her out to my car, I'd have my first catch.

'Listen,' I finally said. 'I have something real pretty in the car for you. I'll let you pick what you want.' It was a done deal. She took the bait right away. I walked through the back door, gently guiding her with my hand, keeping her close to make sure she wouldn't run if she got suspicious.

'Where the hell's my present?' she asked.

'Oh, it's in there,' I answered, pointing into the front seat. I knew it was too dark for her to see. She cupped her hands to her eyes and leaned in. Before she could get too close, D.B. pushed the passenger door open. I gave her a quick shove and hopped in next to her. It all happened so fast, she barely had time to react. I leaned over the chick to give D.B. a high five. It was too damn easy.

I was half-asleep when my phone rang at home. I was surprised to hear the voice of one of the Disciples I'd come across at the diner. He was asking if I had seen or heard from the chick I picked up earlier that night. He said he was worried some bounty hunter might have snatched her. I told him I talked to her, but I didn't know anything else.

I tried to go back to sleep, but my mind was racing. I no longer saw myself as Dog the Disciple. I had a new identity. My life was in a total turnaround. I liked the way it felt. I was good at this. I knew I could make a career out of it. I lay in bed for the next two hours dreaming of my future as Dog the Bounty Hunter.

I was more motivated than ever to make a name for myself in the business. When I walked into Lucky's office the next morning, he said, 'Here comes the bounty hunter.' I just smiled. Chasing fugitives turned out to be exciting. I felt like I was right back in the days of planning big scores and rolling hippies, except now I was on the right side of the law.

Lucky told me he had a client who skipped out and ran to Vegas. We hopped on a plane later that afternoon. I figured I would get settled into my room and rest for a while before we hit the town. I clicked the television on and listened to an evangelical preacher give a sermon while I unpacked. As I reached for the remote to change the channel, I heard the preacher say, 'I have a feeling there's someone out there whose very existence is about to change. He has a chequered past, perhaps a criminal. You never thought you could turn your life around, but you can. I am here to tell you the Lord has raised His hand and said, "Be healed. For you shall serve Me, as a messenger of My word and faith." If you can hear me, son, the Lord has asked me to tell you to trust His mighty plan. You must honour His wishes, and you shall be greatly rewarded for your service.'

That message was for me. I could feel it through the TV. The hand of God had touched my heart. The Lord was telling me to stay righteous. I couldn't wait to tell Lucky about what I had just heard and went round to his place.

I woke up the following morning to the sound of Lucky banging on my door. I thought he was playing around, trying to get me back for interrupting him the night before. When I opened the door, Lucky was in his underwear in a full-blown panic.

'I ended up passing out last night, and I got robbed!'

This was a major problem, since I didn't have more than seven bucks in my pocket. Neither of us had credit cards, either. Since we flew to Vegas at the last minute, we had only bought one-way tickets. We didn't know when we'd be coming back. It all depended on whether we caught the jump.

Lucky said we had to find the guy we were looking for so we could get the hell out of Vegas. We knew he had skipped town without a cent to his name. My instincts told me we should hit all the soup kitchens in the area around midday. I figured the fugitive had to eat. Sure enough, we found our guy standing in line with his tray at one of the first kitchens we rolled into.

While I was busy cuffing the skip, I noticed Lucky went off to make a call at a nearby pay phone. I put the guy in the backseat of our rental car and smoked a cigarette, waiting for Lucky. When Lucky got back to the car, he told me he had a way to get some cash. He wanted to call the car rental's insurance agent and file a claim for stolen jewellery.

'Are you crazy? Someone robs you blind and now you're lying to the cops. I'm on parole, man. I fuck up again and I'm in big trouble. Why don't we just have your wife send us money for the plane tickets?' I had to convince Lucky that what he was doing was wrong. I tried to reason with him, but he wasn't interested in hearing what I had to say.

Lucky took off his sunglasses and glared at me. 'If I called my wife, I'd have to explain what happened with my other money. This way I get the money clean, and my wife never has to know.'

He let out a long sigh and stared off into the distance. He wouldn't even look at me.

'Fine,' he said calmly. 'I'll drop you off.'

And he did. He took off into the heavy Vegas traffic.

I walked the rest of the way back to the hotel. It must have been at least ten blocks. When I got up to the room, he had already split. I didn't know how I was getting back to Denver. I thought about a movie I had just seen and got a great idea.

I took a shower and put on a pair of nice pants, a silk shirt, and a quick shine on my boots.

Before I left the room, I bowed my head and prayed, 'I know this ain't right, God, but I've run into a desperate situation here. It's a one-time only thing, I promise. But I need to go out there and sell my body for money.' I never thought things could get so low. Tonight, I was Dog the Booty Hunter.

I walked the strip and checked out a bunch of different casinos. I must have looked nervous and out of place, because casino security was eyeing me everywhere I went. I finally worked up enough courage to approach an attractive woman standing at the bar. Right off, she let me know that she wasn't interested in my company. Clearly I was not as smooth as Richard Gere in *American Gigolo*. The pressure was on. The women could see the desperation all over my face.

I threw down my last few dollars for a couple of cocktails at the bar. I needed to relax and think of a new strategy. Not long after, I noticed an elegant older woman sitting a couple of seats down the bar from me. She was probably in her late forties. When she saw me checking her out, she flashed me a smile. Jackpot. I got up, walked over, and sat down next to her. The conversation was brief and to the point.

'Would you like some company?' I asked.

'How much?' she said.

'Usually I charge a little more, but for you, honey, how about ninety-seven dollars?'

She wrote something on a cocktail napkin and placed it in my hand. Without another word, she left and walked off into the noisy casino. I unfolded the napkin. It read: 'Room 216. Come at Midnight.' I didn't know what to make of that, but I sure as hell was looking forward to finding out.

I stayed with her until early the next morning. I was dressed and just about to slip out the door when she clicked on the bedroom lamp.

'Don't forget your plane ticket money. It's on the dresser,' she said in a raspy voice.

I didn't remember telling her that I needed the money for a plane ticket. She propped herself up on her elbows in bed and smiled knowingly at me. 'You're no whore, sweetie. Travel safe and have a good flight back home.'

When I got back to Denver, Lucky and I were able to talk things out. We both had had some time to think. The truth is, he was desperate for my help hunting down fugitives, and I needed the work.

When I first started working for Lucky, he'd hand me two or three cases a day. About a month after Vegas, he was giving me stacks of twenty or thirty at a time. I couldn't understand how all these guys were suddenly jumping bond on him. I'd ask, but he wouldn't say much about the sudden increase in activity. It didn't take me long to figure out he was taking on fugitives from other bail bonds offices and passing them on to me. I'd hunt them down, and he'd take a cut of the capture.

Lucky taught me many things, but he made it painfully clear that everyone in the business only looked out for their own self-interest. I learned not to expect anyone to do me any favours. I had to watch my back at all times.

I am eternally grateful to Lucky for giving me the opportunity that he did. He took me under his wing and showed me the ropes of bounty hunting. It was a trial by fire and a damn good education. In the end, though, I didn't let my appreciation of him cloud my judgment. Going into business for myself was the next logical step. I could see that Lucky was on a one-way road to destruction. Somewhere down the line, his drinking was going to land him in prison, or worse. I didn't want any part of that. It was time for me to distance myself from him for good. I opened an office that combined my vacuum business, Brighton Kirby, with my new company, AAA Investigations. I had big plans, huge aspirations, and a drive that would somehow get me there, come hell or high water.

# CHAPTER NINETEEN

# Zebadiah

By Christmas 1979, I worked up the courage to call Jim Darnell and say I wouldn't kill him. There's great freedom in letting go of rage. Once I uttered those words to Jim, my life completely changed. All of my anger and bitterness towards him and LaFonda disappeared. I was still upset that she had taken Duane Lee and Leland from me. I wanted my boys back in my life in the worst way. Reconciling with Jim allowed me to move through the world as a warmer, kinder, more understanding man. Besides, I was now remarried, to Ann, who was pregnant with our first child. The baby was due soon. I didn't want to bring my kid into this world while I was filled with rage. My unborn child deserved more than that.

Nine years after that call, I heard that Jim's mother put a gun to her mouth and pulled the trigger right in front of him. Poor bastard had to watch his mommy eat a gun.

I wanted Jim to pay for what he had done, but his mother's suicide was too much. My mother always told me, 'The Lord sayeth, "Vengeance is mine, I shall repay."' I thought His vengeance was too severe.

'Lord, enough,' I prayed. 'He has paid. Please, Lord. No more pain for Jim or me.' I meant it, too. A heart filled with anger has no room for love. My heart was wide open with the Lord's spirit. I didn't want to see Jim suffer any more than he now already had.

Twenty-six weeks into the pregnancy, Ann went into labour. It was too soon.

Our son, Zebadiah Duane Chapman, was born on 1 January 1980. The doctors warned me that, because of his premature birth, he was very small. Zebadiah weighed slightly over one pound. There was a lot of doubt as to whether he was strong enough to survive.

At the time, I still hadn't reconnected with Duane Lee and Leland. I missed my boys so much. For that reason alone, Zebadiah's birth was terribly emotional. For the first time since before going to prison, I again had a son I could reach out and hold. The connection was instantaneous. For a moment, the gigantic void from losing Duane Lee and Leland was filled by my little baby boy.

Zebadiah's story captured the attention of local news media. They reported he was one of two babies born on New Year's Day. The other child was the son of the great former Denver Bronco quarterback, Craig Morton.

Doctors worked around the clock to help Zebadiah live. He had tubes coming out of his mouth and nose, and a heart monitor no larger than a credit card was taped to his chest. Despite their efforts, Zebadiah suffered an unexpected injury to his lung, which collapsed from his lack of strength. Once again, the doctors said they doubted a child born so prematurely could survive such an injury. I disagreed. He was a Chapman. He was strong. He was a fighter. He had a will to live. I ordered the doctors to do everything humanly possible to keep my boy alive.

For thirty days and nights, Ann and I sat by Zebadiah's side. The bills were enormous. I didn't have health insurance. I thought the state would pay the expenses. When the hospital informed me I would be financially responsible, I actually thought about robbing a bank. But if I got caught, I'd have to go back to jail. I knew I couldn't help Zebadiah if that happened. I prayed to God to help my family through this. I needed a miracle. A few days later, a local reporter called to tell me that their television station had set up a Zebadiah Duane Chapman fund to help offset the costs. I was moved to tears by the generosity the good citizens of Denver showed my family.

A month after Zebadiah was born, I heard God say, 'Can I have him back now? He's a miracle baby. His name will go down in history. He's in a lot of pain. It's time for him to come home.'

Giving my son up to the Lord was a tremendous sacrifice, but I knew He was right. Ann held Zebadiah in her arms until he slowly faded away. Sadly, my son lost his battle for life on 31 January 1980.

Ann and I were terribly distraught. All I wanted to do was make love to my wife. When something traumatic happens in my life, it's a natural instinct to make love to help numb my pain. I needed to be with my wife. During this period of grief we conceived our son Wesley, who was born nine months after Zebadiah passed away.

By the time Wesley was born, however, my marriage to Ann was over. Initially there was no animosity. We were two people who didn't belong together as man and wife. After our divorce was final, Ann and I continued to see each other from time to time. We unexpectedly conceived a third son together – J.R. Since I had custody of Wesley, Ann wanted to keep J.R. I had no problem with that.

And then one day, I got an unanticipated knock on my door. Ann and her parents had sent the cops. They literally were pulling Wesley out of my arms.

I held Wesley in one arm and shouted, 'You pigs!' Next thing I heard was the sound of guns being cocked next to my head.

This wasn't a battle I was going to lose without a fight. I had already lost three sons. I wasn't about to lose another. When we went to court, however, the judge awarded custody to Ann. He felt that a child belongs with his mother. I didn't agree. Luckily, he made sure we set up visitation rights for both babies for me. Despite the court order, Ann moved back to Utah. I've never heard from her again.

Years later, J.R. called me.

'Is Duane Dog Chapman there?' Right away I knew it was my son.

'I was hoping we could be father and son, Dad.'

It warmed my heart to hear his voice.

He asked me if I knew he had been born with some mental challenges. I knew, but it was never an issue for me. I love all of my kids the same. I wanted to set his mind at ease, so I said, 'That's OK, son. So was I.' He laughed a precious, wonderful, childlike laugh. We haven't met yet, but I hope we do soon. I'm told he looks a lot like his old man. Not long afterwards, Wesley reached out to me too. It was the first time he and I had spoken since the cops took him out of my arms.

# CHAPTER TWENTY

# Salesman of the Year

Two short years after getting out of Huntsville, I was doing great. I was bounty hunting part-time at night and on the weekends. I continued selling vacuums ten hours a day, six days a week. I was keeping up a pace that would take down a well-seasoned prize fighter in peak condition. I could have just sold vacuums; I was making enough money. In fact, a couple of guys from the home office called and asked me if I wanted to go to work for them. They offered me a starting salary of $100,000 dollars a year. I was floored. I could make my mom and dad so proud. But I loved the bounty hunting. The money wasn't nearly as good, but the thrill of the chase was almost as much fun as the good old days as a Disciple on the other side of the law.

I destroyed my competition at Kirby. I became the number one salesman in the company. In 1982, I was awarded the prestigious President's Ring award as Salesman of the Year. A couple months before that, however, the president of Kirby died. The new president was a man named Norm Mahoney, whose son Brian was best friends with Jim Darnell. I'd soon find out that that wasn't a good thing.

The company's annual sales-award banquet was held in Chicago. I was so excited, I called my mom and asked her to accompany me as my guest. She had never been to Chicago. The company put us up in a high-rise hotel. Neither of us had ever been up so high. I am afraid of heights, so I slept on the floor because I was too scared to look out the window from my bed.

Everyone who sold Kirbys in the world was at the ceremony, including the new president and his son. Mom and I found my name listed in the programme as the third award to be given out. She was so proud to see my name in that booklet.

The first two awards were handed out. Each recipient went up to the podium, gave a short speech, received the award, and had a picture taken with the president of the company before sitting back down. I've always liked public speaking, so I prepared a short speech for myself just in case I had the chance to say thanks. I wanted to acknowledge what Herman Cadillo had done for me. I was a broken man who found purpose and meaning when he plucked me from my parents' basement. I wanted to tell the audience that God showed me the light and led me from my darkness. If I could change my life, anyone could. That was the message I hoped to share.

I heard the master of ceremonies introduce my award. I straightened myself, sat up with pride, and took my napkin from my lap when he announced that the President's Ring was being awarded to Duane 'Dog' Chapman. I was about to get up to accept it when I heard him say, 'And now, for our next award . . .'

Mom and I were in shock. I didn't know what happened. I was embarrassed and humiliated in front of everyone I worked with. Worst of all, I was ashamed because this took place in front of my mom. At the end of the ceremony, I went backstage where I first met Brian Mahoney.

'Dog, I hate to be the one to break this to you, but the company found out about your record. They don't want you out selling our product or affiliated with our good company name.'

'But I won the Salesman of the Year award, and I'm supposed to negotiate my contract to start training salesmen in the main office . . .' I was dumbfounded. I didn't see *this* coming. I felt completely blindsided and betrayed. I had served this company with years of hard work.

'Yes. About that job. That offer is null and void. Jim Darnell has told me everything about your past. I know who you really are. You're a convicted murderer.'

I wanted to grab that smug son of a bitch by the throat and strangle him. Then an absolutely horrifying thought occurred to me. I had $200,000 worth of Kirbys in inventory back in Colorado. I wasn't just a salesman any more. I had become the youngest factory distributor in the history of the company. They couldn't do this to me. But then, I didn't think the great state of Texas could convict me for murder one.

I punched Brian in the chest. Hard. *Blam.* I told him to eat shit and die.

I turned around and realised a small crowd had now gathered around us. I could hear people whispering, 'Oh, my God. They were right. He *is* a killer.'

I turned to my mom and said, 'Let's go.'

I saw all of the salesmen I had worked with over the years standing and staring. Not a single one stuck up for me. I didn't give a crap any more. I was better than these guys. The Lord had been preparing me for this moment. He kept saying, 'Get ready. Your life is going to change very soon. You're going into something else.' I tried to head Him off, outsmart God. Ha. Good luck. When the Lord calls your name, you come running.

I flew back to Colorado feeling down, but not out. Brian told me I could liquidate my inventory, but I couldn't sell them door-to-door. It would be a loss, but not a total wash. At least I still had my dignity, even if I didn't have my job. For some reason, I didn't feel desperate. God had my back. I had kept my word, my promise to Him. I didn't ride Harleys. I knew He wouldn't let me fall. I wasn't the same man who went to Huntsville and surely wasn't the same guy who came out. One thing was very clear after Chicago. I would forever be branded a killer. My conviction would haunt me for the rest of my life. I hadn't made that connection since getting out, because things had been going great. I had an awakening in Chicago. No matter how successful I became, no matter how hard I tried to change, the world would always see me as a convicted murderer. That bothered me a lot more than losing my job.

When I got home, I got down on my knees to pray to God.

'Lord, is this what You want? Because of You, I became the best vacuum salesman in the world. But now, that's no longer an option. You have shown me over and over that You have a plan. I need to know that this is what You want me to do. I need a sign, Lord. I don't want to fall back into my darkness or turn back to a life of crime. I am not desperate, but I need Your help, Your guidance.'

My biggest fear in what the Lord was telling me was that I would become a rat. A rat drops a dime, collects his money, and runs away laughing. That wasn't who I was. I couldn't accept the fact that people would see me that way. The Lord kept showing me that bounty hunting was the direction He wanted me to take. He kept giving me instant signs. I ignored Him for as long as I could. The Lord assured me I would not be a rat. If I became a bounty hunter, I would become a collector, an enforcer. To be a true Christian, you have to do your best to be Christ-like. I wanted to live that way. I couldn't be a saint, but I knew I could be a soldier.

'Show me that *this* is Your will. I need to know that I won't fail You.

I guess we're going to do things the hard way, huh?'

The Lord spoke to me and said, 'I will make you fishers of men. Follow Me, Duane. Who was the greatest bounty hunter of all? Jesus Christ.' I was up to the task. I knew my true calling was bounty hunting.

# CHAPTER TWENTY-ONE

# Getting My Boys Back

After Zebadiah died, I yearned to see my sons Duane Lee and Leland. I wanted to be their father again. I heard LaFonda and Jim Darnell had moved to Colorado Springs, about ninety miles south of Denver. It wasn't fair to them or to me that LaFonda separated us. Every time I asked her to visit, she turned me down. I'll never understand her anger towards me. I know I let her down by my actions in Pampa. She needed a husband and a father for the kids, and I couldn't be there. As much as I wanted to be – Lord knows I loved my family – I had to pay for my crime.

I didn't know where LaFonda and the boys were living. All I had was a phone number. I became like Sherlock Holmes trying to track them down. I even called the Colorado Springs Department of Water and Power to see if I could come up with an address. It was late at night, so the guy who answered the phone was the janitor. I explained my situation, hoping he was a father too, praying he would understand my need to see my sons and find it in his heart to help me out. He was an angel on earth. Ten minutes later, I had their home address.

I thought about straight-up knocking on the front door. I dreamed about Duane Lee and Leland jumping into my arms, hugging and kissing their daddy. Leland was a baby, barely nine months old, when I went to prison. Duane Lee was a toddler. I missed out on so many blessed moments of their lives, moments I'll never get back. I have to take the blame for that. Even so, I hoped they still loved and missed me as much as I did them. It took me months to do anything more than watch them from across the street.

Christmas was coming. I asked my mom to drive me down to Colorado Springs so I could leave a telescope for Duane Lee and a toy truck for Leland on the front porch. I dropped the hand-wrapped gifts, rang the bell, and ran like a bat out of hell. I was still too scared to make direct contact. I was afraid they'd reject me. That would be the worst possible outcome, given how much my heart ached to have them back. Mom burned rubber pulling away from the house like we had just robbed the joint. Her little Volkswagen Bug began swerving and jack-knifing on the icy back roads. When we finally stopped, I pounded my fists on the dashboard and let out a cry. I knew in my heart LaFonda was pointing to our car and telling the boys, 'There goes your deadbeat dad.'

Even though I never loved Ann, I was hurting because she took my babies away. I was out looking for another woman. First I met a beautiful girl named Penny. She had long sexy black hair and dark eyes, and she dressed like a cowgirl. I took one look at her and thought, *Mmmmm*. Later that night I met a bushy-haired, sexy Barbra Streisand-looking woman sitting at the same bar. She wasn't my usual type, but something about her drew me in. She told me her name was Lyssa and her husband was an Assembly of God minister. Screech! So much for that girl. Well, not so fast. I was intrigued that the minister's wife was sitting alone in a bar, so I struck up a conversation. I asked her if she understood the Spirit of the Lord, the Holy Ghost, and what giving God His glory meant.

'Of course I do! I went to Rama Bible College with my husband.' She told me her husband, the minister, was unfaithful to her, so she kicked him out and filed for divorce. Blam!

Ann did not share my love of the Lord. I thought about a particular scripture from the Bible that says, 'Be ye not unequally yoked together with unbelievers.' I was unequally yoked with Ann. It would be like a Bible-loving choirboy falling for an atheist drunk. It just doesn't work. When Lyssa told me she understood the Lord, I offered her a thousand bucks on the spot to have my baby. I was serious, too! I promised her she'd enjoy the experience, and even told her she could visit the baby whenever she wanted. Believe it or not, she said yes! It took me a week to finally get her into bed, but by then, we were already in love. We got married by an Indian chief in the Colorado mountains.

Lyssa got pregnant right away. She laughed at all of my jokes and was smarter than me. I love smart women. The more intelligent they are, the greater my desire for them. I thought Lyssa was my perfect mate.

I wanted to name the baby Geronimo if it was a boy. Up to that point, I had only fathered boys, so it never occurred to me that Lyssa could have a girl. But she did. On 8 June 1982, Lyssa gave birth to my darling

Barbara Katie. Our son Tucker was born one year later and Baby Lyssa came along in June 1987.

By that time, we both knew our relationship had changed. I was getting restless, looking for a woman who could walk alongside me on the same path. I thought Lyssa was the one. Lord knows I loved her. But her dreams and mine were no longer headed in the same direction. She wanted to spend the rest of her life living in a secluded cabin in the woods. I wanted the bright lights of Hollywood. Lyssa knew she could never match my yoke.

It took me five years of fighting LaFonda in court before I was finally awarded visitation rights to see my boys on weekends. As happy as *I* was, the news wasn't exactly music to *their* ears. By that time, Lyssa and I had welcomed two more children into our lives, but Duane Lee and Leland were absolutely frightened to be alone with me. In many ways, I was a stranger to them.

It took time for all of us to get know one another again. It was a slow process, sometimes frustrating and heartbreaking, but eventually we began to bond. I showed them affection, giving them lots of hugs and kisses whenever they'd let me close enough.

I tried to instil a sense of faith in God into their lives. I knew the value that had added to my life as a young boy. It was all I knew, and it was the greatest blessing I could offer as a father. Every night, I prayed to the Lord to help me show my boys I was a good man and a worthy role model. I needed the Lord to help guide the boys back into my life at their own pace. I had waited seven years to get my boys back; I could wait until they were ready.

I had finally begun to connect with the kids, when I almost blew us back to square one. Leland came to show me a loose tooth. When I was a boy, Grandpa Mike used to tie one end of a string around a doorknob and the other to my tooth. When the tooth was good and loose, he'd yank it out by slamming the door! I thought that was how teeth got pulled, so when Leland came to me, I did what Grandpa Mike did. The problem was, Leland's tooth wasn't quite ready to come out. He went flying off the stool I had him sitting on and tumbled on to the floor. Duane Lee cracked up watching this debacle unfold as his brother lay on the floor crying more from fear than pain. I tried to console the poor boy, rubbing his head and holding him in my arms. I felt awful, but I have to admit, I thought it was pretty funny too. Years later, we all still laugh about that night. It was a breakthrough moment for us, one I'll never forget.

Eventually, the boys moved in with me. I was married to Lyssa, and we were living in a pretty tough neighbourhood just outside of Denver. Grandpa Mike left me that house when he died. We were living there free and clear. It wasn't a bad area when Grandpa first moved in, but now it was infested with gangs. I had six children living in the house, Duane Lee, Leland, Lyssa's son Jason, Barbara Katie, Tucker, and Baby Lyssa. Everybody knew that Duane 'Dog' Chapman lived in the house with the green paint sprayed around the perimeter and the words NO COLOURS! on the sidewalk. I had six kids who played outside and rode their bicycles in the streets. If anyone tried to mess with them, they messed with me. I didn't want any criminal stuff going down in front of my house. Those days were over.

# CHAPTER TWENTY-TWO

# Meeting My Soul Mate

I first met Beth Smith in 1988, when she was just nineteen years old. I was thirty-five. I've always had a thing for smart women – especially smart women with big tits. The moment I met her, I knew there was a hell of a brain behind those breasts.

I met Beth at the county lock-up, when her father called me to post her bail. He said she was arrested for shoplifting a lemon.

I thought, *Huh?*

I explained to her dad that I never did bail for less than five thousand dollars. Her bond was only twenty-five hundred. I took my time going to the jail that day. The $250 fee was hardly worth my time.

It turned out Beth was actually wanted for more than stealing a lemon. She was standing on line at the grocery store waiting to pay for the lemon when she received a page on her beeper from her boss, a Colorado state senator. Whenever he paged her, she had to respond right away. This was before cell phones, so she got out of line to use the pay phone, still holding the lemon. Store security nabbed her on the spot for shoplifting. That alone would not have been enough to arrest Beth, but she also had a gun in her pocket. She had taken it away from her dumbass boyfriend before going to the store. He was drunk and shooting at birds. She didn't want him to get into trouble, so she put the unlicensed, unregistered gun in her pocket. Before the cops came to get her, she told the security guards she had the gun. They had no way of knowing if Beth was dangerous. They sure knew she had a concealed weapon and was allegedly 'stealing'. When the police arrived, they ran a routine check and discovered there was an arrest warrant on her for unpaid parking tickets. So they took her in.

I called Beth to come down to my office to fill out her paperwork like all clients I bail out. It's standard procedure. I need to know who these people are and where they live. I need family contact information and stuff like that. I ask all sorts of questions other bondsman would never consider, like shoe size or whether they have a twin. It might seem trivial, but it makes all the difference if they try to run and hide. That information will help me hunt and find anyone.

I called and called, but Beth flat-out refused to come in. That's Beth. You can't tell her what to do. Never could. Still can't. I finally threatened to put her back in jail if she didn't show up.

Blam. In she comes. I knew she was young – too young for me. I was never one of those older guys who went for the young girls. But damn. Those breasts. I know what you're thinking. I'm an idiot, right?

Beth loves to tell people that the minute she laid eyes on me in the office that day, she knew I would be her man. 'Oh yes, he will be mine.' That's what she said. But I was still married to Lyssa, wife number three, so Beth wasn't an option. Not then, anyway.

Beth grew up in Denver the youngest of five kids, two boys and three girls. Her dad, Garry L. Smith, played first base for the minor-league team the Kansas City Athletics in the late fifties. He was one of the most relentless competitors in the minor leagues. Her mom, Bonnie, was a tough, abusive, abrasive woman who never took no for an answer.

Beth lived a pretty good life in Harvey Park, suburban Denver, until her father left home when she was eight. Bonnie was left to raise five kids as a single working mom. Beth grew up pretty fast. She left home at eighteen to work for Don Sandoval, a Colorado state senator. It was a really good job for a young girl right out of high school. She did his bookkeeping and later became his executive assistant when the legislature was in session. Beth soaked up information like a sponge, learning the judicial and legislative process from the inside. Her years of experience would later help us combat the system in ways she could never have imagined as a young girl just starting out.

I tried to dodge Beth, avoiding her like a bad cold. I'd be driving around Denver, and out of nowhere, there she was, right behind me. She was literally stalking me. She had a friend at Leo Payne Automotive, and one time she took a car from the lot on a test drive so I wouldn't recognise the vehicle following me. She shadowed me all over Denver. Sometimes I knew she was behind me, but this time I didn't. She decided her friend's car was a great way to keep an eye on me, so she took her time returning it. The car dealership reported it stolen, and Beth was busted for car theft, though the charges were later reduced to a misdemeanour, joyriding. I had to post a $25,000 bond to get her out. I couldn't believe it! Judge Palmieri sentenced her to six months' probation and a fifty-dollar fine.

Much like her attitude in coming to see me after her first arrest, Beth didn't much like being forced to check in with her probation officer. She is the kind of hard-headed woman who needs to make all decisions herself. At the end of her probation, her officer recommended she do a little time. He didn't feel she had learned her lesson. When Beth went before Judge Francis Jackson to plead her case, the judge listened with deaf ears. He wasn't much interested in her point of view. He ordered her to be incarcerated for forty-five days in the Jefferson County jail. Case closed.

Even behind bars, Beth was an uncontrollable force. She spent her entire stay threatening to expose the county for corruption and the inhumane conditions of the facility. Judge Jackson even called me for advice on how to handle her. I had to laugh. I barely knew the girl, but I understood her well enough to say, 'How do you handle Beth? That's easy. You don't! My suggestion is you run for cover and wait for the storm to pass. You gotta let her out if you want her to stop harassing you.' The best part of Beth's being in jail was she made me more money inside during those forty-five days than I could have dreamed of. She sent me all the criminals so I could write their bonds.

In spite of her protests, Beth emerged from the Jefferson County jail a changed woman. She realised that life was too short to waste behind bars. She didn't want to end up like the people she met there. She decided to turn her life around. The judge did her the greatest favour of her life. Had she not done time, who knows where she would be today. Also, by the time she got out, Lyssa and I were separated, and I had started dating my new secretary, Tawny.

I first met Tawny in 1988 after arresting her on a possession of narcotics warrant. Three years later, in 1991, she walked into my office and said, 'You owe me a job, Dog Chapman.' I had no idea who she was. She had gained a lot of weight and looked pretty good. Tawny told me she had been working at Beneficial Finance, so she had the kind of bookkeeping experience I needed. I was looking for a secretary, so I offered her the job. She was great.

I was raising all of my children on my own. I was depressed and lonely. One night, I had a few too many and did the wild thing with Tawny. The next day, I felt terrible about sleeping with my secretary. I didn't want to mess up our working relationship. I just got horny. When I tried to explain to Tawny that I just wanted to be friends, she pretended to hear what I was saying, but she had her own ideas. Later that night, I went to Tawny's house to take her out to dinner. She had all of her bags packed.

'Where are you going, honey?' I thought she was headed on a vacation or something.

'I'm moving in with you. The kids need a mom.' All of my children liked Tawny and didn't have a problem with her moving in. Reluctantly, I let her live in a guest room. We screwed every now and again. That lasted a few months, but it wasn't enough to satisfy her.

Not long after, Tawny came to me and said she would go to the media if I didn't marry her. She said she was going to tell all of Denver I was doing my secretary. The day wasn't starting out the way I had planned. It went from bad to worse when I got word of a new Colorado statute saying a convicted felon can't be a bondsman for ten years after discharge of parole. Sixteen Denver bondsmen ended up losing their licences. I was off parole in 1981. They had me by one year. This meant that I would either be unemployed for a year or somehow had to convince the Colorado lawmakers the new law shouldn't be retroactive. Until we could prove this, I lost my licence.

Lucky for me, I had Gary Lozow on my team. He's the same Denver attorney who's been handling all of my legal work since I was a fifteen-year-old hood throwing rocks through windows.

We presented my case to the honourable Judge Hiatt, the same judge who took great pride to see me get my bond licence four years earlier. I felt he was a fair and decent man who would listen to the facts and decide the merit of my case based on all that I had done for the community. Lozow asked Judge Hiatt for more time so he could effectively argue my case. He also wanted to get my records from the Texas Department of Corrections. He promised he'd move as quickly as possible, so he wouldn't hold up the courts. Hiatt agreed to give Lozow the time. We and the court moved so slowly that we burned off the entire year and the law didn't impact me. The statute became null and void as it pertained to me. I kept working.

Since Beth lost her job working for Senator Sandoval when she went to jail, she also needed work. She decided to get into the bail bonds business – she was determined to make me her man. Anytime I called, she came running.

One night I called Beth from a Denver biker bar where I was trying to get some information for a case I was working on. I had gone to the bar with Tawny, but she left me to run an errand. I wasn't sure where she went or if she was coming back. I was getting pretty drunk trying to keep up with the bikers, so I called Beth to come get me. I didn't think I'd turn up any leads, and I wanted to go home.

At the very last second, I came up with a pretty solid lead. I had to check it out.

'Beth, honey, drive me to this house. I think the girl I'm looking for is there.'

'No way!' Beth has a way of making things harder than they need to be.

'Drive me to the house, damn it!' I was getting pissed and was too drunk to care that I was yelling.

Beth agreed to go by the address once. The car slowly crept up. We were just passing by when I spotted the woman I was looking for. I leaped out of the still-moving car and started chasing her. She ran into the house and out the back door. She finally locked herself in a corner apartment down the block. I had her. When I kicked the door open it accidentally hit a friend of hers in the head. The woman ran again. This time, she went out the back door and into a junkyard behind the apartment complex, where she hid in a doghouse.

'I'm outta here, Duane. I want no part of this!' Beth was yelling at me as I went to grab the woman.

Just then the police showed up and told us to freeze. They wouldn't let me capture the fugitive. Instead, they arrested both Beth and me. 'Who cares? They're bounty hunters. Book them for burglary.'

'You're nothing but trouble, Duane Chapman,' Beth said. She wasn't in the bond business yet.

In Colorado, the law states that anyone who enters and remains in a dwelling to commit a felonious act is guilty of first-degree burglary. Beth and I were booked and thrown in jail. I was so drunk that, in the back of the police car, I kept telling Beth, 'I told you we'd have fun times.' I didn't remember much the next day.

Beth didn't have as much to lose as I did. For her, the arrest was just a felony. But for me, my bail bonds business and bounty hunting career were at stake. To make matters worse, I was arrested with Beth – something I didn't think Tawny would understand. I kept Beth real close after that night. I knew she could rat me out and make things hard at home.

She threatened to tell Tawny everything, but she never did.

When we went to court to face the judge, Beth's charges were dropped to a 'dog at large' offence. No joke. It amounted to walking a dog without a leash. I don't know if the DA was trying to be funny or was just sending me a message. My charges were reduced to trespassing, which wouldn't affect my career.

# CHAPTER TWENTY-THREE

# My College Education

After starting AAA Investigations, I began networking and meeting lots of other people in law enforcement. I've always been a pretty good matchmaker of sorts. I don't mean boy to girl; I mean FBI to police officer, private eye to firefighter, narc to CIA, and so on. I learned the importance of those relationships early in my career. As a bounty hunter, I get to meet all types of defenders of the law. I have a sixth sense about introducing friends to other friends. Sometimes those meetings come from the strangest of circumstances.

In 1982, I was chasing a fugitive who was supposedly affiliated with a well-known crime family from New York. I was out looking for the guy all over Denver when I spotted his car outside a very fancy restaurant he was known to hang around. I let the air out of two of his tyres by pricking the valve stems with the ends of a couple of wooden matches. I waited for the son of a bitch to come out so we could nab him. When he stepped out of the restaurant, he immediately spotted his flat tyres. He realised someone was on to him. He tried to get away in his car, but he wasn't going to go very far with two flat tyres. I grabbed the guy, got him out of the car, threw a pair of cuffs around his wrists, and told him he was going down for running on his bond. Before I put him in the car, I couldn't help but notice he had the softest hands I ever felt on a man. His hands were perfectly manicured. Clearly he was a man of means, if not connections.

'There's a mistake. I'm in the Witness Protection Program. Contact the feds. Go ahead, check my story.'

Now, I've heard a lot of guys tell me a bunch of b.s. stories over the years, but none had ever said they were in witness protection. My curiosity got the best of me, so I called to verify what he was saying. I wasn't going to hand my fugitive over to the feds without a receipt.

Without one, I couldn't collect on the bounty.

I spoke to an FBI special agent in the Denver office who agreed to meet me at a local coffee shop. This was very unusual, at least in my limited experience. A half hour later, three men dressed in standard-issue dark suits, crisp white shirts, blue ties, and overcoats walk through the door at the White Spot coffee shop. One of the agents introduced himself as Keith Paul. When they showed up, the feds took my guy in the parking lot.

Keith Paul was only a couple of years younger than me, but he looked like he should be in class at the local high school. He had a closely shaved crew cut, pasty white skin, and a baby face that barely looked like he ever had a need to shave. Despite his youthful appearance, he was taller and bigger than me. His presence must have been daunting for most, but to me he looked like a choirboy who had lost his way.

I liked Keith from the start. He and I spoke the same language. He was a no-bull kind of guy who liked to get things done as much as I do. A couple of days later, Keith called to get together. He said the guys at the Bureau were curious about me. I didn't know what to think. It wasn't in my nature to trust the feds. The idea of working together went against my personal preferences in law enforcement. But that's what we decided to do. It made a lot of sense for both of us.

A few days after meeting Keith again, I was out making a bust. This time I was chasing a Colombian woman. I found her hiding at home not far from Aurora, just outside of Denver. When I busted her, I noticed a large package on her kitchen table. It looked like a shirt box wrapped in plastic.

I pointed to the package and her, 'What's that?'

'Coca.'

I wasn't there to bust this woman for drugs, but I could tell this was a pretty big load of cocaine. My gut reaction was to call Keith Paul and hand it over to him.

'Keith, it's Dog Chapman. If you're interested, I've just stumbled on to twenty-five pounds of blow.' I told him where I was. He said he'd be right over.

As a bounty hunter, my concern is getting my prey. I don't give a rat's ass about busting people for matters that don't concern me. If someone has drugs, is high, or has hot goods, it's not my place to call them out. All I want is my fee for the return of someone who runs from the law. That's how I made my living then and how I continue to make money now. As long as I get a body receipt saying I caught the fugitive, I can take it to court and get paid.

However, Keith and I had a terrific understanding of how one hand washes the other. We made each other look good. He asked me what being a bounty hunter was like, and I soaked up all I could about his life as a federal agent. That's what our relationship was all about. I took meticulous notes, teaching myself everything I could about legitimate law enforcement.

I always carried documentation that clarified my rights as a bounty hunter. It wasn't always easy to explain that I was an agent of the bondsman, empowered to bring back fugitives – especially since, in some states, a bounty hunter has rights even the police don't have. Back then, cops often had no clue about the laws applying to bounty hunters, so I was often viewed as a rogue vigilante out for my own good. My notebook was as important to my survival in business as my instincts, because it got me out of situations where cops thought I was the criminal.

The more I got to know Keith, the more we both realised we could really help each other's career. He'd show me warrants for criminals they were seeking, and I'd unofficially go out and find them. Keith never asked me to help or specifically gave me instructions. He simply told me that, if I ever came across any of these guys, I should give him a call. Sometimes we were going after the same guys anyway, so it was no big deal for me to let him know if I found one or two along the way. Plus, I'd learned early on how helpful it can be to aid law enforcement agencies whenever possible.

I was never a rat. Never. But I knew how to get information to the right people, especially the FBI. I never expected favours in return, but it was nice to know I held that chip if I ever needed to cash it in. Also, I wanted Keith Paul and his co-workers to see I was on the same team. Ever since I left Huntsville, I wanted to right my wrongs. I was determined to get myself even in the eyes of the Lord as much as I was in the eyes of the law.

I was hoping that I'd have the chance to redeem myself for all I had done wrong. I didn't know where or when or how, but I knew I would someday do something so big it would make people see me in a different light. I would no longer be Duane Chapman, convicted felon, murderer, and gangster. I would become Duane Chapman, defender of the law, good guy, and hero. I lived to clear my name. Not just for me, but for my family. I needed to legitimise myself as a bounty hunter and defender of all that is good. Doing favours for the FBI was a very good place to start. But even with all of my good intentions, I still had a lot to learn.

I started by hunting fugitives in Denver on the FBI's Most Wanted list. I immediately found the first guy I went after. I went to his momma's house just as he came walking out the front door. It has always been my experience that when it doubt, go to Momma. Everyone wants his momma when times are tough.

I called him over to my parked Ford pick-up truck. 'Do you have the time?'

He thought nothing of our exchange until I stuck my gun in his belly. I leaned out the rolled-down window to slap my cuffs around his wrists.

He was totally surprised. The guy had had no idea I was taking him down.

I called Keith Paul to tell him the good news.

'Hey, man. It's Dog. I've got your number-one guy.'

Much to my surprise, he sounded angry.

'What? Where are you?'

I gave him my location, still puzzled by his lacklustre response. I found out the next day that Keith was upset because my methods of tracking a fugitive aren't exactly standard procedure for the FBI. Truth be told, I think he was just pissed because I found the guy a whole lot faster than they could. I didn't have to go through all of the bureaucratic red tape. I was a one-man show. I didn't have department heads to answer to or rules to follow.

Every student needs a good teacher, and Keith Paul was one of my greatest. I had a lot of experience on the street, but I didn't understand how an investigation worked or proper protocol with law enforcement. I had learned the bail bonds business from Lucky. Now I wanted to learn law enforcement from Keith Paul.

I wanted to be the best bounty hunter who ever lived. Keith Paul wanted to be the best FBI agent in the world. We taught each other everything we could from our individual perspectives. We couldn't have been more different in our appearance, but deep down, I think we both shared a common goal to be number one.

While working with Keith, I crossed paths with another important teacher who would have a strong impact on my career. Her name was Cathy Carson. I met Cathy after I made a memorable bust, up in Arapaho County.

I'd thrown this large brother in the back of my Z28. He was enormous, six four and at least 240 pounds. The guy actually threatened to put me in a scissors lock and push me out of my moving car.

Who the hell did this asshole think he was? I pulled my car over on the side of the highway, took out my pistol, put the nose of the barrel to his temple, and said, 'You think so?'

He was diddy diddy done done.

'How do you like me now?' I snarled as I told him to get out of the car. I pushed him into the trunk for the duration of our journey to the Arapahoe County Courthouse. When I pulled up, I could tell by the look on Sheriff Sullivan's face that he didn't much approve of my style of apprehension. As I reached into the trunk for this monster of a man, I noticed an attractive woman standing in the distance watching me. I looked up and said hello, completely ignoring the giant in handcuffs. She came over to introduce herself.

'Hi, I'm Cathy Carson.'

'You can call me Dog.' There was a moment there when I thought . . . maybe. But then Cathy told me her husband was a cop. Just then, she recognised my fugitive and smiled.

'I nailed this punk.' She got right in his face and said, 'Hey, dickhead. Nice to see you. Guess you haven't learned much since the last time I got ya!'

Cathy and my guy were standing chest to chest. 'Fuckin' bitch.'

I gave the guy an elbow to the ribs. 'What's wrong with you? Respect the lady.'

I turned to Cathy and asked, 'You a cop too?'

She laughed and said, 'No. I'm a bounty hunter. I work for the Arapahoe County Sheriff's office.'

A female bounty hunter. Well, why the hell not? I'd never thought of it before, but looking at Cathy, it made perfect sense. I've always had a thing for tough chicks. I liked Cathy from the moment we met.

I began spending time with Cathy to learn more about how she worked at the county level versus how I made my living on a per-capture basis. Cathy's job was similar to how the U.S. Marshals work when they hunt for fugitives. Both are salaried positions, so it doesn't really matter if she catches her guy or not. Either way, she still gets paid. My income was strictly dependent on bringing in my man. As we began to swap information, we realised that both of us were often looking for the same guys. It made a hell of a lot of sense to work as a team. No sense in both of us going after the same catch, because I was always going to get there first! At least, that's what I told her.

We worked well together, because there weren't two competing male egos involved. Even so, bounty hunting is still a numbers game. If numbers count, then Cathy was the champ. We tipped each other off all the time. It was a win-win for both of us. I have to give credit where credit is due. In the first twelve months after we met, Cathy bagged 639 captures to my 635. It was a close race, practically a photo finish. But a win is a win, and she won by a nose.

Cathy and I worked together for several years, but by the end of 1985, I had lost touch with both Keith and Cathy. Cathy got out of the business altogether to spend more time at home. The last time I heard from Keith, he was working as an FBI supervisor down in Florida. I owe much of my success to Keith and Cathy. It was their professionalism, integrity, and love of what they do that inspired me to continue to strive to be my best.

# CHAPTER TWENTY-FOUR

# Meeting Tony Robbins

Aside from all that Keith Paul taught me about law enforcement, one of the greatest gifts he gave me was his suggestion that I meet his friend, Anthony 'Tony' Robbins. It was after a long night chasing a fugitive with Keith and some other G-men.

*Boom. Boom. Boom. Boom. Boom.* Five shots rang out. After the fifth, I stood up and told the guy to come out with his hands up.

'Get down, Dog. The guy's armed.' I wasn't sure which FBI agent said that to me. I didn't care. The punk just capped five shells from a six-barrel shotgun. I knew he didn't have any left or else he'd keep shooting.

'Slide the gun across the floor, put your hands on your head, and get out here, NOW!' I yelled.

Sure enough, the gun came flying out, spinning and sliding, practically landing at my feet. I had just seen a movie where General Patton was in the field leading his troops while bullets went whizzing past his head. Old Indian women have often told me I'm Cochise or Geronimo reincarnated, so a white man's bullet is never going to touch me. I've been told I would never die a violent death, because I have the spirit and blessings of the great Indian chiefs. So I stood right up, grabbed the guy, and handed him over to the feds in cuffs.

Later that night, Keith Paul and I went to the White Spot diner, as we often did, and talked about the capture.

Keith was curious. 'How'd you know he didn't have any more bullets?'

'I didn't know. I just had a feeling.' I get feelings about things a lot. Most of us do, but we don't know how to tune in and let those gut feelings guide us in everyday life.

'You know, I just met a guy who came to the Academy to train us. He talks like you, only he uses bigger words. I think you should meet him. His name is Tony Robbins.'

I had never seen Keith so worked up about a guy. Keith isn't an easy man to impress, but he genuinely seemed awed by the experience. If this Tony Robbins guy got the attention of Keith Paul, I was definitely interested in meeting him.

This was back in 1985, when Tony was enjoying tremendous success with his first book, *Unlimited Power*. He was a private consultant to movie stars, politicians, athletes, and business leaders around the world. Companies like IBM, AT&T, and American Express paid Tony to teach their executives to be the best. Sports teams, including the Los Angeles Dodgers and Los Angeles Kings, hired him to help athletes achieve peak performance. His aim was to help people find their strengths and conquer their weaknesses, to help them discover and develop their own unique qualities of greatness. He sounded like the perfect guy for me to meet.

I had previously heard of Tony in my Kirby sales days. Guys like Zig Ziglar and Norman Vincent Peale were big motivational speakers back then. They changed people's lives with their lessons and insights. People were saying that Tony Robbins was the next great leader in helping people captain their destiny.

I told Keith I was very interested in meeting Tony. I didn't hear another word about it until one day a few weeks later, when I received a call from the Tony Robbins organisation.

'Mr Chapman, please hold for Mr Robbins.' I was stunned.

'Hello?' It was him. I could tell by his very deep voice.

We spoke for a while. He asked about my murder one conviction, except he had been told it was manslaughter.

'It says here in my notes you were convicted of manslaughter, is that correct?'

I felt compelled to be honest with the guy so I said, 'Uh . . . no. It was murder one.'

'I see. Well, tell me something. How would you feel if I asked you to come to Texas and speak at our next seminar about your life and overcoming your adverse experiences?'

I had to laugh. There was no way I was ever going back to Texas.

'Not on your life, buddy.'

But, Tony being Tony, he smoothly, gently, and easily persuaded me into going without my ever knowing I had just been flipped. He said they'd fly me down to Austin and promised me five grand just to tell my story. It seemed too good to be true. I thought it was a set-up – that somehow, someone in the Texas Department of Corrections realised there was an error in my parole and wanted me back in Huntsville. All they had to do was get me over the state line and I'd be back in jail.

I spoke to Cathy Carson. I knew Keith Paul wouldn't intentionally set me up, but my gut was saying something wasn't right. Cathy was a good, solid, clear thinker. She'd know what to do. She said she had never heard of Tony Robbins, but the FBI really believed in him. That was enough evidence to her that the offer to come to Texas was legit. Plus, the money was pretty damned appealing. I'd have to catch a dozen fugitives (or more) to make five thousand dollars. It was worth a shot.

With great caution, I decided to make the trip. When I got to Austin, everything seemed on the up and up. So far, so good.

On my way to the seminar, I realised I was out of cigarettes. I spotted a 7-Eleven across the street. I figured I could pick up a pack of smokes before I went to the conference. I didn't want to be late, so I crossed over in the middle of the block. Just as I reached the sidewalk, a motorcycle cop pulled me over.

*Damn it. I was right. This was all a set-up.*

The cop got off his bike, pulled his helmet off, and said, 'Come here, boy.'

I walked two steps closer to the bike, yet far enough away to run if I had to.

'Where you off to in such a hurry, boy?'

'Well, officer, sir . . . ' I was fumbling with my words a bit, still wondering when the other shoe would drop.

I continued, 'My name is Duane Chapman, most folks call me Dog. I'm in town to speak at the Tony Robbins seminar right there across the street in that auditorium.'

'You don't look like a speaker to me. You look more like a badass biker boy, probably wanted for something.'

'No sir. I am a defender of the law. Here's my badge, just like yours.' I pulled my badge out from behind my shirt. I wear it like a necklace. I handed it over to the officer so he could see we were brothers in the law.

'Well, I'll be damned. Nice to meet ya, *Dog*. Welcome to Texas!' He extended his hand in friendship and brotherhood. I never felt better about myself than I did in that moment of pure acceptance.

A few hours later, I found myself onstage, speaking to thousands of strangers. I was so pumped up from adrenaline, I felt like I was back in the ring, boxing again. I loved the sound of people cheering for me as I walked down the long aisle, offering high fives and shaking hands. I felt like a rock star. These people didn't know me, and I didn't know them, but we loved one another. I had never experienced this type of adulation. It was the greatest sensation. I made my way towards the stage. There was an empty chair next to where Tony Robbins was seated. He stood to greet me. I was stunned by his stature. The guy is practically a giant, towering nearly a foot over my five seven. When he shook my hand, his hand devoured mine. I was blown away by his very presence. He's engaging, warm, and powerful in every way.

Tony introduced me. He said, 'This is Dog Chapman. His story is one of the greatest examples I have ever heard of a criminal gone wrong. Please put your hands together and give Dog a great big welcome!'

What the hell did he mean by 'criminal gone wrong'? Tony later told me that I was the antithesis of what most criminals become after serving hard time. I chose a path to lead by example by making something of myself. I found my strengths and created a life that took my inner criminal out of the equation while still choosing to use all of my knowledge and understanding to aid me in my pursuit of justice. If I was a criminal gone right, I'd still be on the other side of the law.

Tony had a way of helping me see things differently to anyone else. I began to speak – telling the crowd about how I went to prison 'right here in Texas' for a crime I did not commit. I talked about turning my life around, becoming the top Kirby salesman in the country, making more money than I could ever have dreamed. I explained my transition into the world of bounty hunting and bail bonds. The audience hung on my every word as I spoke about captures and arrests. Tony loved it. He could see the crowd was eating it up. He smiled his big, toothy grin, knowing he had found a gold mine in this old Dog.

At the end of my speech, Tony opened up the floor for a Q&A session. I didn't expect that part. I was nervous, because despite how well things were going, I still had it in the back of my mind that this could possibly be a sting.

The first question was: 'Have you ever committed any crimes – like burglaries?'

I was mad as hell. Now I was sure this was a bust. 'What is that supposed to mean?' I growled back.

I could hear soft snickers coming from the audience, which became an uncomfortable sort of murmur.

Tony sensed it too. He jumped right in and said, 'Dog, why don't you tell us a little more about what state you're in when you go after fugitives?'

I looked over at Tony, relieved as hell to get back to business as I knew it.

'Well, Tony, usually, I'm in Colorado, where I live, but sometimes I can go to any state I want if they allow bounty hunting.'

The audience erupted in laughter.

I leaned over to Tony and asked, 'What did I say that was so funny?'

Again with his big smile, Tony looked at me and said, 'What I meant was, what state of mind are you in when you hunt for these guys?'

I felt dumb as a rod. So much for all of that new-found self-esteem! We bantered for a few more hours about mind-frames, the power of mental states, the birth of excellence, motivation, and all sorts of other subjects that got me thinking about ways to improve my life, until I was so drained I felt like I needed to lie down. My brain was spinning with thoughts and ideas. It was incredible. I was exhausted yet invigorated. It wasn't all that different from how I feel after going on a successful hunt.

The crowd loved our interaction. Most people were cheering, but a few were making bull's horns using their first and pinky fingers. Where I come from, that's offensive, so I stuck my middle finger up and said, 'Hey, you too, man!' Tony leaned over and said, 'Dog, that means "I love you" at my seminars.'

'Oh, yeah? Well, where I come from that means crap.'

Tony laughed a deep hearty, throaty laugh. 'Not here. It's sign language. It's all good.

'Dog, if you feel up to it, let's take one more question.' Tony pointed to a man in the audience who looked kind of familiar. 'Yes, you, sir. What's your question for Dog?'

'Hi, Tony. Thanks. Yes, well, I am a Texas highway patrolman who had the pleasure of meeting Mr Chapman this afternoon after stopping him for jaywalking. I came here to listen to your first guest, and to be honest, I didn't get too much out of what he had to say. So I decided to stay to hear Dog's story. I just wanted to thank you because it was the greatest story I ever heard. I want to go back to the station and tell all the guys about Dog, because he is truly inspiring.'

I got a standing ovation after the cop spoke. I could see tears welling up in Tony's eyes. I leaned over and said, 'You cry too, brother?'

I could feel my own tears of joy starting to come. Two giants on a stage – I had to laugh as we both stood there and cried.

I began speaking at Tony's seminars on a pretty regular basis. One day, he asked me why I enjoyed the experience so much.

It was a simple answer. I loved hearing two little words that packed as big a punch as Joe Louis's left hook: 'Thank you.' I went on to explain that no one ever says thank you when I get the bad guy. In fact, for the most part, other people take most of the credit for all of my hard work. I told Tony I wouldn't know what to do if a bondsman actually thanked me.

Towards the end of a seminar in Palm Springs, Tony surprised me by asking everyone in the audience to come up and thank me. There were hundreds of people there. Each and every person came up to me, gave me a hug, shook my hand or patted my shoulder, and said, 'Thank you, Dog.' Once again, tears rolled. I have never been so overwhelmed or grateful. It was a beautiful, practically spiritual experience.

# CHAPTER TWENTY-FIVE

# Mistake

Tawny coerced me into marrying her. I told her I didn't want to marry her because I liked women too much to settle down. I even talked it over with my preacher, who could see I was unsettled by the idea. I knew in my heart that marrying Tawny was a mistake. She was all wrong for me. My kids liked her, though. They were even calling her 'Mom'.

Friends told me that Tawny took speed. When I told her what people were saying, she promised she'd go straight. On the other hand, that girl could rock my world. I was torn between my heart and my head.

Despite my misgivings, I married Tawny. Two months into the marriage, it was obviously a disaster. Even the judge who married us pulled me aside and asked me if I wanted to take a little more time to think about marrying that broad.

Beth was now working for Granville Lee, the first black bondsman in Denver. He was one of the brightest in the business. Other bondsmen continuously warned me about Beth, saying she was tough, ruthless, and smart as hell. Ahhh . . . all the qualities I like in a woman, plus she was rack-tacular. My competitors saw Beth as a threat; I saw her as an asset. Despite my personal feelings for her, I had just got married again. I didn't think I had room for another woman.

One day Beth and I were talking on the street when an old buddy of mine, Keith Barmore, came over to say hello. Keith and I grew up together. We spent most of our youth fighting the Vatos. Keith was a large guy, with hands as big as my dad's. He was physically strong and emotionally volatile. He became known as 'One-Punch Barmore' because he only needed one to knock you down. He was eventually sent away to a juvenile detention centre.

Keith was no better as an adult than he was as a punk kid. He would drink beer heavily. It just about broke my heart when I heard Beth was dating him. When I heard they got married, I got physically sick. There couldn't have been two people in the world who were worse together than Beth and Keith. Friends told me he was abusing her something awful. Beth's a tough girl, but when I heard about what he was doing to her, I wanted to kill him myself. The only good thing that came from their union was Beth's beautiful daughter, Cecily, whom I love and adore as if she were my own flesh and blood.

Truth be told, Beth and I were sleeping together the entire time I was married to Tawny and throughout her marriage to Keith. Beth used to jokingly threaten to take our motel bill to the office and show it to Tawny unless I promised to show up and spend more time with her. I always had Beth book the room in her name, just in case.

Even though we were both married, Beth was still in hot pursuit of my affection. After she got her bond licence, she began writing some pretty sketchy bail so I would have to chase down her guys if they skipped. Now, most bondsmen try to write bail based on a fugitive's word that he won't run. Not Beth. She was looking for high-risk guys to make sure she saw as much of me as she could. It was risky business, to say the least. It would have put her *out* of business if I weren't the Dog. She knew I could find anyone. It was a calculated risk on her part, but a well-thought-out plan. That woman is manipulative but smart. She was making money and making me come to her. She had me chasing guys who weren't even on the run. Better still, she paid me every time!

Sometimes Beth would go with me on bounties when I needed a brain or a beautiful young girl to act as a decoy. The first time I took her with me was one of the funniest hunts I can remember. Beth was trailing my every move. When I finally spotted our guy, I yelled as loud as I could, 'Freeze, motherfucker! Get down on the ground with your hands in front of you!' I turned to check on Beth. She was flat out, facedown on the ground.

'Not you, Beth. Get up!' She wouldn't move. I could see her motioning for the fugitive to get down by patting her hands in a downward direction.

'Beth. You're no conductor. Get your ass up! I'm talking to him, not you!' But she wouldn't budge. She was scared to death I was going to hurt the son of a bitch.

A year after the Colorado statute was announced, Lozow appeared in front of Judge Hiatt again, only this time he argued that the ten-year statute made it possible for me to keep my licence. In spite of the DA's argument that he couldn't confirm what Lozow was saying, the judge had heard enough and ruled in my favour. I dodged another bullet and was able to continue.

Throughout the year, I couldn't help but think the Division of Insurance was trying to push me out of the business. Someone with a lot of power and influence was gunning for me. All of these laws and bills were popping up that were seemingly aimed directly at me, with one goal: to shut me down.

I received a call from an investigator from the Division of Insurance. Not long after I got my licence back from Judge Hiatt, he needed me to post a bail bond for a family member. It seemed a little strange that he came to me, especially since the Division of Insurance was always breathing down my neck. I agreed to write the bond, thinking it was my way of extending an olive branch in peace and good will. The following day, I called the investigator to enquire about the nine hundred dollars he owed me for writing the bond. He hemmed and hawed and then said he already put the cheque in the mail. I just love it when someone tells me, 'The cheque is in the mail.' Translation: You're screwed.

Three days later – still no cheque. When I tried to reach the investigator, there was no getting through. Ironically, I did receive a call from another local bondsman who called to tell me I was never going to get paid. This small bond wasn't going to put me out of business, but it sure as hell was going to send the investigator's family member back to jail.

The investigator wanted to meet for a 'business opportunity'. This was beginning to stink to high heaven of a low-down dirty set-up. I called Lozow to see what he thought. Lozow made it clear he thought something was up, but he told me to take the meeting. I called my mom to tell her what was happening. She became suspicious and thought it might be a good idea to record the meeting just in case.

We met at Copperfields, a bar in downtown Denver near the courthouse where cops and lawyers like to hang out. The investigator walked in looking way overdressed for the joint. It occurred to me he was dressed pretty nice, worth a couple grand, for an investigator from the Division of Insurance. I grew suspicious right away. I clicked on my recorder before we sat at a table, to capture every second of dialogue. Good thing I did.

We got right to the point.

The deal was a 'one-time proposition'. Any complaint from one of my clients would be taken care of. In exchange for that service, I had to pay five hundred dollars per complaint. Once I paid, the problem would go away.

Now, I knew the offer was illegal. If I agreed, I would be out of business for good. I kept saying, 'This is illegal', to be certain the recording proved I wasn't interested. The investigator assured me it *wasn't* illegal. When I asked how will you 'show this' the investigator said it would be considered a 'fine', and suggested I shouldn't talk about our little arrangement. When I enquired about the bond money he owed me, I was told, 'Consider it a down payment for future complaints.'

I didn't commit, but I didn't turn it down, either. I left the bar and called Lozow and told him what happened. A few days later, Lozow called to say it was a shakedown. It was all a scam and he told me to keep the tape. Quite to my surprise, a few days later I received the bond money due me. That was the last I heard about this for a while.

# CHAPTER TWENTY-SIX

# Aloha From Hawaii

I began speaking at Tony Robbins's seminars at least once a year. That became the only real vacation I took. I'd run myself all year long until I was completely exhausted, and then I'd go to a seminar to recharge and refuel my batteries. I'd always come back invigorated in both myself and my faith.

In 1991, I attended a Mastery Seminar in Hawaii that changed my life for ever. These are ten-day intensive courses designed for people like me who are familiar with Tony's philosophy and who attend the one- and two-day seminars regularly. I was excited to be a part of this seminar, because I was there as both speaker and student.

Whenever I spoke at a Robbins seminar, I always entered the room with the song 'Secret Agent Man' blaring in the background. I would walk from the back of the auditorium as it played, and the crowd would stand up and applaud. This time, I walked in to 'I've Got the Power'. The feeling and appreciation I got from that hundred-yard walk would get me over every hurdle, past every roadblock, and through every indignity I had to endure for the next year. On this particular night, I gave the crowd the best of all I had to offer.

Tony spent much of the ten days talking about how life is a struggle, something that my mom always said too. Those words floated in my thoughts the entire time I was in Hawaii.

After I spoke, I took my seat at one of the many banquet tables. The waiter placed two forks to the left of my plate. I called him over. I thought he had made a mistake.

'You're going to lose your job. You gave me two forks.' I was seriously concerned for this young man.

'No, brother. You're supposed to have two. It's good. No worries.'

I wasn't sophisticated enough to know any better. I wasn't ghetto dumb. I just never went to dinner any place fancy that gave me more than one fork, knife or spoon.

I looked up at the waiter and noticed he had much darker skin than I had. He wasn't black, but he wasn't white, either.

'Why did you call me brother?' I was curious to hear his response. I wasn't offended. In fact, I liked the sound very much. But in my world, BRO meant 'Bend Right Over', or else it was a word I heard the black guys use on the streets. The way my waiter used the word, it had a different feel.

He looked at me with a kind smile and said, 'Under the skin, we are all brothers.'

His name was Skip. He was pure Hawaiian. I liked everything about him. I always felt a connection or brotherhood when I was a biker brother, but it had been years since I felt that way. Skip opened a door that had been slammed stone cold shut since Huntsville. Skip was the first to introduce me to Aloha, the spirit of love and welcome.

My ten days at the Mastery Seminar solidified my need for brotherhood. For the first time in years, I belonged to an organisation where everyone around me was a brother or a sister. I met lots of interesting people who felt the same way. I met Martin Sheen and the well-known film producer Peter Guber. I knew Martin Sheen from television. He liked to ask me a lot of questions. He was one of the most positive thinkers I have ever met. He also has an uncanny skill to prophesy. In 1989, he predicted I would someday have my own television show.

I had no idea who Peter Guber was. He and I didn't get along too well at first. I challenged him to climb a sixty-foot pole. Now, I'm afraid of heights, but I wanted to show this guy that I wasn't afraid of anything. Turns out Peter was afraid of heights too. I made it up the pole as fast as I could, but only a little more than halfway before I shimmied back down.

'This guy's no bounty hunter.' Peter was taunting me. I was a convict turned bounty hunter in a circle full of rich, powerful celebrities and businessmen. I felt out of place, but I was there to push myself to places I never dreamed were possible. That's the reason I came to Hawaii – to master my skills.

I had to do the climb again. I had to complete the task, challenge myself to go further than before. I closed my eyes and began visualising myself as a hamster going through a tube. I kept thinking it would be fine if I fell because Tony Robbins was so rich, the lawsuit filed by my family would ensure they'd be set for life! I kept my mind occupied the entire climb until I reached the top. I already knew I could do anything I set my mind to. This climb was just another challenge I had to get through.

Now it was Peter's turn. He began to climb up the pole. I could see he was as panicked as I was. He stopped a few feet off the ground.

I started screaming at him, 'Close your eyes! Tony Robbins is rich. If you die, you'll own a lot of shit!'

All of a sudden, Tony walked over to where we were. He was amused by our exchange. I had no idea Peter was already a very rich man. I also didn't know how heavy he was in Hollywood. I should have been a lot nicer to him!

I met the wife of the late comedian John Candy at the same seminar. She loved to sing opera, and I fell in love with her the moment she began to sing. I'd never heard opera before, but hearing her voice sent me to the moon.

I was filled with a glow that I'd been waiting for all my life. Hawaii felt like home. I felt like I had been searching all my life for a place that had these values, these ideals. The islands took hold of me – the smells, the ocean, the flowers, everything growing and growing and growing – and I realised this was the place I'd always been searching for.

It finally occurred to me why I came. If life is but a struggle, like Tony and my mom said, why not struggle in paradise?

The last day of the seminar, everyone goes around a circle and says what they plan to do, now that they have completed the Mastery programme. When my turn came, I looked at the group and said, 'I'm moving to Hawaii!' I had it all figured out. I would start a bail bonds business and hunt bounty in the Pacific for a while. I was paid five grand for speaking at the seminar, so I had the money to get started right away. I didn't see any reason to leave the island.

Later that day, a couple of the seminar trainers took me aside. 'You know, Dog, you don't have to take it this seriously.'

'I'm staying.' My mind was made up.

That night I called my mom. 'I'm not coming back.'

'But Duane, what about your life here in Denver? What about your home, your kids?'

'For the first time in my life, I feel like I *am* home.' I cried as I shared my truth.

'Are you drunk, Duane?'

I just laughed and said, 'No, Mom. I'm not drunk. I'm just happy.' She could tell I was serious, and she knew I wasn't coming back.

'Just watch the kids for me for a few weeks. Let me get the ball rolling here. I've got a foot in the door. I have to take this chance, Mom.'

I thought my affiliation with Tony Robbins would make it easy to get my bail bonds licence. But as always in my life since Huntsville, that murder one rap defined me. It has always been and will always be something I will need to overcome. I was rejected, considered unsuitable to write bonds in Hawaii. It was an unexpected setback.

I went before the judge to explain my situation. As ammunition, I even held up a copy of Tony Robbins's book *Awaken the Giant Within*. I pointed to the two or three paragraphs where Tony uses my story to illustrate how a man can turn his life around. I used the book like a résumé. My story was compelling enough for the judge to give me special permission to get my licence.

Once the judge gave me the green light, I had barely enough money left over to pay for food and a rental car for another month. With the rest, I had a thousand business cards printed and bought my mobile phone.

I'll never forget that first September living in Hawaii. It was the month that Hurricane Aniki hit. It caused massive damage throughout the islands. And while it raged, I was sleeping and working in a rental car parked under a freeway overpass. I'd spend every precious day at the jail and courts from the minute they opened until after they closed, handing out my cards, trying to get business. Things were a lot tougher than I expected. My Denver offices were very lucrative. I thought I'd be up and running in no time. But Hawaii isn't Denver. The bail bonds business was locked up by a couple of bondsmen who were here long before me. They wanted nothing to do with Dog or my unorthodox methods.

As the month drew to a close, I was down to eating one bowl of Vietnamese *pho* noodle soup a day. I began to wonder if Hawaii was a dream that was just out of my reach or a nightmare that was about to implode.

Within a year, my marriage to Tawny had fallen apart. I was dividing my time between Denver and Hawaii. I had moved Tawny and the kids to the island, but I wasn't happy to be married to her. If we got into an argument, I'd get drunk and find myself a whore. Eventually, I told her to pack her bags and go.

I travelled back and forth between Honolulu and Denver a couple of times during my first year. I was trying to get settled in my new environment and get the business off the ground. Thank God the Denver offices were doing well, because I needed all the help I could get to subsidise the new Honolulu office. After my first few months, I barely had enough money to pay for the minimal overhead.

I was down to zero. I bought a Charlie Brown Christmas tree for the family that year because it was all I could afford. The kids and I were sharing a bottle of ketchup, pretending it was spaghetti sauce.

And then my phone rang. It was a guy named Folia. He needed a bond for fifty thousand, and he had a cousin named Malcolm Flores who needed one for a hundred grand. Blam. I made fifteen grand on the spot. The timing couldn't have been better. It saved my life and my business was off the ground.

# CHAPTER TWENTY-SEVEN

# Mirror Image

I was living in Hawaii when I won the 1991 Hero of the Year award from the *Rocky Mountain News* in Denver. Life was pretty good. I had just finished my first Tony Robbins Mastery Seminar and was trying to live my life in a righteous and proud way. Tony's wisdom and words flowed through me, inspiring a new perspective on life. I was eager to get my office set up in Oahu. The promise of paradise kept me motivated to make a name for myself in Hawaii.

Just as I began to get settled, I received a phone call that I wasn't expecting from the mother of one of my first girlfriends. I hadn't thought about Patty Coffee in years. We began dating when I left home in 1968. She was nineteen when we met. Patty had one eye that was a little bit crooked, but she was beautiful to me. I was working for my dad in metal fabrication, slaving my ass off to make four hundred bucks a week. She was a stripper. I've always had a thing for strippers. I knew a little about sex when we met but not enough to truly satisfy a woman. I'd screw any girl with big tits who'd take her top off. I had no idea they had to have a brain, too.

Patty taught me where to touch a woman, how to touch her body, and all sorts of other wild things I never knew I could do. She read sex books to me out loud so I could remember everything. I wasn't even sixteen years old. For the first time in my life, I was a very eager student. Her approach was a little mechanical at first, but once I got the hang of it, sex was better than I had ever imagined it could be.

When I turned sixteen, I started screwing every woman I met. I loved making love. Patty understood I wanted to see other women. I was young and sowing my oats.

I met a girl named Debbie White, whose family owned a successful florist shop in Denver. The last time I saw Debbie I noticed her tits were a little bit bigger and her tummy was a little rounder than usual. I didn't think anything about it at the time.

By then I needed to leave Denver for a few reasons. For one, I had too many girlfriends. I heard Debbie committed suicide just before I got out of prison in 1979.

It had been more than twenty years, so as you can imagine, I was rather surprised to hear Debbie's mother's voice on the other end of the phone. She always hated me. When I was a kid, she chased me out of her yard, telling me to get my biker ass off her property. There was no love lost between us.

'Duane Lee, I have something to tell you.' My heart stopped. I knew what she was going to say. I was certain she was going to tell me I had AIDS. I thought about it for a moment and realised it had been too long. I would have known by now if I had AIDS.

Just then, Debbie's mother said she had to call me back.

'Wait. Stop.' She hung up before I could hear why she called. Whatever it was, it couldn't be good.

The next day, she called me back. She was direct and to the point. 'Duane, you have a son.'

'Oh, my God!' It was the last thing I expected to hear. But then I remembered my mother once telling me about bumping into Debbie after I moved to Illinois. If Mom would have told me about Debbie while I was with LaFonda, I probably would have wanted to be with Debbie. I loved both women. Mom knew I would never have left Denver if I had known about the baby.

'One day you're going to be very happy, son.' That is all she said. Mom knew a kid would heal me from my wrong ways. But she also knew Debbie wasn't the right girl. Debbie and I shared drugs together. She tried to keep me away from hard drugs but couldn't do it.

'Shut up and sit on the back of the bike, bitch.' Like Patty, she was also a stripper. I never met a stripper who was filled with self-esteem, and Debbie was no exception. We shot pure crank – speed, methamphetamine – together. All us bikers shot crank back then. We were outlaw bastards. We'd get into wild, crazy fights and wouldn't care. I never felt a thing from being on that stuff. I never got hooked, thank God.

'His name is Christopher Michael. He's in jail for committing a hate crime.'

My heart sank thinking about Christopher. After all these years, I finally discovered I have another son, and he's behind bars. It was more than I could bear. I knew what it felt like to be a young man who made foolish choices. Prison is no place for a boy.

I called Tawny to give her the good news. She didn't see it that way. I asked her to go with my mom to the jail to meet Christopher.

She called me right away. 'Oh, my God, Duane. His hands, his features, he's exactly like you.' In a way, I was hoping she might come back saying there was no resemblance, but I love kids so much it wouldn't have mattered. I was so happy to have another son.

'Mom, did you see him too?' I asked.

'He's your kid, Duane. No doubt about it.' Whenever Mom used words like 'might have' or 'must have' she was lying, but in a Christian way. She never wanted to hurt me. When I asked her one final time if she'd known about Christopher, she said, 'Well, I might have had my suspicions.'

I saw the addition of Christopher to my family as a blessing. The Lord was smiling on the Chapman family. I had a brand-new boy. Granted, he was twenty-one years old, but he was my baby boy. I felt like my karma was all good. I was getting my office set up in Hawaii, living the dream.

First chance I got, I flew back to Colorado to meet my boy. I went down to the county jail. By this time, I was already well known in Denver as the Dog. I had a love-hate relationship with the cops there. Since I had just won the Hero of the Year award, the lieutenant showed me a great deal of respect. I told him my story about Christopher. He was understanding and sympathetic. 'Let's go see the boy.'

He took me to the third tier of the jail.

'Daddy!!' I saw a scrawny little white boy running towards me. He cut in and out of the black guys, like he was running for a touchdown. Christopher jumped into my arms like he was a little kid. He was a mirror image of me at that age.

'Daddy! I knew you were alive.' He was a child stuck in a man's body. I had to get him out of this place. I posted his bond that same day. I took him to my mom and dad's.

Flash looked at him and said, 'That's the boy you will always have around because he will be lost without you.' It's true that Christopher is needier than my other adult children. He's extremely immature for his age, but I love him as much as any of the others. His adoptive mother told me he was diagnosed with ADD/ADHD. That's bullshit. The only thing Christopher suffers from is SAC – Stubborn Ass Chapman.

After his mother killed herself, Christopher was put into foster care. The woman who adopted him hated me. In a strange twist of fate, my grandpa Chapman lived across the street from the family that adopted my son. When Christopher was four and five years old, Grandpa bounced him on his knee, unaware he really was his great-grandson. By the grace of God, he was never without his real family.

Christopher was charged with committing a hate crime and burglary. He was facing forty-five years in the joint. The judge presiding over his case was a guy I knew when I first starting writing bail in Denver. At the time, he was just a lawyer named Frank Martinez. I wrote a lot of bail for Mexican clients in the early days. I told them they couldn't run, and they hardly ever did. We shook hands like blood brothers. I used to suggest Martinez's firm to my clients because he was so honest.

I met Martinez in a funny way. I passed him one day in the hallway of the courthouse and we bumped into each other on purpose.

We snarled at each other for no other reason than our machismo.

'What's your problem, essa?'

'What did you just call me?' Thank God, Dick Jordan, another bondsman, stepped between us. He told us we were just alike and would actually like each other.

Two days later, Martinez called me. 'I've never met anyone like you, Dog. You defend my people. You're not Mexican. Why would you aggressively defend my people?'

My explanation was simple: 'They're my people too. I'm a bondsman. I don't care where my clients come from. They're all my brothers.'

Martinez must have appreciated my candour. 'Well, Dog, I'll send you all of my clients if you send me yours.' By law, I wasn't allowed to recommend a particular lawyer, but I could affirm a client's choice. From that day on, I sent all of my Mexican clients to Martinez.

A year later, I heard someone call my name as I was walking in a courthouse corridor.

'Dog, I want to show you something.'

I turned around and saw Martinez pointing to a courtroom. I walked through the double doors and saw a nameplate reading JUDGE FRANK MARTINEZ on the desk in the centre of the room. I was so happy for my compadre. He became one of the smartest, fairest, sternest judges to preside in the Denver court system. Whenever I walked into his courtroom, Martinez got a big grin on his face.

'Well, if it isn't the Mighty Dog.' He had a deep, hearty laugh.

'Dog, tell everyone about working the chain gang in Texas. I want my courtroom to hear how you turned your life around.'

I'd tell the story of being in Huntsville and the gruelling days of working the fields, hoping my journey would help convicts go straight.

As luck would have it, Martinez was the presiding judge for Christopher's case. I called him up to let him know my son was on his docket. I told him Christopher wasn't a gay basher. He's just a redneck who didn't know any better. My son was weak-minded and didn't have the capability to know what he was doing was wrong. Martinez heard me out. He told me to come to court with Christopher and his lawyer. When I got there, he asked me to repeat what I'd said on the phone. The judge found mercy in his heart to drop the hate-crime charge and reduced his charge to robbery. Christopher took a nickel, which equals five years in prison, for his crime. He got very lucky.

# CHAPTER TWENTY-EIGHT

# My Darkest Day

In a sense, I am the biggest mama's boy ever. My mom meant the world to me. She taught me to appreciate the ladies, treat them with respect, to embrace their loveliness, and adore their companionship. Women weren't allowed to run with the guys when I was in the Disciples. They could hang out with us, but never, ever could they go on a robbery or a score. But I always have to have my lady with me. I worry about her when we're apart. It's not a jealousy thing so much as it is deeply caring for her well being. There's nothing like holding a woman close and always having her near.

It was very hard for me to accept that I caused my momma pain when I was growing up. No matter what I did, what mistakes or poor choices I made, Mom was always there for me. She loved me unconditionally, in a way no other woman can.

In late 1993, my sister Joleen called from Denver to tell me Mom was dying of emphysema and severe angina. I didn't believe it until Beth called me and said my mom really was dying. She bought me a plane ticket to come right home.

Eleven hours after receiving Beth's call, I was at my mother's bedside at St Anthony North Hospital, in Northglenn. I held her hand, trying not to show my own fear at the thought of losing her. I gently brushed back her hair with my fingertips, speaking in a tone just louder than a whisper. 'When you get better, I'm going to move you out to Hawaii so we can be closer.'

I could see Mom's eyes light up at the thought of spending the rest of her life in paradise. She squeezed my hand so tight. Now she had a reason to get better, a motivation to live. I prayed over Momma and asked the Lord to help heal her from her disease.

'Lord Jesus, bless us with your great gift of healing. We need you now more than ever, Lord. I need my momma, her strength, her spirit. Please, Lord. I beg you to heal her from her illness and allow her to stay here with her family just a little while longer.' Tears streamed down my face as I begged the Lord for my momma's life.

Just then, my mother's doctor pulled me aside to talk about options. I stood listening to him with my dad and Joleen. In an effort to relieve her discomfort and prolong her life, the doctors wanted to perform a tracheotomy. But Mom wasn't the kind of woman who could stand living with tubes or holes in her neck.

When he told me that, I turned to my dad and asked, 'Does he know who I am?' Reluctantly, Dad told me he did. I got right in the doctor's face and told him, 'If my mom dies, you die. Got it?' The doctor looked at my dad to see if he was going to jump in. He didn't. Dad, Joleen, and the doctor stood silent, knowing damn well I meant it.

Her eyes lit up and she straightened herself in the bed. She squeezed my hand and nodded. With Hawaii in her future, Joleen said, her spirit and health improved with every passing day.

The day my mother arrived in Honolulu was a truly blessed day.

She said, 'Son, I don't know why I didn't raise you here. I am so sorry. You are right. This is beautiful!' I don't think I ever saw my mom look happier than she did in that moment after stepping off the plane.

Mom came out first, while Dad worked in my bail bonds office in Denver. As soon as he could, Dad came out and joined her. My plan was for them to take it as easy as possible, to just relax and fish. For once in their lives, I didn't want them to worry about a thing. I was able to get her and Dad an apartment just above ours on Oahu at the Waipuna. That way, Mom had the chance to play with the grandbabies whenever she wanted, and I could spend time building up the business. Although she loved the kids, what Mom really wanted to do was help me out. She did all the bookkeeping, while Dad learned the bond business. With their help, for the first time in my career, all of my bills were paid, and there was money left over in the bank. That cushion gave me room to grow. I began looking for other office locations right away.

I checked out the other islands, but no location seemed as logical as or more appealing than Kona, on the Big Island. The Big Island is so called because it is more than twice the size of all of the other Hawaiian islands combined. The terrain ranges from high mountains to sandy beaches, from dense tropical rain forests to vast pastures. The moment I landed in Kona, I thought I would spend the rest of my days living in that particular tropical paradise. I envisioned my parents moving in with my family and me, so we'd all live together in one huge compound.

Despite Mom's illness being in remission, I was well aware of her fragility. She had been on oxygen for so many years that she had developed a wrinkle where the tube went around her face. She was very meticulous about her appearance, and she hated that damn wrinkle. A month after arriving in Hawaii, Mom was off the oxygen. It was a miracle.

I had no idea how much time we had left together, but I knew damn well I wanted to make every minute count. Even though I appreciated her help around the office, I wanted her to live a comfortable and easy life. Once I brought my parents to see Kona, they fell in love with it about as fast as I did.

That was it. I immediately began searching for a home where we could all live. At the very least, I wanted Mom and Dad to have their own place. One day, I found the most beautiful house high on a hill above Kailua. The views were breathtaking. I could see the mountains and ocean from every room in the house. For twenty-five hundred dollars a month, the house could be mine.

Crash. That was the sound of my dream falling to the bottom of the sea. I couldn't afford that kind of money for rent. It was out of the question. The owner asked me why I looked so sad.

I explained who I was and why I was looking for a home in Kona. 'I brought my mother to Hawaii to live the rest of her life in paradise.' The house was exactly what I imagined. Unfortunately, I forgot that paradise comes with a price.

The owner and I sat and talked for a while longer. She told me Elvis Presley had done the same thing for his mom. She looked at me and said, 'You know, my mortgage is only $850. If you were able to cover that, I would be satisfied.'

I was in shock.

She smiled and asked, 'So . . . deal?'

How could I refuse? Two weeks later, my parents moved in. I felt so proud.

Mom and Dad ran the Kona office for me. Things were going pretty good. Mom flew to Honolulu whenever I couldn't make it to Kona.

About a year after moving to Kona, Mom called and said she wanted to come for a visit. I picked her up in my MG Midget, and we spent the next three days driving all over Oahu. We talked endlessly about our family, my Indian roots, and my dreams, hopes, goals and passions. I told her about my need to follow the sun, my heart and my visions. Mom explained that was the way of her people. She was very exact when she spoke to me on that trip. She wanted to make sure I understood who I was, where I came from, and my path towards the future.

Mom and I loved shopping together. I never got tired or bored while she browsed. She was always filled with such wonder, as if she was trying to soak in as much information as she could. For some inexplicable reason, on that particular visit, I felt like she was running some type of race. At the time, I had no idea why. She even put a red, decorative clown mask on layaway, as if to say she would be back to pay for it in full sometime soon. Just before leaving to go back to Kona, we stopped at a flower shop to buy a gardenia plant. She loved gardenias. The fragrance always reminds me of her. She put it in my living room before she flew back, deliberately picking a spot I could see each time I came into the house. Every gesture, each word she spoke, every gentle touch filled my heart with joy and my eyes with tears.

When we got to the airport, Mom handed me a card but told me not to open it until after she was gone.

That was odd. She said 'after I'm gone'. Driving home, something struck me about the way she turned and waved goodbye. It felt different to usual, as if it was a final farewell.

I opened the card when I got home. In her beautiful handwriting, the note said:

> *Dear Duane,*
> *I know you want this to say I loved you more than everybody, but I didn't. I loved you all the same. I want you to know that I know that you loved me the most. This is going to hurt you the worst, but no matter what I will always be there. Remember, you are the leader.*
> *Love,*
> *Mom*

I cried like a baby. Was she saying goodbye? What did she mean? Later that night, my phone rang.

'Hello, Duane. It's Mom. What are you doing?'

The truth is, I had a girl there who wasn't my wife. I wanted to get off the phone, if you know what I mean, so I hurried the conversation along.

Mom softly said, 'I just called to say goodbye . . . '

I was completely oblivious and too preoccupied to hear what she was saying. 'Well, OK, Mom, 'bye.' I hung up.

The next day, Tim 'Youngblood' Chapman, my long-time friend and bounty hunting associate, came over to tell me to call my dad right away. When I did, Dad said, 'I can't wake your mother.'

'What do you mean, Dad? Shake her!'

'Duane, your mother's dead.' There was no cushion, no sensitivity. Dad just blurted out those words as cold as ice. I didn't want to hear what he was saying. I refused to listen.

I became very angry and belligerent. Just then, Tawny called me from my dad's house. I told her, 'You better put my bible on her chest, and raise her from the dead. If you don't bring my momma back, I don't know what I'll do!' I was out of control. What made me think my soon-to-be ex-wife Tawny, of all people, could bring my mom back from the dead? I wasn't making any sense at all.

'Duane, she's dead. She passed away. I can't bring her back.' Tawny tried to stay calm, but I was a wreck. No one could get through to me. I'd just lost my mommy. I wanted to kick myself in the ass for having that whore over the night before. I should have taken the time to talk to my mom.

I spent most of my life putting Mom through hell, and now she was standing at the gates of heaven. Sixty years of stress killed her. The doctors told me she died a peaceful death. No pain or suffering. She just quit breathing. They wanted to do an autopsy. I wouldn't let them. I wasn't going to let anyone slice open my mother.

I don't remember much after getting off the phone that day. Youngblood came over for a while, but there was nothing anyone could do to ease my intolerable pain. I left the apartment and started walking. It was a hot and humid September morning. I was wearing my cowboy boots and jeans, no socks or shirt. I don't usually drink hard alcohol. I was never the kind of guy who turned to the bottle. But all I could think about was finding a fifth of whiskey and getting drunk. I wanted to dull the sharp ache in my heart. I drank as I walked more than twenty miles from Waikiki Beach to Diamond Head and then on towards Sandy Beach.

Sometimes I feel like there are two guys who live inside of me. There's

Duane and then there's the Dog. I tried to pull Duane out that day, but it was Dog who emerged. When I drink, I'm not the same man. Duane can't handle pain or significant problems. That's when the Dog comes out. He's got a hardened heart. He's capable of handling anguish and agony. He's the boy who was kicked around in the seventh grade.

I finished the entire bottle before collapsing on a curb alongside the highway. I began to cry – no, make that *wail*. My feet were rubbed raw, stuck to the insides of my leather boots. When I pulled the boots off, a stream of blood dripped on to the gravel. My feet were unrecognisable, swollen way beyond their normal size. Blisters had given way to open sores. Whatever skin was left was inflamed and on the verge of infection.

I looked up and saw a cop pulling over. I am sure I looked like a homeless person or a strung-out junkie.

'Brother, what's the matter?'

'Get lost, copper!'

Again, the cop said, 'Brother, what's the matter?'

'My mommy died . . . ' Once again I began to cry.

'Come on, get in the car. I'll take you home.'

'Naw. Get lost.'

Thank God the cop wasn't taking my anger personally. He finally coaxed me into the car.

I began to tell him about how my mom came to Oahu the day before and how she wore her little scarf over her head driving around in my car.

'All the things we talked about, I had no idea she was saying goodbye. For real, man. Now I can look back and see God was telling me something but I wasn't listening.'

The officer stayed silent as I spilled my guts.

'She waved her hand this strange way when she left. She said, "Goodbye, son."' On the ride home with the cop, it occurred to me that I wasn't walking close enough with God to know when He was giving me messages. I needed to start paying more attention to Him. From that day on, I've never been far from His side.

# CHAPTER TWENTY-NINE

# Cracking Up

After my mother died, I spiralled into an unfamiliar world of darkness. Throughout my life, the Lord has challenged me in ways I was always able to overcome. Beth was back in Denver, still married to her first husband, Keith. Everyone she saw told her to stay far away from me – that I had changed. Beth kept trying to find me to see what was happening. She was hearing things about me that didn't make any sense. She wanted to come to my mother's funeral, but Tawny wouldn't let her. Beth and Tawny were the best of friends and worst of enemies. Do you know the old saying, 'Keep your friends close and your enemies closer'? That is a perfect description of Beth and Tawny's relationship.

Tawny and I officially separated in 1994, but our marriage was over long before that. I was having such a hard time after Mom died. Tawny finally hit a wall. She showed me some Halcion pills. I wasn't thinking straight enough to know what I was doing. I took the pills. Had it not been for Baby Lyssa and Barbara Katie, I would be dead. They kept me awake until the pills were out of my system.

After I broke up with Tawny, I began a relationship with a woman. I met her after placing an ad in the local paper for a nanny to help take care of my kids. I thought she was wonderful. She cooked, took care of me, and looked after my kids like they were her own. I was shocked that thirty or forty women responded. I'd meet them in a bar or have them come by the house for an interview.

Almost every time, the girls wanted to screw. They'd say things like, 'When I read your ad, I could tell you were really just looking for love', or 'You're looking for a mom for these kids, aren't you?'

As hard as it was for me to believe, they were right. When I placed the ad, I didn't even realise what I was really looking for.

It was great. I was getting laid all the time, but I couldn't find an appropriate woman to care for my children.

You know the old saying, 'Love is blind'. Well, if that's true, I was a regular Ray Charles, because the woman I fell in love with was anything but perfect. In fact, it seemed as though everyone could see her for who she really was – except me.

The first time I introduced her to Youngblood, I was so proud. In my eyes, she was attractive.

Right away, though, Youngblood pulled me aside and said, 'She's a druggie. What the hell are you doing?'

I was almost offended by his comment. 'No way, man. She's no druggie.' I found myself defending this woman in a way I had never had to in previous relationships. She wasn't as smart as most of the women I'd been with, but that didn't make her an addict, at least not in my mind.

'Duane, she's a drug addict.' Youngblood stood firm in his conviction. He knew me better than anyone. It wasn't like me to be so naïve. I make my living by reading people. How could I have been so wrong?

I waited a few days to ask her if she was doing drugs. When I did, she denied it. A couple of weeks later, I began to notice she was a little hyper. She was zipping around the house, cleaning up, and getting stuff done at a much quicker pace than usual. She wasn't lazy, but she wasn't usually a great housekeeper. Once again, I asked if she was on drugs.

'I do a couple lines of coke every now and then. It's not a big deal.'

'Well, it's a big deal to me, honey. You can't do that any more.' I was adamant. Since I got out of Huntsville, I didn't do heavy drugs. I smoked pot, but coke, crack, ice, Ecstasy and heroin were all off my radar screen. They are a no-no for Dog the Bounty Hunter. I tried to explain how I could lose my bail bonds licence if I got caught with drugs in my house. As a convicted felon, it wouldn't go down well if that shit was a part of my life.

I decided to let the subject go. I didn't understand her need to do cocaine, because I didn't need it. For six months, I didn't connect the dots. By now, we were living together. One night, she came to me and said, 'It's time we take our relationship to another level. I'd like to see you do the wild thing with my girlfriend.'

'Cool!' What guy wouldn't dig his lady coming to him and saying she wanted to get it on with another beautiful woman? I was totally into the idea, but I knew I had to get drunk, stoned, or take a Valium to go there, because I wasn't normally the kind of man who wanted to share sex with anyone except my old lady.

'OK, call your friend.' I began to drink before she got to the house. I wanted to loosen up, be cool, you know how it is. I didn't want to be the nervous dorky guy. I thought a few drinks would help calm me down. To be honest, I was as nervous as I was excited.

When her friend walked through the door, I thought I had died and gone to heaven. She was spectacular – long reddish hair, big tits and full hips. She took off her coat as I poured her a drink. She reached into her purse and pulled out a pipe. At first, I thought it was a regular pot pipe. After taking a closer look, I realised there was something yellowish-white in the pipe.

'Wanna try some?' She purred like a kitten.

'What is it?' I had no idea what she was smoking. I thought it looked like speed. If it was speed, I wanted nothing to do with it. I hate speed. You can't eat, screw or sleep on that drug. Shelly told me it was the opposite of speed. She said it was an aphrodisiac. Whatever it was, I wanted it.

The only thing I knew about smoking cocaine was what I read about Richard Pryor blowing himself up and catching on fire while freebasing. I had never heard the term *crack*, because that wasn't something anyone I hung around with was into. I didn't need any help feeling like a Spanish fly, but what the hell. I was willing to give it a try. I didn't have a clue what I was smoking, nor did I understand the danger.

The girls lifted the pipe to my mouth, lit it, and blam! After one hit, I lost my inhibitions. I ripped off all my clothes and began to live out my wildest fantasies. I kept asking, 'Why don't people market this shit? This is the greatest feeling I've ever had!'

Eight days later I finally came up for air. I had lost a tremendous amount of weight. One of the side effects of smoking cocaine is a lack of appetite. I hadn't eaten or slept for more than a week. I didn't leave the house or bathe. Girls kept coming over, bringing more coke. In a little more than a week, I went from Dry Dog to Drug Dog. I was snorting, smoking, freebasing, and drinking. I was hooked. Bad.

I no longer wanted to be Dog the Bounty Hunter. Duane was nowhere in sight. I began to call myself Kawani, which is Hawaiian for Duane.

I was addicted. While I hid out in my room getting high, Leland and Baby Lyssa tried to get rid of my girlfriend. They wanted her stone cold out of my life. I remember Baby Lyssa coming to me one day and telling me there were maggots in the kitchen sink. It hadn't been cleaned in weeks. My girlfriend asked me to send the kids back to live with their mother. There were times when I thought she might be right, but I didn't want to live without my babies. I was in deep. Too far. One night, out of pure desperation, I called Beth.

'Where have you been, baby?' I began to weep like a child as I confessed to Beth I'd been freebasing. 'I smoke it out of a pipe.' I have no idea how long we were on the phone, or what else we talked about.

Beth was on the next flight from Denver. I was too high to pick her up from the airport. Though I was a complete jackass, Beth wasn't ready to give up on me yet. She came to Kona to reclaim the house as hers. The first order of business was to get rid of my girlfriend. Beth could see I was a wreck so she handed me a couple of sleeping pills to take the edge off. Once I was asleep, Beth told my girlfriend to get out and never come back.

The house was an absolute disaster. Beth changed all the sheets, did mountains of laundry, cleaned the kitchen, scrubbed the bathroom, and stocked the fridge. I never even realised I had been sleeping without sheets on my bed, on a naked mattress, for weeks, if not months. Beth looked through my chequebook while I was asleep and discovered several cheques had been written to my girlfriend's drug dealer. That bitch was robbing me! Even though I knew Beth was coming from a place of truth and love, her brutal honesty hurt me. Beth has always been the one person in my life who slaps me in the face when I need to wake up and see how things are. She helps me come back to my senses when I've slipped or messed up.

I am an optimist. I think the best of everyone. Beth is a realist. She sees people for who they really are. I think that's why seeing me with a strung-out woman was so hard for Beth to understand and accept. She was literally and utterly in shock from the conditions we were living in. My physical appearance was almost as appalling as the mess she found around the house. Everything I had spent the last six months sweeping under the carpet was about to be revealed.

When I came to, Beth stood over me and said, 'Duane, your mother would roll over in her grave if she saw how you're living.' Beth is good that way. She knows just the right things to say to get under my skin fast and furious. Beth wanted to get me out of the house before my girlfriend came back, so she took me out for dinner. She thought I looked as though I hadn't eaten for weeks. I was unrecognisable, nearly emaciated. I was down to a hundred and forty-three pounds.

'Where's my Duane? Where's Dog?' Beth's voice sounded as broken as her heart.

'Dog is dead, Beth. I'm Kawani now.'

I remember hearing Beth say, 'Oh, my God' over and over.

'Dog is buried. He died with Mom. I'm different now. There's nothing you can do. It is what it is.'

'Kawani? You're Kawani? You're no flipping flower child, Duane. You're not a doper, either. What you're doing is a crime. It's illegal.'

That seemed like a pretty good moment to pull my crack pipe out of my pocket and light it up – right there in the restaurant.

Beth rolled her eyes and said, 'So, for our next trick, we're going to jail for possession of an illegal substance? Is that what you're telling me?' Hell, she and I had already been to jail for burglary. Why not? But Beth wasn't going to stand there and watch me go down in flames. No way.

'That's bullshit!' Beth was mad as hell. She grabbed the pipe and my dope right out of my hand. She wanted to beat the crap out of my girlfriend for getting me involved in this shit. She wanted to kick that chick's ass in front of me so I could see what a bad influence she had been. When we got home, the girls began to rumble, rolling around on the floor and beating on each other. I had to break up the fight before someone got hurt really bad . . . or worse.

'Take your crap and go, Beth.' I threw her out of my house. She was crushed. I had resisted drugs and other temptations during at least three thousand arrests of hardened criminals and four wives who were all users. I never slipped. Not once. Once my girlfriend started bringing other women into the bedroom, between the girls and the feeling I got being high, I was confused and unable to make rational decisions. I lost track of everything that was important in my life. I didn't care about work, my business, or myself.

# CHAPTER THIRTY

# Rock Bottom

Beth flew back to Denver the day after I threw her out. Six weeks later, I was begging her to come back.

'I can't live without you. You have to come back, honey. Come help me. I need you to help me.' I must have sounded pitiful.

Beth hopped on the next plane. She got to the house and found my girlfriend sitting on the sofa, all messed up in her pyjamas. I was thirty pounds thinner and had let my hair grow. I didn't have a pompadour any more, I just wore my hair shaggy around my face. She hardly recognised me. She asked if we could have sex so she could be sure it was me.

By now, Beth suspected there were problems with my business in Honolulu. She has that same sixth sense that I do. She kept telling me she thought something funky was going on. And, as it turned out, there was.

She flew to Oahu to check on A Hawaii, the Honolulu branch. I had ignored it for months. For the first time since I opened there, we were losing money. It didn't make sense, because that office was busier than ever.

Beth started investigating. I thought it was errors in bookkeeping or lack of management. Two days later, Beth called me and said, 'Duane, you've got problems.' I was hoping she was going to say it was no big deal, she'd handle it, and everything would be fine.

Wrong. She said, 'Your employees are stealing from you.'

There was no way what Beth was saying could be true. These were two of my closest and most trusted friends. Why would they steal from me? I put them into business. I gave them their jobs. It made no sense at all. We were like the three musketeers – all for one and one for all.

'That's not all. Both of them are taking their bail bonds test.' This wasn't good news.

Age 19 with Duane Lee

Boxing career

Denver, 1997, with Cecily and Bonnie Jo—her first camping trip

With Gary Boy, 2001

Cecily, Bonnie Jo, and Gary Boy at the Waipuna in Honolulu

Me and my boys at Tony Robbins's in Kona, Hawaii, 11 September 2001

The first day of the Luster hunt. Four Seasons Hotel, Beverly Hills, California, 5 January 2003.

Malibu, the home of Elizabeth Luster. Looking for her son, February 2003.

On Luster's trail

Shiner from Mexico

News conference in Mexico with Leland and our first lawyer, George Garza

Beth and I were invited to the Mansion for Independence Day, 4 July 2003, two days after returning from Mexico *(Reproduced by Special Permission of Playboy magazine. Copyright © 2003 by Playboy. Photo by Elayne Lodge)*

With Beth and Conan O'Brien

With Chuck Norris

With Beth, Lyssa, Leland, and Jay Leno *(Photo by: NBC Universal Photo Bank)*

With Beth in front
of our billboard

'Snap out of it, Duane. It's time to get back to reality, Big Daddy.' Whenever Beth calls me Big Daddy, I know she's being sincere and I'd best pay attention.

'From what I can see, the guys have been writing bail behind your back with your powers and pocketing the fees. They're skimming a few hundred bucks here and there, but from the looks of it, it's adding up to thousands of dollars.'

As hard as it was for me to believe, it was true. While I was lost in space for six months, the guys wrote two hundred eighty-five powers, signing my name to the cheques, and stealing eighty-five. A bail bond power of attorney, or 'power bail', is an instrument much like an oversize cashier's cheque from a bank. The bail bondsman signs this power and gives it to the jail or court official who will accept it and release the defendant from custody. This means they failed to report those bonds to the insurance company, Amwest. I was aware that the Honolulu office was consistently coming up short, and owing the insurance company money. Whenever that happened, I usually wrote a cheque to cover the deficit, because I knew I had payments coming in. I was only out-of-pocket for a short period.

This time was different. The insurance company became as suspicious as Beth after she saw their agent Richard Heath in Las Vegas at the bail convention in February 1997. Heath told Beth he'd heard I was doing drugs. Although she refused to answer him, she did suggest he come out to Hawaii to pay me a visit. Before Heath left, she said, 'Do yourself a favour. Don't call him first.'

Richard Heath came to audit my books in early March. In spite of Beth's suggestion, he did call to let me know he was coming. He told me to come to Honolulu to answer any questions he might have. I was writing four million dollars a year with that punk. I had to prove my innocence so I didn't take the fall. This business was all I had left. My sister Jolene was now running my Denver office. Kona wasn't netting a profit. If I lost Honolulu, I was done.

After a couple of days, Heath was convinced that I wasn't the one who wrote the powers. I could easily prove I was in Kona when they were written. Also, the paperwork was all done in someone else's handwriting, so I couldn't have been stealing from my own company. It was obvious who stole the money. Nonetheless, I promised Heath I would make up any deficit, so he could go back to his office and say it had all been worked out. After all, I didn't have a history of falling behind. I even had $200,000 in my 'build-up fund', which is like a slush fund the insurance company keeps on account to make sure they don't lose money if you don't pay.

My offer to make good wasn't enough to appease Heath. He sat me down and suggested I take a break from the business, take a year off to get my life together. He even offered to 'take over' my business and clean things up while I worked on getting my personal life in order. As added 'encouragement', he told me the two guys stealing from me were not convicted felons. He was quick to point out that I was. He said everyone in the business hated my guts.

He had the ability to rescind my powers by cancelling my insurance, but he didn't have the right to take my business. I was furious. Who the hell did this guy think he was?

'You will never take my business. Never. Do you hear me, Heath? I will never let you take my business away.' I stormed out of the office, headed straight for the airport, and flew back to Kona.

The next day, I received a call from Heath. It was 11 March 1997. I remember the date, because it was my mom's birthday. After school that day, the kids and I were supposed to go visit her grave in Hilo.

Heath was angry. He was in my office, still trying to get some answers. Apparently he didn't like whatever he was finding. He ordered me: 'You need to come back to Honolulu now.' No one tells Dog what to do. I had plans. It was my mom's birthday. Heath coldly said, 'Let the dead bury the dead', but I wasn't about to jump just because he told me to.

'Go to hell, Heath. I'm on my way to get my kids. I'm not coming.' I slammed the phone down like I was killing a bug. When I got to school, I was met in the parking lot by the principal. He told me the police had just come to pick up the kids. Social services had received a phone call from someone who said that my children were in danger and asked that they be removed from my care. Though he didn't have a lot of details, he did say something about my being a drug addict who was endangering them.

My whole body went numb from the shock. At first, I felt weak in the knees. That quickly gave way to a rush of adrenaline that washed over me like a tidal wave. I went berserk. I wasn't a doper. I wasn't an addict. Who were they talking about? OK. I have to admit that, at the time, I didn't know I was in as deep as I was. I was oblivious to the reality of my use. While I don't think I ever put my kids in a dangerous situation,

I can't say for sure, because I wasn't thinking clearly. All I knew was that I had to find my kids. They were all I had. Without them, I had nothing.

I drove home, hoping and praying this was all some terrible mistake. I was living a nightmare, one from which I couldn't awaken. When I got home, my phone was ringing. I thought for sure it was one of the kids.

'Hello?'

'Duane, it's Richard Heath.' He was suspiciously kind. 'Everything OK?'

I played dumb.

'Well, then. Can I expect you back in Honolulu tomorrow to resolve this?'

'Yeah. Sure.' I just wanted to get off the phone in case one of the kids was trying to call.

The moment I hung up, the phone rang again. I thought it was Heath calling back, so I answered tersely. 'Hello!'

'Dad? It's Lyssa.' My nine-year-old baby was crying. 'They're saying you're a heroin addict, Dad. Why are they saying that?'

'Lyssa, honey. Calm down. Where are you? Are you hurt? Are you OK?' I just wanted to find her, wrap my arms around her, and never let her go.

'I'm fine, I ran away. I climbed out of the window when they weren't looking. I'm at McDonald's. Can you come get me?'

I ran like greased lightning. Fifteen minutes later, Baby Lyssa and I were on our way back to the house when my cell phone rang. It was Tucker and Barbara Katie. They had also split from social services. Tucker kicked the window out of the room they were in so he and Barbara could climb out and run away. They weren't very far from where we were, so Lyssa and I drove to pick them up. I had all three of my kids back. I was relieved to be reunited, but I couldn't shake my gut feeling I was heading for a fall.

# CHAPTER THIRTY-ONE

# Getting Out of Hell

After discovering that all three of my children had escaped, a woman from social services showed up at the house with a couple of cops. They were demanding I take a drug test. If I refused, they threatened to take my kids away for good. While I talked to the woman, I could see the cops asking the kids if they were OK. I heard one of them ask if they ever saw me doing drugs. Did I ever hurt them?

My blood boiled at the thought of anyone suspecting I would ever hurt one of my children, but I had to stay calm so the cops wouldn't see me losing my temper. I agreed to take the drug test, even though I knew it was a risk. I *had* been doing drugs, lots of them. But if I didn't take the test, I would lose my children. By agreeing, there was a possibility of testing negative, because it had been a couple of days since I did my last hit of cocaine. I didn't know how long that stuff stayed in your system.

I decided to fly to Denver to wait it out. If the test came back positive, the kids and I would be far away from their jurisdiction. I was pretty sure social services couldn't touch my family in Colorado. It was a calculated precaution to preserve my family. I was sweating bullets for three days until the results came back. Negative. Dear Lord, that was close.

All the while, Richard Heath was still applying pressure for me to get to Honolulu. He and I had some unfinished business. After social services cleared me, the kids and I flew back to Hawaii so I could deal with Heath.

'Duane, I am not going to press charges against your employees. In fact, they have both agreed to testify against you, saying you stole the money.'

I was speechless. He must have had some idea that they could be lying. I was innocent, but he didn't seem interested in the truth. I was a convicted felon. My signature was on the cheques, even though it was forged. If this went to court, Heath told me that a jury would probably take me down for ever. He said, at the very least, I was looking at doing time. The thought of going back to jail took my breath away. The pain in my chest was unbearable. I thought I was having a heart attack as he went on and on about my options. If I went to jail in Honolulu, who would bail me out? None of the local bondsmen, that's for sure. They all resented and hated me because I had swooped into town and changed the way everyone had to do business.

My mind wandered; I began to worry about my children. If I couldn't make bail, what would happen to them? Who would take care of them? I had no way of knowing how long I'd be gone, but I knew my absence would mean they'd end up in foster homes or worse. Heath could tell I was scared. And I was. I was in a corner and he knew it.

'So, what are my alternatives?' I asked.

'Well, Duane, I'm feeling generous today. I will agree not to press charges against you if you agree to get out of the business for a minimum of two years. What I'm saying is, you're done.'

Once again, I was going down for a crime I didn't commit. I had no choice. I couldn't fight it. I didn't have the money, and I didn't have enough friends in high places. There was no one in my corner but me. I was down, and this time I was definitely out.

I took the deal. Life as I knew it was over. I had no job, no income, and no savings. Word spread like wildfire. Rumours swirled. I heard people saying I had embezzled millions of dollars and tried to kill a man. I heard whispers whenever I walked into the court.

'I told you about that guy.'

'I told you he was a no-good felon.'

'I knew he was full of it.'

Every syllable, every utterance, every word, cut me like a knife.

I had to give up my house in Kona. I could no longer pay the rent. The kids and I moved into a one-bedroom shanty down near the Minini Beach. It wasn't fancy, but it was still near the ocean. Without income or any prospects for work, I was forced to apply for welfare and food stamps. For forty-plus years, no matter how bad things got for me, I never had to face welfare. It was the most humiliating decision I had ever made. But I had to think about the children. Social services were still looking over my shoulder too. If they'd got word I had no money to feed and clothe my kids, they'd take them away in a New York minute. They were all I had left. It didn't take long for word to get out that I was on welfare.

The Mighty Dog had finally fallen. I was facedown in the dirt. I felt worthless – like I had let so many people down. Welfare was paying me $895 a month; the one-room apartment the four of us shared cost $850. That didn't leave me much money for food and other necessities. We were living on cat food and mayonnaise. I told the kids it was tuna salad. I went to the shore and tried to catch our dinner every night. When I came up empty, we went without a meal. The children never complained, not once.

When it all became too much for me to bear, I broke down and reluctantly called my sister Jolene to ask her for an extra hundred bucks so I could feed the kids. She had all but forgot about us. She didn't want our problems to cause her any grief in Denver, so she distanced herself as far from our situation as she could. If it weren't for the children, I would have been as good as dead to her. She sent the money but called the welfare department to tell them. When they got word of the extra cash, they threatened to take away my benefits. Instead, they deducted the hundred dollars from my next month's cheque. When I asked Joleen why she called them, she said she was fearful of being party to welfare fraud. Can you believe it?

I had never been lower in my life. Even my family had to get in a kick or two while I lay on the ground broken and bleeding. But I couldn't wallow in my grief. I had to pick up the pieces. I was the leader of my family. It was my responsibility to provide for them. I was feeding my kids cat food pretending it was OK. It wasn't. I had to start thinking of ways to get myself back on track.

My first stroke of good luck in months came in early September 1997, when I heard my old friend Tony Robbins was coming to Hawaii to do a seminar. He was going to be on the Big Island, just outside of Kona. I called him up to see if we could meet.

'Of course,' he said.

For the first time in nearly a decade, I realised Tony hadn't asked me to be one of his guest speakers. I was worried, because I was certain he must have got wind of my troubles. I couldn't think of any other reason he would have excluded me from the seminar. Tony was always a good listener. More important, he was very sage with his advice. For years, he was one of my most trusted mentors. During one of the breaks, I cornered him so we could talk. I told him everything that had happened since my mother's death.

'My God,' he said, 'I can't believe it.'

'I can barely believe it myself, Tony,' I said. 'But I am trying to fight my way back. I need some help.'

I watched Tony stand stoic and silent. He listened carefully as I expressed my shame and guilt. I was reaching out for a helping hand. So far I didn't see his extending halfway to meet mine.

'How can I help you, Duane?'

'I have an idea. I thought you might consider hiring me as head of security for you, just until I can get back on my feet.' There was a long, awkward silence. Finally, he said, 'Dog, I am going to help you . . . '

Inwardly, I felt a huge sense of relief. 'Thank the Lord. Tony, you have no idea how much this means to me–' I was in mid-sentence when Tony jumped in.

'No, Duane, I won't give you a job. But I will give you some advice.'

Wherever that weight on my shoulders had gone, it was now back, and heavier than ever. While I always appreciated his advice, it wasn't going to pay the rent or put food on the table for my family.

'You are overqualified to work for me. Security isn't what you do, man. I wouldn't be doing you a favour. If I can be direct, I think it's time for you to hear the harsh truth. Quit telling people about what's been done *to* you. Quit complaining about how other people have hurt you and all of the wrong things that have happened in your life. You lost your edge, let your guard down, and clearly, you've trusted the wrong people. These choices were your own. It's your fault, *your* responsibility. You need to accept full responsibility and move on.'

Tony's advice was harsh but spot-on.

'Duane, you've been through enough of my seminars to understand that you are the only person who can change your circumstances. You're one of the strongest, most remarkable people I've ever met, Dog. You have overcome far worse circumstances than what you have just described to me. You are a survivor.'

He was right. There was no easy way out of my predicament, but I felt I had been kicked around enough in my life. Tony Robbins graciously offered me an out, in case I wanted to pack up the kids and start again in Denver. He told me to go back to Denver, sit on a rock next to a stream, and go back to my roots. That was the last thing I wanted to hear!

In retrospect, I think he could tell I was in pretty deep. My physical appearance was a dead giveaway that I was drugging pretty bad. He didn't want to be involved, but he wasn't the kind of guy who would let me rot, either. He told me to get as far away from my girlfriend as I could. 'Duane, she's dragging you down.' As many times as I heard that from other people, it seemed to pack the biggest punch coming from Tony.

I was forty-four years old. I didn't want to start over, but what were my choices? Failure is never an option. Giving up, throwing in the towel, letting the bad guy win, that isn't how I lived my life. I had to face my truth. I had to accept that my mom was dead. She wasn't going to be there to pick up the pieces. She had been my best friend. When she died, I felt like I died too. When people said bad things about me, Mom always told me something good. Every time I needed a friend, Mom was there. Every time I went to jail, Mom welcomed me home with open arms. The greatest lesson she taught me was to always have faith and never give up. She used to tell me that everything happens for a reason.

I can still hear her say, 'After the storm comes more rain, but then another storm comes. Only after that storm can things begin to blossom and bloom. But son, remember, there will always be another storm. If you make it through one, you can make it through all of them.'

After the seminar, I sat by the ocean for two straight days, not knowing what to do or how to change my life.

I spent hours thinking about my mom, the kids, Beth, my girlfriend, the Lord, my life, my mistakes, and my options. I had this overwhelming feeling that my mom was watching me. I knew she was saying, 'C'mon, Duane, you've been through this before. This isn't the toughest battle you've ever fought. You've done it before; you can do it again.' I looked up and noticed footprints in the sand. As far as I knew, no one had walked by. I leaned over to take a closer look. They were my mom's footprints. They started where I was sitting and ended at the ocean's edge. She was telling me to leave Hawaii. It was a message of hope and inspiration to get myself together and start over.

My life has been filled with trying moments when my faith gets tested. Tony Robbins used to say there was great power in positive thinking and positive confession. The words you speak are crucial to how you live. Your mind believes whatever you tell it. If I felt like a deadbeat, I acted like one. If I moved through the world like a leader, people would see me as one. I realised that every challenge is an opportunity to strengthen my faith, to learn how to make it stronger, and to use that situation to learn and grow. If you keep making the same mistakes, you keep getting the same results. I needed change. I had to make some hard decisions. I thought about the story of Jesus raising Lazarus from the grave. He believed He could bring him back to life when all of His disciples doubted Him. Jesus led His disciples through fields of doubt. Sitting on the beach that day, I felt like Lazarus. With Jesus' love and strength, and an unshakable belief in my own faith, I, too, was resurrected.

As hard as it was for me to concede, I had been beaten. Game over. I stood up on the beach, cupped my hands around my mouth, and shouted, 'I'm going back to Denver! I will start over, I will succeed! I am the Mighty Dog!' I yelled until my throat was raw and my voice was shot. I stood for a moment as the sun set over the Pacific. This day was done. Tomorrow would be a new beginning.

# CHAPTER THIRTY-TWO

# Kidney Stones Saved My Life

I packed up the kids and moved back to Denver. One of the conditions my sister Jolene placed on our staying with her was that she really didn't want me to see Beth. Jolene warned me I would be on the street if she caught me with her. I should have been able to come back into town and walk right into my old bail bonds business, but I had already handed it off to my sister before I moved to Hawaii. That would have solved my money problems and helped me get back on track. She did give me work as a bounty hunter, but the business belonged to her. She and I have a long history of not getting along, but now was not the time to be so harsh. I opted to stay in a motel near Jolene's house. The only way I could bounty hunt for her was if she gave me a car to use, which she did. If I caught two guys a day for her, I made a hundred and fifty bucks. I didn't have a lot of extra money for food, so most of my down-time was spent just hanging around the motel.

Although I had left my girlfriend behind in Hawaii, I brought all of her bad habits with me to Denver. I was still getting high from time to time. I hadn't spoken to Beth since she turned me in to Richard Heath six months earlier. Everywhere I went, people brought up Beth's name. For the most part, everyone thought it was best that we didn't get together. They all warned her to stay far away from me. I heard she had a boyfriend who shot steroids. Because of the drugs, he'd go into rages and beat her.

We managed to avoid each other for a few weeks. Then one day, we were both standing in the alley behind the houses on bail bonds row. It was like a scene from a movie. I looked at her and she at me. By the time Beth got to the back of the alley I was already by her side. I grabbed her and put the most passionate kiss on her.

'Meet me in an hour.' I told her where I was staying and took off to make sure the kids were otherwise occupied for a while.

I am an extremely sensual man. When I kiss a woman, I want to envelop all of her in my mouth. I like to lick her face and neck, and I want to feel connected in my love. I'm not in it just for myself. I'm not satisfied unless my partner is happy. Making love to Beth was always hot, and the moment I saw her in the alley that day, I knew we'd be together for ever.

My sister had warned me she would take away the car if she caught me with Beth. Well, later that night, Jolene saw the car parked outside Beth's house. She came up to the front door with her husband, who is a federal police officer. They asked for the car keys. I couldn't believe my eyes as I watched them drive away.

I don't know why I went to Beth's that night. Our afternoon of passion was the stuff that dreams are made of, but I was still angry with her for ratting me out to the insurance company. A part of me was mad at her, but I needed a place to go. I had my babies; they needed a home. A small motel room wasn't the right place for them to be. Then, one night, the kids and I were over at Beth's for a meal. Her daughter, Cecily, was there, and all the kids were passed out around the house. I'd picked up two tough bounties that day and could barely keep my eyes open.

Beth said, 'Why don't you all just stay here for now? Don't worry,' she laughed. 'We'll just take it one day at a time and see how it goes.'

Beth and I decided the time had come for us to join forces – romantically and professionally. At the time, she was working for Bail City, whose insurance company was Pioneer General. When they found out about us they called Beth and made it very clear that it was either Duane or her job.

She accused them of blackmail, and in typical Beth fashion, she told them that they didn't run her life. They fired her.

A few days later, we all moved into Beth's house for good. It wouldn't be easy, and we were certainly no Brady Bunch, but we loved each other. That love would get us through any challenge that lay ahead, and there would still be a few doozies.

'I've waited so long for you, Duane. I waited through your marriage to Lyssa, and then Tawny. Now I have you, and you're a drug addict son of a bitch.' She'd been through the bullshit before. Since prison, I was always the guy who didn't do drugs. Beth began to cry. When she weeps, she ruins me. I looked at her, tears also now streaming down my cheeks, and I realised she was right. I remember thinking, 'I'm her hero and now I've let her down, too. It's time to snap out of this.'

Throughout my six months of being on drugs, I avoided looking in any mirrors. I knew God wasn't standing with me. Once in a while, I felt him check in, but I was too ashamed to ask the Lord into my life during those months. I was terribly ashamed of my behaviour. I never prayed, something I normally do all the time. I felt like my prayers would hit the ceiling and bounce back down, so I didn't even try. Instead, I took another hit off the pipe.

God gives us all free will. I had a choice to get high or not. For years, I hadn't understood how someone could choose to hit that stuff, smoke, snort, or do any kind of drug. I just saw them as weak-minded. They were garbage, trash. How pathetic do you have to be not to have control over your urge to get high?

Well, now I know first-hand. Whenever I talk to someone about drug problems, I tell them, 'We have to get through this', because every day is a struggle for an addict. Once an addict, always an addict. I've been there. I know how hard it is to kick an addiction.

One day, Beth forced me to look into a mirror. She said, 'Look at yourself. You've lost so much weight. You're sick, Duane. If you don't quit doing drugs, you will die.' When her soft-love approach didn't sink in, she began humiliating me.

'You're a crackhead.'

'You ain't the Dog any more.'

'Your dad's at the door. He wants to talk to you.' That one really got me, because I never wanted to disappoint my dad. He always said I was a nothing. I never wanted to give him the satisfaction of being right.

'I'm coming back, Beth. I swear, baby. I'm coming back.' I promised what I couldn't deliver. I couldn't kick the habit.

Kidney stones saved my life. The pain was excruciating. I thought I was dying. I went to the doctor and told her I was in agony. I explained I was a drug user.

'Let me take your blood pressure.' While the doctor examined me, she began asking me all sorts of questions.

'Why do you take drugs?'

'For the sex.'

'Are you living with a girl now?'

'Yes, that's her in the hallway.'

'Do you love her?'

'No.' The confession was a relief.

'Who do you love?'

I couldn't answer. My blood pressure went off the charts.

The doctor diagnosed stress and depression. She prescribed Prozac and blood pressure medication.

Beth took one look at the prescriptions and was mad as hell. She didn't think I needed Prozac. I took the pills anyway.

I was in a tunnel-like state from the Prozac. I had a hard time telling fact from fiction. One day I thought Beth had packed her stuff and left. I got up that morning earlier than usual, and she was gone. I opened the closet to see if her clothes were still hanging there. They were. I sat down on the bed and realised I was falling in love with Beth. I started to love her in ways I never imagined or thought were possible. My old girlfriend was becoming a ghost from my past. I don't know if it was the Prozac, or if my feelings were genuine and real. I didn't care.

The Prozac seemed to be working, except I couldn't remember the simplest things. For some reason, I wanted to call LaFonda. I had known her number for twenty-five years, but now I couldn't remember it. When I told Beth, she showed no mercy. She didn't want me on those pills in the first place. I called another friend of mine and told her what was happening.

She told me to throw those pills down the drain because they would make me do crazy things.

As soon as I stopped taking the pills, the pain from my kidney stones came back, only this time it was worse than ever. I went back to the doctor.

'You have kidney stones.' The doctor ordered me to rest. I lay on Beth's sofa for a month, waiting for the pain to end. The doctors were scared I might not make it. I had lost so much weight from doing drugs that I was down to a mere 130 pounds. My body was dying. I didn't have the physical strength to fight for my life. In my peak physical condition, back when I was boxing, my weight hovered around 155. I was slim like my son Leland. Today I weigh around 200 pounds. I was a sick, weak shell of the man I once was.

After mom died, I went into a deep depression. For the first time in my life, I felt alone. Mom's presence usually kept me from making poor choices and dreadful decisions. After Huntsville, I had become a pretty savvy guy who avoided doing heavy drugs and lots of drinking. Women were usually my drug of choice. And like a drug, it was a woman, someone I would never have been with if I had been feeling better about myself, who started me down a path of self-destruction that eventually led to the relationship that introduced me to my drug abuse.

I was extremely lonely and not thinking clearly when I chose to participate in smoking cocaine that first night. I didn't know how fast things could get bad. As hard as it might be to believe, I simply had no clue what I was getting myself into. I sank so low that once I was in the bottom of that deep, dark pit, I didn't know how to get myself out. I knew I had let my family and friends down, which made it so hard for me because I miserably failed at getting myself together. It became a vicious cycle. The worse I got, the worse I felt. The worse I felt, the worse I got.

Truth be told, if my mom had been alive, I'd have never given in to that type of temptation. I couldn't have faced her. I was depressed and desperate for love and acceptance. My life had taken a downward turn, the likes of which I had never experienced. I felt I had no control over any aspect of my very own existence.

For a year and a half, I felt as if I had suffered blow after blow. My once strong mind and ego were fractured. I was a broken man. And I was truly alone. My father went back to live in Denver and my sister Joleen, who had helped out with my bail bonds business in Hawaii after mom died, stopped coming. Throughout my career, there was always someone in the office running my business so I could focus on what I do best – writing bond and capturing jumps.

I had such an overwhelming sense of hopelessness. I lost my edge, my spark, my judgment, and my belief that I was better than the way I was living. That's why I know how a fugitive feels when I have to hunt him down. I know the pain that takes a brother to the depths of depression and desperation. I don't want anyone to feel that alone or lost. I have felt it. I have lived it. And I never, ever, want to go back there again.

If Beth hadn't saved me, I'm not sure I would have survived those years.

The first thing I needed to do was get my health back. A different doctor told me to get on a weight lifting programme and put on some pounds. He also suggested that I stop using caffeine and alcohol and that I avoid peppers and a foot-long list of other foods, which he suspected might be irritating my bowels.

I finally passed the kidney stone. The very next day, I was up and at 'em, hitting the gym every chance I got. I began to bulk up almost immediately, gradually putting on sixty pounds of pure muscle.

It took me a month of agony, but I finally emerged drug-free and stronger than ever. It wasn't easy, but I made it through the darkness of those six months. With God's help and Beth's love, I had all the support I needed. Now, all we had to do was to get back on our feet financially, and we'd be set.

But by Christmas of 1997, we had hit the absolute bottom. We were stone-cold broke. The whole bail bonds industry knew we were together as a couple. The thought of the two of us joining forces scared the hell out of everyone.

We signed on to work with Mike Whitlock, who agreed to back us for insurance. He was the first person to give us a break. We weren't making great money, but we were surviving. Beth was writing bail while I was out bounty hunting. For a while, it was slim pickings. We had been out of the game for a few months, so there wasn't a lot of business.

By New Year's, we had committed to each other to make a miraculous comeback. Come hell or high water, we were back in the game. Nothing and no one could stand in our way. We were unstoppable.

Not so fast. By the end of the year, our insurance company came to us and said we were too high-risk. It's true, one out of every three of our clients was running, but I caught each one. Beth and I battled with Mike Whitlock for a while, but it was no use. He dropped us like we were hot.

Beth went through a couple more insurance companies before she found us both a temporary home. By the grace of God, an old bounty hunter named Andy Raff came by to see me. He knew all about me. He was a rebel who just wanted to give me a break.

'What have you got for collateral?' I didn't have much to offer. Beth and I were still pretty much living day-to-day. We were happy just to have the chance.

'Don't tell nobody, but I'm going to sign you up for nothing. How many powers do you want?' Like that, we were back swinging. And strong, too. We became the Bonnie and Clyde of bail bonds. Every time we showed up at one of the local jails, I could hear people saying, 'They're baaack!'

# CHAPTER THIRTY-THREE

# One Step Forward

Once Beth and I decided to join together in business, we slowly began pulling ourselves out of the financial black hole we'd been in since I got shut down in Hawaii. We had to take some large steps back in lifestyle. We moved into a small three-bedroom townhouse. Beth was pregnant with Bonnie Jo while we built our new business. We became a threat to the industry, their worst nightmares.

People started flocking to Free as a Bird Bail Bonds. We jammed music every morning while I walked my gigantic pet lizard on a leash up and down the sidewalk in front of the other bail bonds offices to get attention. We had free coffee and doughnuts. DAs came in, cops stopped by, and everyone loved our very entertaining atmosphere. I plastered a mug shot of every fugitive I ever arrested on a huge wall. Clients would come in just to see who they knew on our wall of fame. It became a status symbol of sorts to be on Dog's board of mugs.

Once business began to build, Beth was more determined than ever to go after the other bondsmen and insurance companies who continuously tried to put us out of business. She was fighting mad and didn't give a damn who knew.

One night we walked into a meeting of the Denver Association of Bail Bonds just to let the three hundred or so members know that Dog and Beth were now a team. Although there were only thirty-eight people present, we knew word would quickly spread. When we walked through the door, every head in the joint turned to see us standing there. It was great. I was dressed in a long black leather trench coat, looking like Keanu Reeves in *The Matrix*, while Beth, well, was Beth. She wore a low-cut, revealing top and high heels that resonated off the linoleum like gunshots with every step she took.

Before the meeting began, someone made an announcement that we were not welcome. A couple of guys stood up, turned their chairs around like protective shields, and hid behind them. Several guys formed a human chain and pushed me right out the door. Beth was still inside. I had to make sure she wasn't in danger. I called out her name as I tried to get back inside.

As Beth made her way outside, one guy lunged towards her. She threw her arm up, caught him in the throat, and bodychecked him into the wall. Several other guys got up too. One sprayed a can of Mace towards my face, but he missed. I had a huge wad of chewing gum in my mouth I was about to spit out. The Mace hit the gum between my teeth. I spit it out and said, 'I'll eat that can of Mace, motherfucker!' The son of a bitch ran away. I just laughed. These guys were pathetic. After those two punks tried to take us down, somebody called the cops. We had delivered our message. We were back in business and no one could stop us. If they didn't like it, too bad. Beth and I laughed all the way home. Suckers!

The next day, we were served with a stack of restraining orders from disgruntled bondsmen. We fought every single one of them in court. It was the Ike and Tina Turner Revue. We won them all. The bondsmen kept telling the judge they were scared of us. He laughed and said, 'They scare me too, especially her, but there's no reason for these orders!'

Being in business was one thing. Staying in business was something else. We had a difficult time finding an insurance company to back us. Most of them viewed us as high-risk. They thought we were writing some bad bonds that would lose them a lot of money.

Beth and I set out to effect positive change in the otherwise dishonest world we worked in. Because of her background in the legislature, we consulted with several state senators on creating bills to reform the industry. Most of our time was spent trying to regulate the insurance companies, who were as crooked as the thieves they insured. At the time, an insurance company could write as much insurance as they wanted. If the company went out of business, the bondsman was stuck holding the financial bag. He had to pay the full value of the bond if his client skipped. It was a very big problem for the bondsman, who might have put his house up for collateral.

We saw that imbalance in business practices as being completely unfair to the bondsman, and we spent an enormous amount of time working with local government in Denver to get those laws changed. We were successful on every level. Not only were our rights better protected, but also, within three years, our provisions in the new laws essentially put the Colorado Department of Insurance out of business. Success is the best revenge.

But it was short-lived. In February 1999, the Colorado legislature passed a new law stating that convicted felons could not bounty hunt. How did this law slip in? We were friends with all the lawmakers. We knew what was happening on the state level before anyone else.

I was making a bust when Beth called to deliver the bad news. I threw up. I remember standing on the street next to my car asking the Lord when He was going to cut me a break. I couldn't help but feel that the state was purposely coming after me. Someone with a lot of power and influence was at it again. My assumption was that the guys from the Denver Bond Association were behind it. They must have paid a lobbyist to quietly try to push the bill through without word ever leaking. Every time we thought we won a battle, it turned out we hadn't even begun to fight the war. It was only a matter of time before they would be permanently successful.

I've always been a fighter, but I have to admit, I was losing my stamina. Because of my situation in Hawaii, I wasn't able to write bail, but I could still bounty hunt. And now, because of this new law, it looked like I might lose that right too. I have fallen and risen from the ashes so many times in my life; I wasn't about to get burned again. I spent the past twenty years trying to live a good, honest life. But throughout that time, I was constantly answering for that one horrible night in Pampa. That damned murder one conviction haunted me everywhere I went. I could run, but I couldn't hide.

I had to stop the madness. Tony Robbins taught me to always use your resources, use who you know. You have to have something for people to buy before you can sell. I paid a visit to Senator Joyce Lawrence, the sponsor of the new bill. Beth put together a presentation to show her all of my accomplishments as a bounty hunter. We had dozens of letters from clients and other members of law enforcement singing my praises for the work I had done.

I was extremely nervous. If the senator didn't like what she saw and heard, I would be out of business for good. After I gave her a long speech about how her bill would end my career, she was somehow unaware that the new law would negatively impact me. She told us she would amend the bill so I could go back to work – if Beth and I could collect enough signatures of support from other state senators.

One thing I knew for sure, we had our work cut out for us. But I also knew I could sell grass to a golf course, so I figured convincing a bunch of conservative senators to let me do my job couldn't be all that hard.

Beth and I spent the following two weeks meeting all thirty-five senators in the state of Colorado. Some were on board right away. Others, well . . . not so fast. Senator Ken Clover didn't even want to take the meeting. His grandmother had been murdered by an ex-con. When I walked into his office to shake his hand, he stood cold and still. He told me he hated all ex-cons. I was startled by his generalisation, especially because I have seen so many felons eventually make something good out of their lives.

I did the only thing I could think of. I engaged the senator in conversation about something other than crime. I said, 'Senator, do you hate pie?'

He said he only hated lemon pie.

'Well, then, let me ask you something, Senator. Do you hate all pie because you don't have a taste for lemon pie?'

He looked at me for a moment, clearly trying to figure out where I was going with all my talk about pie.

'No. I only hate lemon pie.'

Blam. I just closed the deal. Made the sale. I was out selling Kirbys again, only this time I was selling my life, my career. I begged the senator to give me a chance. I told him I was a good guy. I gave him the scrapbook Beth made of all the articles written about my accomplishments. I wasn't the felon who killed his granny. I was the guy out there chasing down those scumbags.

Nearly all the senators we met agreed about one thing: they couldn't pass a law for a single man. The consensus was that a law had to cast a wide net. Fair enough. But I was quick to point out that laws do affect a single person each and every day. I told the senators a story about how I was recently out driving on a two-lane highway in the middle of the plains when I came to a four-way stop. I could have kept cruising right on through that stop sign. No one was around to see me. But I didn't. I stopped. I obeyed the law. Why? Because it is the law. I wanted the senators to see that laws are as individual as their interpretation.

After I won the battle to keep my bond licence, I began spending more time with a bunch of the other bondsman's kids who were pretty much a fixture on bail bonds row in Denver. They ranged in age from eighteen to twenty. They were all adults, but they were young and immature. Tim

'Youngblood' Chapman was the son of one of Denver's best female bondsmen. I liked Tim from the moment we met. At the time, I didn't have my oldest sons, so I kind of took Tim under my wing as a surrogate son. He was smart, educated in bail, and fearless. He knew the business cold. He is the same Tim Chapman I work with to this very day. One of the other boys was Max, who was the son of the vice president of the national motorcycle club, the Outlaws, and little Lee was the son of another bail bonds family, and David Bautista, whom I brought into the bail bonds business from selling Kirbys.

I began noticing these kids were constantly getting into trouble. They all knew the bail bonds business from watching their parents over the years. When their parents were tossing them out of the house, I recognised the benefit of their knowledge and presence right away. I was the guy who always caught their parents jumps, so to them I was 'cool'. They wanted to be around me because I wasn't their dad, but I could lead them in a way that kept them out of trouble. I began using these kids to help out around Free as a Bird Bail Bonds. I gave them all badges and radios so they felt like they appeared 'official'. They loved it and it worked well for me because I needed the help.

I read *Billy the Kid* and wanted to have a gang of 'Regulators' like he did. These neighbourhood boys fit the bill. I even took them all on a road trip to visit to Wyoming where Billy the Kid once hung out with his guys so we could connect like a true gang. We built a big campfire one night and I swore each of these boys in to my version of the Regulators. We made a pact that night to commit ourselves to fight for truth and justice together. The following Monday, we started our crusade to wipe out the city of Denver's 'wanted'.

I trained the Regulators to be my eyes and ears. I sent them out on fact-finding missions, bounties, wherever I needed help in the pursuit of a client who jumped bail. Everyone knew who I was, so it was becoming harder to go unnoticed. These young guys were virtually invisible to the bail jumpers. It was easy to send them over to see if someone's car was in front of a particular house or if the person was at a local bar. The Regulators could slip in and out without the fugitive knowing. That helped me nab my man every time.

These kids took their oath to the Dog very seriously. They were always on time and never missed a day of work. They respected me because I was the guy who used to be them. I turned my life around. They could see the opportunity to become something more than a petty criminal by working with me to get the bad guys off the streets. I talked to them about life, God, and living a good life all the time. I offered the promise of a better plan if they followed in my footsteps and stayed clean. Whenever they had personal setbacks, I'd be there to encourage them to keep moving forward. I showed them love and acceptance by always giving them another chance. I felt like the Pied Piper trying to lead these boys who had mostly been degraded and belittled their whole lives by living my life so as to be a positive example. Two years later, all of these boys were as well known in the community as I was. It made them feel great knowing people saw them doing good things for the community by getting criminals off the streets. These days, my wife and children are my Regulators. I still do the master planning, but they are all as loyal as my original gang.

Beth and I did suggest that a felon be required to wait a certain number of years before being allowed to bounty hunt, much like the law for bondsmen. Senator Lawrence got behind that idea. She pushed the amendment through so I could get back to bounty hunting. The final vote was thirty-one ayes, two nays, and two abstentions. And, just for the record, Senator Ken Clover voted yes. I guess he likes most types of pie after all!

Do you want to know why there's a group of bounty hunters out there who make it their full-time job to discredit me and destroy my reputation? It started in the mid-nineties, just after Beth and I joined together in the business. People were scared of us. We were seen as a threat to the way all of the other bondsmen in Denver were doing business. They took advantage of their clients in ways we would never, ever consider. They were afraid we would blow the lid off of their unsavoury practices.

Two things to know about Beth and me: First, we don't believe bounty hunters should carry guns. There are lots of other non-lethal weapons that can stun, stop, or sedate someone without killing them. My weapon of choice is Mace. Second, Beth and I consider most of our clients to be human beings who simply made bad choices. We want to help them overcome their lives of crime. We will counsel them, guide them, and talk to them like they're friends. In our eyes, they are all our brothers and sisters. We are honest about their situation. We will tell them they're screwed but also reassure them that they can get a good lawyer and rehabilitate their lives if they want to. Unlike most other people in our business, Beth and I genuinely want to see our clients change their lives.

One day I was out collecting a thousand dollars from one of my clients in the parking lot of a 7-Eleven in Denver. We were making the exchange when I noticed a couple of guys approaching us wearing camouflage jackets and baseball hats that had big bold letters on the front: BEA. They both carried two guns strapped to their hips. When I first caught a glimpse of them, I thought their hats said DEA. I'm sure the exchange of cash looked like a drug deal was going down. To make matters worse, I didn't have my badge on me.

One of the two approached me and asked, 'What are you guys doing out here?'

I took off my sunglasses, handed them to my client, and said, 'Here, honey, hold these for me.'

As I turned around, I realised their hats said BEA and said, 'BEA. What the hell does that stand for?'

'Bail bonds Enforcement Agent.'

I asked the guy, 'You got any Vaseline on you? Because I'm Dog Chapman and those guns you've got are going up your ass.'

When I started walking towards them, they turned and ran to their cars screaming, 'Run, it's the Dog!!'

Anytime I see the BEA guys carrying guns, I do whatever it takes to stop them. These guys are not qualified to carry weapons. They're not cops. Cops are trained experts who shoot to kill. That is, they're taught to fire only when deadly force is necessary to save lives. They don't shoot to wound in order to bring someone in.

A week later, I was in the jail booking another fugitive when another BEA guy walked in wearing an empty holster and bragging about pistol whipping a client. He saw me sitting there with my fugitive but refused to acknowledge me. I stood up to confront the guy, got into his face, and said, 'You know who I am. You know I don't like that kind of talk. Why are you even carrying a gun?'

This guy said to me, 'I don't care if you don't carry a gun. I'm gonna dance on your grave.'

I was about to rumble with him right there inside the courthouse. I didn't give a shit. Beth is a bondsman, I knew she'd get me out. He was a chicken shit and wouldn't take my bait. Later I saw him outside in the parking lot talking to his wife. I waved him over to talk, towards where I was standing.

'Come here, brother. Let's say a prayer together.' I'm sure he thought I was about to eat crow.

'Dear God, give this pussy-packin' punk some balls. I'm going to beat his ass to the ground right now. I want you to give him the strength Joshua had at the Battle of Jericho, because he's going to need it after this ass-whipping.' I took a step back, spit at both of my clenched fists, and said, 'What was that you said about dancing on my grave, white boy?'

He was shaking like a nervous Chihuahua. I turned to his wife and said, 'You see that, honey? You married a pussy. You see the punk you got here, baby?'

I turned back to the guy and said, 'C'mon. Show me how you're going to dance on my grave', as if he was going to Fred Astaire his ass in front of me.

Just then, his wife stepped in between the two of us to stop the fight. She was yelling, 'Stop, Dog. He's legally blind. He's got 40/90 vision!'

I was out of my mind at the thought that this gun-toting Stevie Wonder had a weapon permit! Why would a man who is legally blind be allowed to carry a gun?

The next thing I saw was his skinny little ass hiding behind his wife as they ran towards their car.

To this very day I fight with the guys from the BEA. I hate them, and they can't stand me. I'll continue my crusade to ban bounty hunters from carrying guns until the day comes that we are all on the same side of that subject.

# CHAPTER THIRTY-FOUR

# Going Hollywood

Hollywood has been knock-knockin' on my door for several years. A few years before the Luster case plastered me all over the front pages, I met a man on a flight from Los Angeles to Honolulu. He was seated next to me in first class. I hardly ever talk to people on planes. I don't like flying. The young man asked my name and what I did for a living. For some unknown reason, I was an open book that day.

He was engaged before wheels-up. For five and a half hours, he asked me question after question about my life. How'd I get started? Have I ever been hurt? What was prison like?

I don't believe I've ever talked more on a plane than I did that day. A couple of hours into the flight I asked the guy his name.

'Chris McQuarrie.'

'Oh yeah? Well, nice to meet you, Chris. What do you do?'

'I'm a screenwriter.'

'Ever have a movie produced?'

He smiled in a way that made me feel kind of stupid for not recognising his name or something.

'Yes, I have had a movie produced. Maybe you saw it. *The Usual Suspects*?'

I love that movie. I was practically starstruck. We exchanged phone numbers and talked about getting together while Chris was in Hawaii. I didn't expect to hear from him, but I hoped he would call.

Later that night, I told Beth about my new friend.

'Who the hell was she, Duane?' She was suspicious as hell, thinking I met a woman.

I let out a boisterous laugh. 'No. No. I met this guy, Chris McQuarrie, and . . . ' Right away she knew who he was. Beth knows that kind of stuff. She was leery as I told her how he talked about wanting to write a movie about my life. Beth is always pragmatic in my otherwise overly optimistic world. Before she could tell me she thought he was full of it, the phone rang. Thank God.

'Hey, Dog. How ya doing? It's Chris. Let's get together and talk a little more about the movie idea.'

I smiled and laughed. For once, I could hand the phone over to Beth before she called me a liar or fool. I wanted Chris to confirm what he told me right in her ear.

'It's for you, honey.'

It's true, Beth and I had become very wary of Hollywood and its players. There had been lots of guys before Chris who promised big-money deals and never delivered. Hollywood is a lot of smoke and mirrors. You never know who you're talking to or what they are really all about. One thing you can count on is that everyone has his own agenda. You are merely a pawn to move around to promote whatever that plan is. It's hard to tell players from liars. I'd been drawn in many times by seemingly reputable people; I never knew when I was being played.

So, when this crazy Russian named Boris Krutonog called me in 1995, I was already so jaded I didn't pay him a lot of attention. He'd read about me in Tony Robbins's book, *Awaken the Giant Within*.

'Dog, I am so fascinated by your story.' Even though Boris is Russian he sounded a lot like Arnold Schwarzenegger in *The Terminator*.

As long as I can remember, people have been telling me I'd be famous. I always believed that one day people around the world would recognise the Dog for something good. There have been plenty of times in my life I've dreamed of seeing my name up there on a marquee. But I'd had so many calls like the one I got from Boris, I was practically numb listening to him speak. I was void of emotion. I couldn't get my hopes up again, just to have someone lie to me, use me, and mislead me for their own purposes. I thought it was all a bunch of horsecrap.

'Yeah, thanks for the call, brother, but I have to hang up.' I was nice, but quick to get off the phone.

'Yes. I understand. But remember, you are now a reflection of your mother.'

Oh, no he didn't. He did *not* just bring my momma into the conversation.

'Say what?' I was confused. How did he know my mom had died a few years back? How did he know that would push my buttons? Before I could ask, he was gone.

I called him right back.

'How do you know about my momma?'

He said, 'I know she raised you to be a brave man. This is the time for you to demonstrate all she taught you. She is dead, I know. But who do you think looks over you in heaven?'

'*She* does. Every damn minute of my life.'

'So . . . what's the holdup?'

I stood silent. He was right. Boris had hit my soft spot. He found a way in, a door that no one before or after has ever dared to open.

I later discovered that Boris is one of those Hollywood guys who started out acting in movies, including *The Hunt for Red October* and *The Italian Job*. He also had connections to get things done and deliver. All I had to do was give him the sign I was interested.

I was in.

Boris was successful right out of the gate. He contacted his friend Lucas Foster, who was running Columbia Pictures. Foster had produced several hugely successful movies, including *Dangerous Minds*, *Crimson Tide*, and *Bad Boys*.

I had met Peter Guber at the Tony Robbins seminar in 1990. At the time, he was running his own film company, but later he went on to become the studio chief of Sony Pictures. I had no idea who he was when we met, and he didn't seem to care much about me. All I knew was that he had produced a couple of movies I'd heard of, including *Midnight Express* and *The Deep*.

Both men agreed my life story was filmworthy, but Lucas Foster won, scooping up rights to the story for a modest sum. I was blown away.

Now, for those of you who don't know much about Hollywood, there's a little something in the movie business called 'development hell'. That's when your project, which everyone was so jacked up about in the beginning, sits around for months or years, waiting to get off the ground. That's exactly what happened at Columbia Pictures.

When the rights were released, we went back to Peter Guber. He commissioned a script, but it sucked. Every time Beth and I read a draft, we thought it was crap. I wouldn't approve it for production, so that deal died as well. Eventually, the rights reverted back to us, because their time ran out too. Boris and Beth then took the project to Les Moonves at CBS, who bought it on the spot. Different day, same story.

Boris could see I was disappointed. The up-and-down roller-coaster nature of the movie business made bounty hunting feel like a safe and stable gig. But I didn't give up hope in my Hollywood dream.

'You're an American icon. You're a real-life superhero. Perhaps Hollywood just doesn't know that yet.' I thought *icon* sounded a hell of a lot better than *ex-con*. I wanted to believe Boris was right. I have spent every minute of my life since Huntsville trying to redeem myself for that night in Pampa. I know God sees the score as even, but I wasn't sure the rest of the American people do. My one goal is to find redemption. Tony Robbins once referred to me as the most 'human' human he'd ever met. I wasn't sure I understood what he meant, so I asked him why he thought that. He explained that people can relate to me. The rich, the poor, the good, the bad and the ugly. They can take one look at me and think, *If that seventh-grade dropout son of a bitch can do it, so can I.*

I always tell my kids that I graduated with honours from the seventh grade. I'm not proud that I left school so young, but I'm not ashamed of it either. I'm not a stupid man. Don't confuse my incorrect grammar or mispronunciation of words with being dumb. I have a better education than most. My education, my best teacher, has been living a very full and demanding life. If Hollywood couldn't see that yet, I knew in my gut that someday they certainly would. I kept telling myself that I am an all-around good guy and a slayer of dragons. I couldn't give up hope. The Lord kept telling me, 'This isn't your time. I will fulfil your dream in my own time. Be patient.'

# CHAPTER THIRTY-FIVE

# A Chase to the Grave

Larry and Jerome Bernstein were career white-collar criminals. They weren't the type of cons who would be found making midnight deals in dark back alleys with drug dealers and prostitutes. They were into big business crime, and before the law caught up with them, they made plenty of money off of their elaborate pyramid scams. Despite the fact that they were raised in a wealthy family in an upper-class area of Denver, they decided to take a criminal path in life. They portrayed themselves as businessmen, but when it came right down to it, the Bernstein brothers were just glorified street hustlers with expensive wardrobes. I had captured a few wealthy fugitives before, but white-collar crime was new to me.

When the Denver police finally closed in on them, Larry and Jerome were running a Ponzi scheme called Bernstein Oil and Gas. Their business plan was based on creating a false pretence of profitability for their clients. They would produce unbelievably inflated drilling production numbers and use these to attract wealthy investors. The only thing these people were investing in was a worthless plot of land. The Bernsteins pocketed all of the money. If one of the original investors wanted to cash out, they would pay him from someone else's investment so the money machine kept moving. It was an endless hunt for new investors and new money.

The Bernsteins came into our office on a Friday afternoon to fill out applications for $175,000 in bonds. One was for a hundred grand, the other for seventy-five. They were very well-mannered and nicely dressed in matching suits. It was obvious that they spent top dollar on their wardrobe, even though it might have been paid for with *other* people's money. We knew their family was wealthy, but we wanted to be certain they were bondworthy, so I called them in for an interview before I would agree to write the bond. When they came in, they began to interview me. I caught on right away. I recognised their tactics as old-school Zig Ziglar stuff, like answering questions with questions. They had no idea whom they were talking to. Larry was more curious than Jerome. He demanded to know why I needed to know what size shoe he wore. He couldn't figure out why I needed that type of information. I looked down and saw he wore a size thirteen. That's a large footprint to track, right? I told this rich, smart, college-educated son of a bitch I needed to know his shoe size so I could track him down if he ran.

'Well, if I ran, how long would you chase me?' This was a very important question. Without hesitation, I looked them in the eyes and said, 'To the grave, brothers.' Jerome looked at Larry with a 'whoa no' expression, because they knew I meant business. Without hesitation, they gave us a cheque for $17,500, the standard 10 per cent deposit on their bond.

The weekend came and went. On Tuesday, Beth started getting phone calls from the brothers saying they were scared to go to court. We kept reassuring them we already posted their bond. For the moment, they were safe. The courts couldn't do anything to them until their appearance, which was scheduled for the following Monday. Little did we know that the cheque they gave us was hot. That's what they were scared about. It was only a matter of time before we discovered their cheque bounced. Every time they called, they actually wanted to see if we knew yet.

On Monday, Beth went to court to make sure the Bernsteins showed. They did not. One of our attorneys was representing them. He said they were always early for their previous court appearances. They were never late. Beth and I began to panic. The attorney told the judge he was genuinely concerned for their welfare and asked for more time. The judge agreed their absence was unusual but refused to grant the lawyer his request to meet later that afternoon. He issued new warrants for $300,000 cash – no bond.

Beth called me right away so I could start the hunt. An hour later, we got word their cheque bounced. This did not look good. I had an immediate sinking feeling in my stomach. Larry and Jerome were used to country clubs and cocktail parties. They were privileged and came from a nice Jewish family. The idea of doing serious jail time shook them to their core.

The clock was officially ticking.

Beth went to see their dad. We needed any possible information he might have. When I told him the cheque his sons had given us bounced, he was shocked. He insisted he had at least two hundred grand in his account and he'd make good on the cheque. Beth made the trip to the father's bank with him that afternoon so she could collect our money.

The news wasn't good. According to the bank, the old man had just a little over six hundred dollars in his account. Apparently, Larry and Jerome had cleaned out their own father's life savings.

They had linked their accounts to his, so if there were any overdrafts or fees, money got sucked out of the father's to cover bad cheques.

This all didn't sit well with Beth. She absolutely can't stand to see innocent people get ripped off, especially elderly folks. How could the old man's bank transfer those types of amounts and never once contact him?

Beth decided to bring Mr Bernstein by Jerome's wife's house. The older Mr Bernstein was only concerned that his two sons were safe. Jerome's wife, on the other hand, didn't seem all that distressed about the situation. Apparently, she and Jerome were going through a separation. Beth and I were amazed by her total lack of concern for her husband. She acted as if the whole thing was just a big bother to her.

When I spoke to his wife, she told me the last thing her husband said was that he wanted to commit suicide. She seemed so blasé about the thought. She didn't think he was serious. When I asked if he had ever threatened suicide before, she said he hadn't. She thought nothing of it. I called Beth into the house to interview the wife, woman to woman.

I went into the backyard and began throwing a ball around with their little boy. As we tossed the ball back and forth, an image of Jerome flashed into my head. I could hear him say, 'I didn't know you were like this, Dog. You're playing with my little boy.' I turned back towards the house to find Beth. I knew the Bernstein brothers were dead.

Something told me to go check the other brother's house, but I refused because I didn't want to believe those sons of bitches had killed themselves. After we left the house, I got a lead from a local cop that the brothers had chartered a private jet and were planning to leave town. In a weird way, I was relieved to hear that news. Within a couple hours, I had all of the airports covered. The closest one was Centennial Field. By the time I got there, the cops were convinced the brothers had already fled to Brazil. I spoke to a worker on the field who told me he was certain the Bernsteins hadn't been out there. He said there was no way they took a plane from Centennial, because the plane they usually chartered was still in its hangar.

Before the end of the first day, I made an appearance on the local six o'clock news and told people to keep an eye out for them. I must have called every number in my Rolodex – hotels, bus stations, train stations, airlines, and car rental places. It had been a very long day and I was exhausted. I went home, though I couldn't shake the feeling about Larry's house.

The following morning, I got a call from a security guard who was watching Larry's house, telling me to get over there right away. Beth and I hopped in the car and rushed over. When we turned on to Larry's, street everything suddenly seemed to be happening in slow motion. Ambulances and police cruisers lined the street. There were cops gathered in the driveway of the house. Paramedics were rushing around with medical equipment.

The double garage doors were open and I could see two gold Jaguars parked side by side. A few of the cops in the driveway started making their way back to their patrol cars and I got a clear view of the two bodies sprawled out on the black pavement of the driveway. They were covered by white sheets – except for their feet. I could see a size thirteen shoe sticking out from under a blanket. They were both wearing the same shoes as the first day I had met them in my office.

The cops told me later that Larry and Jerome had got into their Jaguars, closed the garage doors, and started the engines. They left a suicide note that read, 'We knew we couldn't outrun Beth and the Dog.' Beth and I have always tried to hold the hands of our clients to get them through the dark days. They didn't have to kill themselves.

Because of the tragic circumstances, I felt we should be the ones to break the news to the dad. He wasn't in the best of health. When he saw us, he immediately knew something was wrong. I told him the police had found his sons, that they had committed suicide. We tried to comfort him. He looked at me and asked, 'Both of them? Both of my sons are gone?' He was confused and brokenhearted. I felt terrible to be the one telling him this news. I had just stepped into this family's life. I was their bondsman, but something more was happening. The old man needed me to be strong so he didn't completely fall apart as his world caved in all around him.

I guess Mr Bernstein appreciated our involvement on the case, because he invited both Beth and me to his sons' funeral. First we went to the synagogue for the service and then to the grave site. Not many people attended, mainly close family and friends. Jerome's wife didn't even bring their little boy.

I spotted Mr Bernstein walking over towards me. My heart ached for the old man. His sons had put him through so much. He shook my hand and said, 'It looks like we don't have enough men to carry the caskets. I hate to ask this of you, but could you help carry my sons to their final resting place?'

I was overcome with emotion. It was the end of the hunt and the end of two men's lives. Now this frail old man standing before me was going to live out the rest of his days with a broken heart. There were many questions running through my mind. Did I do enough to help Larry and Jerome? Could I have done more? I couldn't help the tears. I asked God to forgive them for their sins and to watch over their souls. I joined the others and carried the casket that day. I asked which of the brothers I was carrying. The funeral director told me it was Jerome. I was carrying his feet. As I lowered his casket to the ground, I heard Jerome say, 'Dog, you chased me to the grave.'

Later that day, I told Beth I wasn't sure I could do this any more. I seriously considered quitting bounty hunting.

A few weeks later, I had lunch with the father. He thanked me for helping him carry his sons to the grave. He said I gave him the greatest gift during his darkest days. Much to my surprise, a relative paid us everything the Bernstein brothers owed, plus a few extra dollars for our expenses. The Bernsteins are a good family. They are kind and righteous people. We stayed in the father's life for another six months so Beth could help him retrieve his money from the bank that wired his life savings to his two sons.

In a strange way, the Bernstein brothers put us back on top in the Denver bail bonds market. The local news had covered the story, but the publicity worked both for us and against us. It boosted our business, but it also brought unwanted attention from the detectives who worked on the case. Later they started popping up on all the chases Beth and I did. They were convinced we had to be crooked.

# CHAPTER THIRTY-SIX

# Ivan Van Thompson

For a short time, Beth and I were writing bonds for Capitol Bail Bonds, owned by Vince Smith. He started using my bounty hunting skills and sending me all over the country to find fugitives. Thanks to Vince, I collected the highest price of my career, six thousand dollars for a sly character named Ivan 'Van' Thompson.

Van was a crafty African-American con artist who was well respected on the Denver streets. He was known for being sharp, a fast talker, and as clever as they come. At one time or another, he was involved in every type of major scam known to man. He was writing bad cheques all over Denver. His forte was stealing other people's identities and credit card numbers.

Beth and I were a little freaked-out about writing a bond for Van. It was set at $100,000. We hadn't been working with Vince long enough to know if he was good for the money. Van was also facing a lot of jail time, which made him a high flight risk. When his ex-girlfriend Kim agreed to co-sign, we wrote the bond. She appeared stable enough because she owned her own home and worked full-time as a nurse. However, I had a nervous feeling in my gut that I could not shake. Something told me Van was going to run.

Just as I suspected, when Van's court date came, he was a no-show. Later that night, my phone rang. I knew who was on the other end of the line.

I played it cool. 'Not a smart play on your part, brother. You've got two choices: either you come into the office first thing tomorrow morning so we can settle all this, or I hunt you down and drag you in crying and screaming.'

He had already started laughing before I finished my sentence. 'Hunt me down, huh?' he asked. 'You one stupid motherfucker, man. I ain't scared of the DA and I certainly ain't worried about your cracker ass. I *won't* be caught because I *can't* be caught. You ain't shit, man.'

Without another word, he hung up.

First thing in the morning, I began my hunt. I started by banging on Kim's front door before the sun came up. I needed to shake things up and apply as much pressure as I could. I leaned on his known associates and staked out his former hangouts. One thing I knew about Van: his ego would be his downfall. I'd seen it time and time again. Guys like him are master criminals in their own minds, always looking to show everyone how clever they are. I knew Van wasn't leaving town. He enjoyed the game too much. What's a performer without an audience? I spent my first day looking for him at all of the local fried chicken fast-food joints. Word was out.

A couple of days into my hunt, an investigator named Grundinger from the DA's office contacted me. I agreed to meet him at a bar one night to discuss the case. Grundinger was your typical conservative tough guy Denver cop. His hair was silver and buzzed supershort. He wore a polyester suit with cowboy boots. I was suspicious of his motives right off the bat. I never thought he had a whole lot of respect for me. He thought I was some low-grade hack that he easily could manipulate. He wanted to compare notes and 'share' information, which meant he would tell me nothing and I was expected to tell him everything. Typical.

Let the competition begin.

By now, Beth and I had started videotaping every single bust, because people were always making accusations about things that never happened. They threatened to sue all the time. Within the next week or two, Grundinger and I crossed paths on countless occasions. I think he was shocked to see me show up at scene after scene. He'd be pulling into a parking lot to check out a lead and I'd be pulling out, or vice versa. Sometimes the two of us were just minutes behind each other. From the start, I think Grundinger and the rest of the Denver cops had disregarded me as another incompetent bounty hunter. Their attitudes changed pretty quickly as we got into the hunt. They couldn't understand how I was able to run neck and neck with them.

My secret weapon was Van's ex-girlfriend, Kim, who was now dating our receptionist, Benji. As the days melted into weeks, Kim began to reveal bits and pieces of information about where Van might be hiding. She often mentioned she needed to go by her place to check on things or swing by home to drop something off, but we all assumed she was meeting him. Even with the tips we were getting from Kim, we seemed to always be a step or two behind Van.

A week or so later, I got a call from Grundinger.

'Dog, I'm sitting here at the station with one of your employees. We've arrested her and charged her with aiding and abetting Van.'

I was shocked. She worked in my office writing bonds for Beth. We showed her the ropes of the business. I never suspected she was a rat. But after I gave it some thought, it all came together. She once dated my son Christopher. I remembered a conversation we had about a month prior, right after they broke up. He told me they split because there was some slick pimp daddy living with her. Of course, I didn't pay much attention to that small detail at the time. But now, it all made sense.

When I hung up the phone, I was pissed. I went off on the most vicious tirade I can remember in a long time. I felt used and betrayed. Beth and I had taken her under our wing, and she stabbed us in the back.

Van was using both women. He hit Kim up to bail his ass out by co-signing the bond, and then he used our employee for information. He actually got her to sign a consent of surety for him. With that document, he could go to the court and use it to get the warrant for his arrest dropped altogether. Lucky for us, he didn't make it that far.

By the time I got to her house, Grundinger and the rest of the Denver cops had already worked the place over. They found machinery to manufacture fake credit cards and discovered a stack of fraudulent cheques he was in the process of printing. We didn't come across anything special, until Beth spotted a small note on the end table next to a phone. There was a girl's name and a street address on it.

'I know this address,' Beth told me. 'It's a Motel 8 right outside of downtown.'

Grundinger and the boys already had some girl up against a cruiser and were patting her down when I drove into the parking lot. Apparently, she was one of Van's cronies.

I was standing next to Grundinger when one of the cops pulled a pistol out of the chick's handbag.

'Look what we have here,' Grundinger said. He looked over at me and said, 'This changes the entire direction of the case, Dog. We've got a known associate with a concealed weapon, which means we have to believe that Van is packing. Basically, your road ends here.'

'What exactly does that mean? No way am I dropping out of this chase.'

Grundinger raised his voice. 'This case is now strictly a police matter. Understand? You've been riding my coat-tails long enough.'

I had to laugh. 'Riding *your* coat-tails?'

'You will receive no further cooperation from my office.'

'I'm crushed,' I shot back. 'I was getting so much from you before.'

I wasn't going to let some stiff Denver cop tell me what to do. I wasn't going anywhere. I had a large bond on the line. I wasn't about to let Van slip through my hands.

I overheard the girl tell the cops that Van had dropped her off at the Motel 8 earlier that morning and then took off. I managed to slide up next to her while the investigating officers were having their own discussion.

'Van dropped you off earlier?' I asked quickly and quietly.

'Yeah,' she answered. I had a feeling that she'd rather talk to me than the cops. If anything, just to spite them.

'Where'd he head off to?'

She looked back in the direction of the cops and then back at me. She obviously hadn't told them anything.

'He said he was going to the Western Motor Inn at I-70.'

A smile came across my face as I walked away. I knew the area well. It was the same neighbourhood I had moved into when my grandpa had given me the old house on Steele Street. This Western Motor Inn was a major hangout for pimps, hookers, and drug dealers.

I took off across the lot to where my truck was parked. Behind me I heard Grundinger say, 'Where the hell does he think he's going?'

I walked into the lobby and immediately noticed a dark figure running at full speed towards the end of one of the corridors. It was Van. He looked right at me and said, 'Fuck!' I stomped my foot on the ground, knowing I couldn't catch him. He exploded out one of the far exit doors that led to a rear parking lot. I followed him, but he was too far ahead of me. By the time I got through the exit and into the lot, he was gone.

I was no longer days or hours behind him. It was a matter of seconds. I was closing in, and he knew it.

When I got back to the office, I told Beth the whole story.

'Now what do we do, Duane?' she asked. I could tell that she was really discouraged.

'I'm going to sit right here in this chair and smoke a cigarette,' I said to her. 'Van's going to call. Trust me.'

Beth let out a long sigh and started shaking her head at me. 'Perfect. We'll just sit here and do nothing. That's just great.'

Suddenly, the phone rang. Beth froze in her seat. When she answered, her jaw dropped to the floor. She looked over at me and pointed at the receiver in her hand. When Beth asked him who was calling, he asked, 'Who has been awake as long as he has?' I jumped up and took the call.

'I am so damn tired.' And I was, too.

It almost sounded like he was still out of breath. 'You motherfucker, Dog! How'd you know where to find me?'

'I was just on my way home. I live right across the street.'

'They got all my shit. They got all my bitches. I ain't got nowhere to go. Everyone I know don't want to talk to me because of all the heat you been putting on them.'

'I told you, Van; there were only two choices.'

'If I come in, Dog, I'm looking at some hard time. Like forty years, man.'

'You got nowhere else to go, Van. You know it and I know it. I'm gonna get ya.'

'Yeah . . . ' he said slowly. His voice trailed off. I knew he was mentally and physically exhausted. This was the end of the line for him.

By the end of our phone call, I had convinced Van to walk into the Denver police station the next morning and surrender.

When I told Grundinger about my little phone conversation, he didn't believe a word I said. He was laughing at me on the other end of the line.

'Yeah, OK, Dog,' he said. He yelled to the other cops in the room and said, 'Dog says Van's coming in tomorrow and turning himself in.' I could hear hooting and hollering erupt in the background.

'Listen to me,' I said. 'He's gonna be there at 10 a.m. sharp. You'll believe me when he walks up those steps, won't you?' We had taunted each other for weeks chasing this guy.

I almost started laughing out loud when Grundinger called me later on that night at home. He must have had time to think about what I told him and started getting nervous. His spoke softly. 'Seriously, you believe Van is going to turn himself in just like that? After all the games?'

'Like I already told you, he's gonna walk right up to us at the station tomorrow.'

Grundinger thought something over for a moment, then said, 'Not exactly, Dog. I can't have you there. We'll take him into custody. This isn't your case any more.' It didn't matter, because Vince Smith told me he'd pay my fee anyway. I made the catch whether Grundinger wanted to give me the credit or not.

Van did show up at the Denver Police Department's offices the next day. Grundinger nabbed him in the parking lot. I wasn't there for the bust, but I caught a glimpse of him being taken up the police headquarters steps. When he saw me, I stopped, saluted him, and mouthed the words, 'Thank you, Van.'

# CHAPTER THIRTY-SEVEN

# Two Steps Back

Now that I had my professional problems ironed out in Colorado, Hawaii was next. One of the conditions of my deal with Richard Heath in 1997 was that I surrender my bond licence during our two-year non-compete agreement. Since I had no licence, my insurance company essentially threw me out on the street overnight. As a result, several complaints were filed with the Hawaii Department of Insurance. There were lots of people who needed my services and who already paid me in advance to oversee their bail and bond. When I was forced to leave Hawaii, many of them lost a lot of their collateral in bail forfeiture. What this boiled down to was, the co-signers were losing everything because the people they were backing skipped out on their bail and I couldn't retrieve any of them. They ran with no threat of the Dog coming after them. By running, they put the screws to their families and loved ones. Nonetheless, my company still had to pay the insurer for the full value of the bond. During that two-year period, that meant liquidating my collateral to make good on the money owed. I hated doing it, but I had no other choice.

Most of the complaints were settled outside of the system. As to the others, my problems started when the Department of Insurance began sending me notification letters to the wrong address. The letters went to an address of mine that was five years old. The strange part is that, prior to my deal with Heath, I always received letters from the department at my current address with no problem. It was my legal address on every document filed with the state. It made no sense that they couldn't reach me through my correct address.

I was patiently waiting for the two-year noncompete to run out so I could get back to Hawaii and start all over again. That would have been the perfect plan, had it not been for those damned complaints I never received. The problem wasn't the complaints; my trouble stemmed from not answering them. Failure to answer was a violation of my licence. If I didn't adhere to all of the rules and regulations, I was in danger of losing my rights as a bondsman. It's a little like ignoring the IRS. Sooner or later, they're going to get you.

In October 1997, my sister Jolene called to tell me she'd heard there was a problem with my licence in Hawaii. That was the first I had heard of any such thing. I called the Hawaii Department of Insurance to give them my forwarding address in Colorado. I wanted to be certain I was getting every letter they sent. On 27 December, I received a certified letter from them informing me that my licence was in jeopardy for failure to respond to complaints. The hearing was set for 29 October. There was no way I could be there to tell my side of the story, because the hearing had been two months earlier. In my absence, the commissioner revoked my licence for five years.

I couldn't believe I was fighting for my job again. I felt Hawaii was where I belonged. It was home. If I couldn't write bonds in Hawaii, all I could do was bounty hunt, but I wanted to do both. I tried to appeal the decision, but the Hawaii Supreme Court refused to hear my case. The penalty for not answering a complaint is generally a thirty-day suspension and a five-hundred-dollar fine. The revocation of my licence for five years was extreme and unfair.

Once again, I couldn't help but feel the Lord was testing me. From August 1997 to August 2000, it sure felt like I was on the wrong side of a machine gun. *Ratta tat tat tat tat*. Challenges just kept coming without a chance to dodge a single bullet. In addition to all of my troubles with work, I lost my dad to a heart attack in August 2000. Although he and I rarely saw eye-to-eye, we had grown much closer. I'll never know what it feels like to have a father love me like I love my kids, but Flash taught me a lot of skills that helped me get through life.

Not long before he passed, Dad and I went to visit his father. During that visit, I came to see Flash in a different light. As we stood in the backyard of Grandpa's house, I noticed Dad became a little uneasy. I could see tears well up in his eyes as we got closer to the woodshed. Flash walked ahead of me so I couldn't see him cry. In all my life, I thought I'd never live to see the day my dad would break down in tears. I looked at Grandpa and asked if he knew why Dad was crying. Grandpa told me he used to beat the life out of Flash in that shed. He tied his hands above his head and whooped him with a leather strap.

He said that's how he kept all his sons in line. Grandpa was oblivious to the pain and destruction his abuse had had on two generations. It wasn't his fault; he didn't know any better. From that moment on, I understood why Flash beat me. He had his own demons to wrestle with. My heart ached for his pain and suffering. I forgave him that day. I let go of all of the anger and resentment towards my father that I had been carrying for so many years. Now we could both be set free. I knew his secret. He didn't have to hold that burden any more.

Had it not been for Beth and her undying love and devotion, I'm not sure I would have made it through those hellacious years. But we did. Against all odds and attempts to kick us when we were down, Beth and I managed to survive – and eventually thrive.

# CHAPTER THIRTY-EIGHT

# The Big One

Flying used to be something most people looked forward to. It was elegant and sophisticated. Nowadays, thanks to Osama bin Laden, airport security has made us all insecure about flying. It has never been my favourite thing in any case. Being confined to a seat for what feels like endless hours with nothing to do is not how I prefer to spend my time. I'm a fidgety guy. I need to move around. Even first-class seats aren't comfortable. Hell, I can't even smoke. Despite Beth's nagging to quit, I can hardly go thirty minutes without a cigarette. To combat my boredom and need for nicotine, I simply go to sleep. From wheels-up to touchdown, I'm out cold.

On 5 January 2003, Beth and I were flying from Honolulu to Los Angeles to meet some people who were interested in talking about producing a dramatic television show about bounty hunting. I did stints on *The Secret World of Bounty Hunting, Take This Job*, and *The Anatomy of a Crime*. The response to our episodes was so strong, other producers contacted us about doing our own show.

Twenty minutes into the flight, Beth woke me up by hitting me over the head with her newspaper. Waking me on a flight is something she knows not to do unless it's urgent.

'Duane. Duane. Wake up. You gotta see this.'

She pointed to the front-page headline in the *Los Angeles Times* that read something like:

HEIR TO MAX FACTOR FORTUNE MAY HAVE JUMPED MILLION-DOLLAR BAIL.

'Wouldn't it be something if he ran, Duane?' Beth's eyes widened at the thought. I knew exactly what she was thinking.

'Duane. This is it. This is the big case the Lord has spoken to us about. This is your chance to show the world that you are the greatest bounty hunter who ever lived.'

Oh, yeah, her wheels were turning. Beth and I had talked about the 'big catch' for years. For a while, we both thought it might be Osama bin Laden. Lord knows, I wanted it to be.

'If this guy jumps, Duane, you've gotta get in the hunt. You have to go get him.'

In my gut, I knew Beth was right. Andrew Luster was a rich white boy. He was just the kind of high-profile chase I was looking for. No one could find him like I would. I had spent so many years standing on the media sidelines in other cases I had helped solve. The FBI and other authorities always took credit for my hard work. After years of battling for recognition, I knew it would have to be somebody big before I got widespread attention. I was ripe and ready for it. I wanted it more than anything in the world.

The only thing I knew about the Luster story was what I seen on the news. He was on trial for allegedly drugging and raping several women.

I hate rapists, with a vengeance. I have never understood that type of crime. Six years ago, my daughter, Baby Lyssa, was a victim of statutory rape by a thirty-year-old man. She was just thirteen years old. She was living with her mother in Alaska. I thought she would be better off living with her mom as she grew into her teenage years. Every little girl needs her mom, especially at that age. But Big Lyssa set few rules and boundaries. Our kids were allowed to do whatever they wanted. I hoped Baby Lyssa would see she was too young to raise a child on her own. She fought me every step of the way.

'Dad, it's my baby. I want to keep it.'

I thought that was bullcrap. She was only a teenager. I completely disagreed with her decision, but I was thousands of miles away. There was nothing I could do.

I didn't see Baby Lyssa for two and a half years after she gave birth to her daughter, Abbie. Throughout that time, I felt I lost two babies. I hated myself for being so harsh, but, like any rational parent, I wanted to protect my daughter. I finally sent her and Abbie plane tickets to come visit me in Hawaii. The second I saw my granddaughter, I knew I had made a terrible mistake. I prayed to God for forgiveness. The Lord spoke to me and said, 'You are not the giver of life.' He was right. It was not my decision to make. Only God knows His eternal plan.

To me, there is nothing that separates someone like Luster – who used his money, power and influence to lure women into his twisted world – from the rat who likewise manipulated, used and raped my baby girl. Luster seduced innocent victims, drugged them, and videotaped himself raping them. The Ventura County DA offered to cut a deal by which Luster would serve fifteen years. He turned it down. He instructed his lawyers to go to trial, assuming, of course, that he would beat the rap. His arrogance was astounding. But from what I could tell, it looked as though Andrew Luster was going down.

I closed my eyes and pretended to go back to sleep. Beth was wide awake. I could tell she was plotting her strategy. We were only twenty-five minutes into our flight. My head was filling up fast with thoughts of running after this rich, spoiled fugitive. I knew damn well that if Luster ran, he would flee the country. This would become an international manhunt. In a way, it was the last thing I wanted to hear about. I was far too old for this stuff. But how could I let this opportunity pass me by?

I spent the rest of our five and a half hour flight internally battling my need to prove to the world that I am the best bounty hunter who ever lived. I knew I could find this asshole. I saw him in my head. This was my ultimate date with destiny. I knew it wouldn't be easy. I surely knew it wouldn't come cheap – financially or emotionally. That was definitely a concern to me. I was just getting back on my feet after losing my bail bonds business in Hawaii a few years earlier. I never wanted to be that broke again. Also, Beth and I were finally connecting as a couple. After more than a decade of on-again, off-again dating, we were finally together. For the first time in my life, there wasn't anyone else diverting my attention.

I knew damn well that entering the hunt meant placing 100 per cent of my focus on finding Luster and not on my family. It meant eating, breathing, and sleeping Luster. There would be no room for anyone else. It also meant personally bankrolling the search, which I knew could go into hundreds of thousands of dollars, depending on where Luster would run – if he ran at all, of course.

By the time our plane landed in L.A., Luster *was* officially on the run. He failed to show up for his court date. He had removed his court-ordered ankle monitor on 3 January and hadn't been heard from since. Before we claimed our luggage, he was declared a fugitive and a warrant was issued for his arrest.

Beth and I went straight to our hotel. She got on her laptop and began researching the case. We even called our lawyer, Les Abell, to tell him we were thinking of going after Luster.

Abell was very enthusiastic. 'Hmm. That's very interesting. One of my clients is a wonderful writer and a Max Factor historian. Her name is Samantha Hart. She wrote a book about Max Factor. Maybe she could help you.'

What a stroke of luck! I could hardly believe it. Beth and I spoke to Samantha later that night. She knew everything about the Luster family. She told us that his mother, Elizabeth, was the adopted granddaughter of Max Factor. The Factors never much cared about the Lusters, because they weren't carrying on the family name. They were not Factors, they were Lusters. From what I could tell, there was a *big* difference between the two.

When we hung up, we knew that Luster would be a challenge. Everything she said made it clear we were up against a smart, rich, educated, cunning and well-connected fugitive. This piqued our interest more than ever. It had been years since we had hunted someone like Luster – perhaps not since the Bernstein brothers.

# CHAPTER THIRTY-NINE

# Entering the Hunt for Luster

Beth and I were in L.A. to talk about doing our own reality show, and Boris thought it was a good idea to set up a meeting with Chris McQuarrie to talk about it. We sat in the bar at the Four Seasons Hotel, going over our vision with Chris, picking his brain as to what he thought we should do. Chris and I had become friends. I felt I could really trust him to guide us in the right direction.

'Hey, did you see this guy Andrew Luster jumped bail?'

I wasn't expecting Chris to change subjects on me. I was unusually flustered. I said, 'Who?'

An awkward silence fell over the table. It was like that old television commercial when someone mentions that his broker is E. F. Hutton and the entire restaurant stops to listen. More important, I could feel daggers flying out from Beth's eyes towards me, because here we were, out pitching a television show on bounty hunting, and for a second, I failed to recognise the name of one of the most wanted men alive. Then it came back to me that this was the guy Beth was talking about on our flight the day before. I regained my composure, acting like I was only joking around, and said, 'Beth and I were just discussing that punk on our flight yesterday. We're thinking about joining the hunt.'

McQuarrie made a point of saying how awesome it would be if I could find Luster. We all knew I was the right guy for the job. I could see Beth's wheels turning faster than a Ferrari burning rubber. Thirty minutes later, Beth was in our hotel room working the phones. She plugged in her laptop and began to book me on as many news shows as she could to get the word out. I hadn't done a lot of national news media. It was all new to me. But that didn't matter, because I was the right guy to talk to about catching fugitives. The first interview I did was with Matt Bean from Court TV for their website www.crime.com. I had written a few articles on past captures for the site, so they knew me pretty well. Matt mostly wanted to know my thoughts on Luster's bail-jumping.

The next day, Cole Thompson, a producer from Court TV, called and asked if I would be a guest on *Catherine Crier Live*. The producer said, since I was in Los Angeles and the show was live from New York, it would have to be a phoner – a live telephone interview. They didn't have time to get me to a studio or in front of the cameras. Beth wasn't pleased with that at all. She knows my presence makes for good, compelling television.

Beth challenged the producer's decision. 'Excuse me, but are you familiar with what Dog looks like?' She quickly uploaded some pictures so the producer could get an idea of who I was. Ten minutes later, I was in a car on my way to the studio.

On the way, Beth was giddy with excitement. 'This is it, Duane. This is the guy the Lord has been waiting for. This is the big case. I just know it.' Beth spoke with such conviction. She had been trying to get me on TV for years, and now everyone wanted me. It was all happening so fast.

Catherine Crier asked me some tough questions on the air, but the one that stood out was when she dismissively asked, 'So how would *you* catch Andrew Luster?'

I looked deadpan into the camera, my eyes hidden behind my trademark black Oakleys so Luster couldn't see my eyes, and said, 'Run, Luster, run.'

'Obviously, Dog. But if you could say something to Andrew Luster right now, what would it be?' Crier seemed doubtful I was up to the task.

'You better run and hide, 'cause *the Dog* is coming after you.'

The next day I was asked to appear on *Geraldo*. Each of the shows wanted my opinion and expertise on where someone like Luster might run. He could be anywhere, and the truth is, he was probably long gone, which made the idea of chasing him less palatable. And yet I wanted to get this son of bitch. I wanted his ass. I wanted to be the guy who brought Luster to justice. Bounty hunters all over the world were talking bad about me, saying I didn't stand a chance. Those bastards. I began hating Andrew Luster. As my anger grew, so did my desire to join the hunt.

After the Geraldo Rivera interview, I was met in the hallway of the studio by the husband of one of Luster's victims. Now, I've been meeting victims for thirty years. I generally enjoy getting to know the folks I am fighting for. For whatever reason, the victim's lawyer didn't want her to meet me face-to-face, but her husband could.

'Dog, please. You won't understand this, but our whole life depends on you.'

But, of course, I did understand. Painfully so, though I never let on how I personally knew the depth of his family's pain.

'If you catch Luster, promise me you'll drive him by our house. I'd like to see him for five minutes. You don't understand. My wife has been terrified by every little sound.' She thought it was Luster coming back to get her. I could see the torment on his face. The man's wife was pregnant with twins. During the trial, she miscarried one of the babies.

I was used to playing referee, but my heart and soul understood that this man wanted revenge. Not just for his wife but for all of Luster's victims. Lord knows, I truly understood his anger and vengeful desire. I shook my head in agreement, letting him know I heard his plea. If I decided to join the hunt, I promised I would oblige.

After the *Geraldo* appearance, all of the big news shows came calling. Even though I hadn't officially announced I was in the hunt, people were beginning to expect that I would be the guy who was going to get that rapist.

The next day, I was preparing to do *The Rita Cosby Show* for Fox. I bumped into John Ritter in the lobby of the Four Seasons Hotel. At the time, his wife was the head of the Los Angeles Rape Crisis Center. He told me to get Luster and their prayers would be with me. Terry Bradshaw did the same. These two guys inspired me that the time had come to enter the chase.

As I got ready for the interview, Beth and I tried to figure out what I would wear so Luster would know I was coming.

'How about this for the interview, honey?' I stepped out wearing my leather vest and no shirt.

'You look hot, Big Daddy. Absolutely!' She loved the way I looked. I just wanted Luster to know I was no joke. I knew he was watching.

We showed up to the set and caused quite a stir. People were whispering, 'Can he go on the air looking like that?' and 'Are we sure this guy is for real?'

Hell, I didn't care. I was there to tell Luster I was coming for him. I wasn't trying to make friends with the newsroom. The Lord was calling me to find Andrew Luster. The pull was so great, so strong, I knew not to question His plan.

With Beth and our youngest three kids *(Copyright © Timothy White)*

The photo shoot for first-season artwork, with Timothy White *(Copyright © Timothy White)*

This man was wanted by the Secret Service. He was captured while filming for Dutch television.

Covered in dirt, coming in from our last capture before our wedding rehearsal, 19 May 2006

My Indian heritage
(Copyright © 2006 Lucy
Pemoni / Diamond Head
Photography)

With my preacher, Tim Storey, arriving at my wedding by canoe, an old Hawaiian tradition
(Copyright © 2006 AETN. Photo credit: Doug Hyun)

Finally *(Copyright © 2006 AETN. Photo credit: Doug Hyun)*

Wedding pose at sunset
*(Copyright © 2006
Lucy Pemoni / Diamond
Head Photography)*

Reflections on Barbara *(Copyright © 2006 AETN. Photo credit: Doug Hyun)*

Group wedding shot *(Copyright © 2006 Lucy Pemoni / Diamond Head Photography)*

Waikoloa, Hawaii: Our fantasy wedding day was missing only one thing—Barbara *(Copyright © 2006 Lucy Pemoni / Diamond Head Photography)*

With Beth at Season 3 premiere, Honolulu, Hawaii, 2006 *(Copyright © Marco Garcia /www.marcpix.com)*

Barbara Katie and her baby, Travis, at my house on his first birthday

Gary Boy and Bonnie Jo at the beach

On the road with Lynyrd Skynyrd, Season 1, 2004

With Beth and kids (*Copyright* © Honolulu Star-Bulletin)

I didn't know Rita prior to this interview. I wasn't sure what to expect. I also wasn't sure why she chose to have me on her show. But we connected from the moment we went live. This was the best interview I had done so far. In fact, it went so well that Rita invited me to stay for the next segment to debate Roger Diamond, the attorney defending Andrew Luster.

The segment started with Diamond trying to establish what a good guy Luster was. He pointed out that Luster had no previous record or arrests and painted him as a classy, upstanding citizen.

I said, 'You'd say anything for five hundred bucks an hour.'

Diamond was rattled by my accusation. 'Excuse me? Who are you? No one even knows who you are.'

'I am Dog the Bounty Hunter. My job is to catch fugitives on the run.'

'Job? What job? Who do you work for?'

'The state of California,' I said. 'When I bring Luster in, he's worth 15 per cent of his bond.'

'You sound more like a bounty hunter seeking the spotlight than you do a bona fide member of law enforcement. What are your credentials?'

'If you want to know about who I am, check out my website, www.dogthebountyhunter.com.' I could see Beth off camera pumping her fist in the air in victory. Just like in my old boxing days, I took this round clean and true.

After the interview, Roger Diamond came over to talk to me in the parking lot. He bet me two bucks I'd never find Luster. I took the bet.

That evening, I did another interview with Rita Cosby, only this time it was for her show on Fox. She asked me similar questions but was far less confrontational than Diamond. I didn't plan on doing it, but during that interview, I knew I had to pull the trigger. I had to enter the race. I told Rita I was going after Luster.

Thus on 5 January 2003, I made it official. 'My name is Duane "Dog" Chapman, and I have entered the hunt for Andrew Stuart Luster.'

God bless Rita Cosby, who believed in me from the start. She always said, 'This Dog can hunt.'

Every bounty hunter worth his salt and several who were just posers entered the chase too. But it didn't matter. I would be the man who brought Luster back to face his crimes. I would see to it that justice was served. There were other bounty hunters popping up all over the place, wearing Hawaiian shirts, practically mocking me, saying I'd never catch the man. I knew for sure if I didn't catch him, no one would. My title was on the line.

I called Tony Robbins immediately following the interview. Sometimes my mouth can get me into trouble, and he always made me aware of making potentially career-ending decisions and comments. I was afraid I had really stepped in it this time. Tony agreed. But he also encouraged me to live up to *my* expectations, not down to everyone else's. He believed that I could and ultimately would find Andrew Luster. Tony helped me spin my announcement into something positive. He pointed out that people were talking about the Dog. They were no longer asking, 'Who is this kook?' They were taking me very seriously.

Holy crap. I prayed, 'Please, Lord. Don't let me fail.'

Later that night, I was with Beth, Boris, and his wife, Maureen. We were all talking about the past few days and my interview with Rita. Maureen was once the publicist for the Rolling Stones among others, so she usually had pretty good insight into how these types of things go.

'Well, now that all the talking is done, all you have to do is catch the guy!' She said it in a very put-up-or-shut-up tone.

Until that moment, it hadn't really sunk in that I was now searching for one of the most wanted fugitives in America. It was time to put my money where my mouth was. I had a lot at stake. By joining the hunt for Luster, I was gambling on my future, my name, and my reputation. But I knew this was my chance to show the Lord I am worthy of His plan, His will. If this was the big one we'd been waiting for, the time had come.

# CHAPTER FORTY

# Carey, Shawna and Tonja Doe

Once I entered the hunt for Luster, I knew I had to use every opportunity to show the world who Dog the Bounty Hunter really is. Practically every journalist I talked with doubted my ability to find the thirty million-dollar man. For whatever reason, they didn't think I was up to the task.

What is impossible for man becomes possible with God. I spent endless hours, days, and nights praying to God to show me the way, to point me in the direction Luster was hiding.

'Lord, this guy is a rapist. If I catch this guy, I can finally redeem myself. I have spent half my life trying to even things up between us, Lord. That's why I need this capture bad. This man is a rapist. Lord, I need your help.'

And I did.

To find a fugitive, you have to think like him, act like him; you have to understand his wants, needs, desires, strengths, and weaknesses. You have to know everything about the person you're looking for. Who are they? Who is their family? Who are their friends? Where do they hang out? More information means greater insight into the mind of the man you're chasing.

From the outside, Andrew Luster seemed to have it all. His mom, Elizabeth, was Max Factor's adopted granddaughter. Factor immigrated to the United States from Russia, landing in Los Angeles in 1909 during the golden era of Hollywood. He created make-up for the movie industry, eventually building one of the largest and most successful make-up companies in history, named after himself. The family sold Max Factor in 1973 for close to a half-billion dollars. After the sale, Elizabeth Luster inherited her share of the fortune. Andrew was just eleven years old, but he was now a multimillionaire.

When he was arrested in 2000, Luster was thirty-seven years old. He was very tall, standing about six feet four inches. Everyone I talked to described him as a good-looking guy, well educated, calculating, and charming. Often referred to as 'Drew' by his friends, Luster was considered a wealthy playboy who spent his days surfing the beaches of Southern California and his nights partying at his beachfront home or the college bars in Santa Barbara. By all accounts, he was living a pretty good life. Although he never married, he did have two sons with a former girlfriend. Luster was a complete womaniser with thirty-one million dollars in the bank to support his party-boy lifestyle.

Beth took the reins in researching Luster. Her role is to help me in my pursuit any way she can. More importantly, she often keeps me focused when I have the potential to get offtrack. She's constantly thinking about all of the possible pitfalls and challenges we might face. In the beginning, Beth wasn't as supportive as you might think. Her tactic is usually to doubt me. She creates a lot of negativity to keep me motivated. Mostly she nags at me, double- and triple-checking that I have looked at every avenue. She doesn't think I know this about her, but I do.

Beth makes sure everything we do is on the up-and-up. She's a tough broad, no doubt about that. She makes sure we don't make critical mistakes when it's time to take someone down. One knock on the wrong door, and I could be out of business. Worse yet, I could end up in jail. The fear of crossing the wrong line always looms over a hunt.

When it came to Luster, Beth and I wanted to make sure we really understood who we were chasing. We viewed him to be an arrogant, rude, opinionated, egotistical punk. But we had to be careful, because his family has a tremendous amount of clout in Hollywood, with friends in very high places. That meant we could expect a lot of dead ends and false leads.

Most of Luster's friends said he rarely talked about his relationship to Max Factor. Although he was financially set, he was stingy when it came to money. He was pretty low-key, choosing to drive a green Toyota SUV and wearing shorts and T-shirts most of the time. Luster used money as a tool to manipulate women. He lived by the 'golden rule': he who has the gold, makes the rules. In fact, Tonja Doe, one of Luster's victims, testified that after she and Luster broke up, he sued her for twenty-five hundred dollars he claimed he loaned her for some medical expenses.

I needed to know more about Luster's victims. Who were they? How did they meet Luster? How did he go about seducing and ultimately raping them? I wanted as much information as I could find. Somewhere there were clues that would lead me to his door, wherever he was hiding. Knowing the details of his crimes, having an idea of the hurt and pain he inflicted on these women, became yet another reason to get this guy.

For their privacy and safety, the victims' identities were kept private during the trial. They were only referred to as Carey Doe, Shawna Doe and Tonja Doe. Despite their secret identities, Beth tracked down two of them, who agreed to share all of the information they had to help us track down their rapist.

Shawna Doe spoke to us first. She described the July morning in 2001 when she awoke in Luster's bed with a throbbing pain that felt like a jackhammer inside her head. She didn't remember a thing from the night before, which wasn't typical for her. She liked to party, but she never blacked out. As she began to get her bearings, it suddenly dawned on her that she might have been raped, maybe more than once. She was panic-stricken. She frantically searched for her tattered clothes so she could get dressed and go home.

When Beth asked Shawna to tell her how it happened, she said she remembered having a few beers with her friend David the night before. Afterwards, they went to O'Malley's bar, where she met a good-looking guy named Drew who kept offering to buy them drinks. She ordered a Long Island Iced Tea and a Cosmopolitan. The last thing she remembered from the bar was taking a glass of water from Drew, who thought she looked thirsty from dancing and partying. Shawna said she couldn't remember ever feeling so wasted.

Next she told Beth that Drew took her to the beach, where they walked on the pier above the thunderous waves. He kept taunting her to get naked and jump into the water until she finally did. The water was much colder than she expected, and the current was very strong. She struggled to make it back to shore. When she finally climbed on to the beach, she was shivering and very cold. Drew scooped her up and took her to his place. Shawna remembered taking a hot shower to warm up.

She told Beth that Drew stepped into the shower and began forcing her to have sex. She was too drunk, or so she thought, to tell him to get out. She couldn't speak. She wanted to scream, yell, tell him to stop, but the words never came.

Later that night, Shawna came out of her blackout to find herself half-naked on Drew's sofa. There were a couple of other guys in the next room, but she had no idea who they were. She had never seen them before.

Drew gave her another drink of what she believed was booze.

Shawna shot it back. Almost instantly, she began to get woozy. The room was spinning. She thought she was going to get sick or pass out.

She slurred her words when she asked Drew what she had just swallowed. He told her it was liquid Ecstasy, something Shawna said she had never done. Once again, she passed out.

The next morning, segments of the night flashed through her head. She remembered Drew forcing himself on her several times. She believed there was another naked man too. Shawna wept as she told Beth her story. It was hard to speak of, and yet she knew we had to hear all of the painful details if we were going to find Luster.

'Liquid Ecstasy' is not Ecstasy but GHB, known on the street as a date-rape drug. It's a clear liquid that is easy to slip into any drink. It has a slightly salty flavour that can easily be hidden in a mixed drink, especially one that contains salt, like a margarita. Mixed with alcohol, GHB is a very dangerous drug. Someone has to know exactly how much to use to avoid an accidental overdose, which can often be lethal. With alcohol, it can render unsuspecting victims helpless, because they commonly pass out. When they awaken, they have little, if any, recollection of what happened.

After her frightening night, Shawna Doe went to the police to tell them she believed she'd been drugged and raped. The investigating detectives convinced her to get Luster to admit he drugged her so they could confirm her story and build their assault and rape case against him. She agreed. While the police listened in, Shawna phoned Luster and got him to admit he'd given her GHB. That admission was enough for investigators to pursue him.

Luster was shocked when detectives knocked on his door and told him they had a warrant for his arrest. He angrily accused Shawna of lying. That was a crucial mistake on his part: the police had never mentioned whose behalf they were acting on. A routine search turned up several vials of a liquid suspected to be GHB – as well as a little cocaine and a collection of homemade videotapes of various naked women who appeared to be drugged. Two in particular, labelled 'Shawna GHBing' and 'Real Hidden Video – Living Room' caught the attention of the detectives. They weren't sure what they had stumbled on to, but it was beginning to look like Shawna Doe wasn't Luster's only victim.

The tapes were graphic. Not only did they show Luster having sex with a number of different women; they showed him sodomising the girls, who were clearly unaware of what was happening. One video even showed him placing a lit joint inside a woman's vagina. Worst of all, every single woman was unconscious, which made a pretty compelling argument that this was not consensual sex.

When I heard about the sex tapes, I talked to a forensic expert who specialised in sex crimes. His analysis of Luster was that he was a necrophiliac, meaning he desired having sex with dead women. He drugged his victims until they were unable to move, simulating the act of necrophilia. In his professional opinion, it was only a matter of time before Luster turned from rapist to killer. His victims meant nothing to him. They were merely practice for his real fantasy – killing and then screwing his victim.

I've seen some pretty sick stuff over the years, but Luster was by far the worst case of cruelty towards innocent, helpless women I had ever been privy to. His case made me ill.

I prayed every day, 'Lord, this pervert is an inch away from becoming a serial killer. Help me find him before he hurts anyone else.' I was working against an invisible clock. Every second that ticked was one second closer to Luster striking again. I had to stop him.

The police were able to identify two additional victims from the tapes. In addition to Shawna Doe, they found Carey Doe and Tonja Doe, both of whom were treated with unimaginable callousness by Luster. Because the three women were willing to come forward and testify against him, police were able to charge him with eighty-seven counts of poisoning, forcible sodomy and sexual assault.

When Luster appeared in court on these charges, he stood in front of the judge and pleaded not guilty on all counts. The judge set bail at ten million dollars.

The case took nearly eighteen months to go to trial. The delays were shrewd tactics created by Luster's high-profile and very expensive defence team. His lead attorney was Roger Diamond, a well-known and highly respected criminal defence lawyer from Santa Monica. He was able to convince the appellate court to reduce Luster's bail to a million bucks. Ironically, my old insurance company happened to be the underwriter for the bail bondsman who posted the bond. The company went belly-up, but when the judge told Luster his bond wasn't good any more, he said he could pay it in cash. The judge accepted $700,000 and allowed Luster time to come up with rest. He made a Dean Witter wire transfer in the last few days of the grace period to cover the remaining $300,000.

With his bail paid, Luster was free until he went to trial. Because of the nature of the charges against him, the court ordered him to wear an electronic ankle bracelet twelve hours a day to monitor where he was during those times. The fact that he was unmonitored during the other twelve made it easy for him to plan his escape.

Luster's defence team did their best to discredit each of the women, even going so far as to claim their client was an aspiring soft-core porn filmmaker. They actually tried to convince the jury these women were acting. The lawyers did their best to paint Luster as a respectable, well-liked citizen. The defence claims about Luster's budding film career were absurd. It was becoming obvious that he was going down.

# CHAPTER FORTY-ONE

# On a Mission from God

Despite the defendant's absence, Judge Riley ordered the prosecution and defence to resume the trial. In the meantime, I had a lot of work to do if I was going to find him. The first forty-eight hours after a fugitive runs are the most crucial. Investigators from the FBI, the Ventura County Sheriff's office and the U.S. Marshals were all out looking for Luster. And now, so was I.

I've always told Beth that if we were ever in a situation where we had to flee, we'd run with only the clothes on our backs. It's essential to leave everything behind that might connect you to your past. When Luster ran, he took all of his warm-weather clothes, his collection of pre-Columbian artefacts, and his dog, Max. Thank God he did. His inexperience helped me find him.

Beth pushed me every day. Failure was not an option. My career was riding on this one. If someone else caught him, I would be the laughing-stock of the business.

I remember Beth saying, 'Prove to me you're the best, Big Daddy. Let's see what you're made of.' She taunted me every day. Besides, we had lost credit for so many cases to the cops and the feds. I didn't want to be shoved aside again.

By 15 January 2003, Andrew Luster was charged with flight to avoid prosecution. That put him on the FBI's Most Wanted List. It also made him 'Dog's Most Wanted'.

I had no time to lose. Every minute mattered. Beth and I went up to the Ventura County Court to get a copy of the warrant. I walked into the courthouse looking like someone straight out of a movie. I was wearing my badge, my dark glasses and my bulletproof vest. I had feathers in my hair and bands around my arms. They had never seen the likes of me in Ventura.

'Hi, I'm Dog the Bounty Hunter. I am here to get a copy of the warrant for Andrew Stuart Luster.' I smiled and acted like this was no big deal. The truth is, I am not a law enforcement officer. Getting a copy of the warrant was impossible. Who was I to ask for that document?

The clerk looked confused, because she knew what I was asking for was something she wasn't supposed to give me. But I could tell she recognised me from TV. I held up the local paper, pointed to my picture, and said, 'You see? This is me. I'm the guy who is going to capture Andrew Luster. I need your help.'

As charmed as I thought she was, she told me to wait in the corridor while she went to see the judge. I looked at Beth. We both knew this was a long shot. A couple of minutes later the clerk came back.

'Here you go.' She handed me a certified copy of the warrant and Luster's mug shots. She was practically still blowing on the ink to make sure it was dry.

I was stunned. Floored.

'What did Judge Riley say?' I had to know why the judge complied with my request.

'He said, "Good luck, Dog."'

We made a call to Samantha Hart at the Hollywood History Museum (formerly the Max Factor Museum of Beauty) to get as much information about the family as we could. She had given us a brief overview when we spoke on the phone, but we needed a more in-depth evaluation of who we were dealing with. I was looking for something to stir things up. I needed an explosive bit of information that would rattle the family. The lack of a blood tie between Luster and the Factor family later proved to be a useful weakness.

It's called shaking the tree.

I remember hunting down a fellow in Denver named Rick Ivy. I kept putting the word out that I was looking for this guy. I spoke to everyone I thought might be connected to him. Eventually, the heat got to be too much. One day, my phone rang. It was Ivy. He said, 'You don't have to keep looking for me.'

'Oh, yeah? Why is that?'

'Because now I'm looking for you.' Ah, the hunted becomes the hunter. It happens all the time, but it hardly ever means a thing except I'm going to get you sooner.

Another time I shook down a fugitive's momma. Within minutes he was on the phone asking me what I was doing at his momma's house.

'I was rifling through her panties. Mmmmm. She smells nice, too.' I'll say anything to get these guys riled up. This one was so mad, he kept calling me back. One time he forgot to hit *67 to block his number. Oops. Fifteen minutes later, I had him in custody.

That approach is a deliberate part of the psychology behind what I do. I want people to think I'm a duck out of water, in a new land, without a clue about what's really going on. Let's start calling his momma names. Let's start saying he's an undercover cop. I will do whatever it takes to get a reaction, because a reaction puts me in touch with the fugitive.

While we were still in L.A., I began thinking about possible clues. There were two big ones that helped me nail Luster, and the first came right away. I knew his dog was missing, and I was certain Luster ran with Max. I had a gut feeling that the proof was in the pooch. I even said that on *Geraldo* a few days earlier. I had to come up with an approach no other bounty hunter would see. So I began hunting the dog, not the guy.

Now, I own a couple of dogs myself. I know how hard it would be to leave your trusted companion behind. For Luster, it wasn't an option. The police claimed they found Luster's dog at his mom's house. My sources were telling me it wasn't the same dog, that Luster had the real one with him. They told me Luster bought a look-alike. That turned out to be a lic. I felt like Sherlock Holmes, never knowing whom I could trust or if what someone said was real. But one thing I did know: find Max, and I would find Luster. Ultimately, Luster did have his dog with him, but it wasn't the break in the case that led me to Luster.

The second clue that helped me find him was his missing car. I found it odd his car hadn't shown up anywhere. I called around for two straight days trying to find his SUV. Beth and I were driving in Malibu, doing fifty miles per hour on the Pacific Coast Highway. A cop spotted us, whipped around the two-lane highway, and pulled us over. He immediately recognised me.

'What are you doing in my neighbourhood, Dog?'

'We're looking for Andrew Luster.'

'Oh yeah? How's that going?'

I explained we were trying to track down his missing automobile, but so far we were unable to locate it anywhere.

'Well, let me call that in for you, Dog.'

The cop walked away to radio in the information we had. He took my cell phone number and said he'd give me a call if he heard anything.

A few hours later my phone rang. It was the Malibu cop. He said he tried to run the information, but the licence plate number I'd given him for Luster wasn't even on the BOLO (Be On the LookOut for) list.

I could hardly believe what I was hearing. It wasn't even a wanted vehicle? How could that be? Luster was one of the most wanted fugitives in America and his car wasn't something anyone was looking for?

I pleaded with the officer to get the car on the BOLO. 'You've got to get that car wanted right away.'

'You got it, Dog. But, we never had this conversation. I never saw you today, got it?'

One of my favourite things that people, especially people in law enforcement, say to me is 'This meeting never happened.' No one ever wants to take responsibility for bending the rules in order to do the job better.

I thanked the cop for calling. Earlier that day, Luster's mother told us she thought he'd gone surfing. If that were true, his car would be parked at or near a beach. I drove around the area for a few hours, scouring beach parking lots, following my instincts. I knew the car had to be somewhere nearby. Beth and I headed east towards Santa Monica. We drove around for a while but found nothing. We spoke to a couple of Santa Monica cops and told them what we were looking for. They told me they would get on it right away.

Time was running out. Beth and I had to get back to Hawaii to shoot our pilot episode of *Take This Job* for A&E, which subsequently became our show, *Dog the Bounty Hunter*. We left Los Angeles later that same day. I was frustrated by the lack of traditional law enforcement emphasis being placed on Luster's disappearance. I couldn't comprehend the incompetence or nonchalance being demonstrated by the authorities.

The very next day, thanks to my getting the car on the BOLO, two Santa Monica policemen found Luster's abandoned vehicle on San Vicente Boulevard. It was immediately towed to an impound yard.

The jury took two days to determine Luster's legal fate. On 18 February 2003, they found him guilty of eighty-six of the eighty-seven criminal counts. They broke it down like this:

Guilty of twenty counts of rape by the use of drugs.
Guilty of seventeen counts of rape of unconscious persons.

Guilty of two counts of poisoning.
Guilty of four counts of drug possession.

The jury was deadlocked on one additional count of poisoning, unable to determine whether he was guilty or not. It didn't matter. Conviction on eighty-six counts was enough to get Luster 124 years in jail. He was sentenced in absentia.

By the time he was convicted, Luster had been missing for more than a month. That was plenty of time for him to undergo cosmetic surgery to change his appearance. He was savvy enough and rich enough to find a way to get a new passport. He could be thousands of miles away or living right under my nose. There was no way to know for sure.

# CHAPTER FORTY-TWO

# Prey

We built a pretty complete profile of Luster. Beth created a website where people could follow our progress and send in possible information on his whereabouts. The site was flooded, mostly with false leads.

> *'Dear Dog. I saw Andrew Luster today on the bus while riding to work here in Honolulu.'*
> *'I just saw Luster on the North Shore.'*
> *'Luster was praying in my church today.'*

We ran down a few leads that felt genuine, but they were all dead ends. Then I got an idea about how to get Luster's cell phone number. Luster looked like the kind of guy who worked out, so I decided to call a few gyms around the Los Angles area to see if I could get it. The first gym I called, I spoke to a guy who was very helpful. I told him who I was and why I was calling.

'I know you from TV!' He couldn't have been nicer. He put me on hold, came back a few minutes later, and said, 'You'll never believe this. He does work out at one of our gyms. I have his information right here.' Blam. I got his phone number.

I immediately called and left him a message.

'Andrew Stuart Luster, this is Dog Chapman. I know you've seen me on TV. I'm going to get you, Luster, you freak.' I wasn't positive it was his voice, so I didn't leave a long message. I did leave my cell number just in case he decided to call me back.

I kept leaving messages until his voice mail was full. That way, I was sure he'd hear me loud and clear. I called back the next day to see if his voice mail was able to accept messages. It was clear. So I did it all again, every day until that number was disconnected.

Meanwhile, I called his cell phone company and said, 'Hi, this is Andrew Stuart Luster, and my kids are in Hawaii. They've got my damn cell phone, and I think they're calling all over the world. I'm at a motel, and I was wondering if you could send me a copy of the bill.' Sure enough, they faxed it to me. I had all of Luster's personal information before the cops had time to subpoena his records.

Once I got his phone bill, I could see numbers he called or received calls from on a regular basis. I began to call each one. His friends were eager to talk. They all belonged to what they called the Bachelor Boys Club. I was working six or seven of these kids' numbers. Most of them were children of famous people or were celebrities themselves.

One of the guys I talked to a lot was a man named Wesley, who was the son of Daryl Dragon and Toni Tennille, aka the Captain and Tennille. One buddy told me about another friend of theirs named Lance, who would turn out to be the weak link in the group. He was vulnerable, because he was mourning the death of his former lover, who was murdered by his wife. Wesley said the wife shot her husband because she found out about the affair. He also said Lance kept the dead man's ashes on his fireplace mantel.

Wesley explained that this friend worked for Ron Popeil, the guy you see on TV selling Veg-O-Matics and rotisseries. He said that Popeil had a big yacht that sailed from California to Mexico all the time, and that Lance may have snuck Luster on to the boat and hid him for the entire trip south. Popeil had no idea Lance had done this. If he found out, Lance would lose his job.

The first time I called Lance, he talked to me for an hour. He spent most of that time mocking me, making fun of me. He pointed out that he was different from the other guys. He didn't drink or party. He said he was too smart to fall for my cheap tactics and trickery.

'You're not going to get me like you did the other guys.'

'Oh yeah? Why is that, Lance? How do you know I "got" them? Do you have something to hide?' I was being kind of rough on the guy. I could tell he was getting upset. He wasn't as strong as the others. He was much softer, not as arrogant. My goal was to keep them on the phone for as long as they would talk. For whatever reason, talking to me made them feel important. I carefully brought up subjects I knew would yield more and more insight and information on Luster.

I flew back to L.A. in early March to pursue Brett, Lance and some other leads. The minute I landed, I called Lance and said, 'I gotcha.'

'Oh, yeah? What have you got?'

'I got you, brother. *You* know it and I know it.'

Again, Lance asked, 'Well, what have you got?'

'My education may only be seventh grade, but I got you, homey. I know you have that famous actor's ashes above your fireplace.'

This guy was talking bull to me for a month. All of a sudden he was out of things to say.

'Now, Lance, I need something from you, son. I need a clue. I need to know where Luster is. Are you going to help me?'

'You goddamned motherfucker.' I could hear the panic setting in. He'd successfully hidden his relationship with his lover from the world. He knew I could blow his secret with one call to the press. He was about to sing like Mariah Carey.

All Lance said was, 'He speaks fluent Mexican.'

Mexican. He didn't say Spanish. He said Mexican.

'Now, Lance. Don't disrespect me. I already told you Luster's momma told me he speaks fluent Spanish. Are you messing with me? – 'cause you don't want to do that.'

'Well, then, I guess that means he could be in Spain or Portugal . . . '

He was as sarcastic as he was acerbic.

If Lance was telling me the truth, he was pointing me towards Mexico. I wasn't convinced his story was valid. Later that night, I heard Lance split town. I have never spoken to him again.

I was getting closer and closer. Luster knew it too. He'd warned his friends not to talk to me, because one day they were as loose-lipped as a nickel whore and the next as tight as a virgin.

Then Luster started emailing me. He didn't identify himself as Andrew Luster. But I knew who it was.

I taunted him in email exchanges that went something like this:

'What's the deal with those rocks that Luster took?'

'What rocks?'

'That means you know something because you read the same article I did.'

'Oh you mean his pre-Columbian art collection . . . He bought this piece in Spain, that piece in Bogota . . . '

'You seem to know an awful lot, which tells me he bought these pieces with you. Tell me more.'

'They're Indian artefacts and they're worth a lot of money.'

To this day, I don't know why he took the rocks or where they're at.

They weren't worth a thing if they weren't together as a set. I thought he took them to trade, but I knew a friend of his had the third rock of the set, so the two Luster carried were essentially worthless.

One thing I knew from the email dialogue was this guy had a lot of answers. He was obviously Luster or someone who spoke to Luster on a regular basis. One day I received an email from a 'Mr X' that read, 'You think your biker attitude will catch Luster? He will be gone by the time you land.'

Land. Hmm. That meant Luster was someplace I had to fly to.

Luster began sending email all the time that were puzzles. He thought he was the Riddler from *Batman*. He was trying to be clever. He was so arrogant, thinking he would show this old bounty hunter he was the greatest fugitive I ever hunted. Then I got an e-mail from 'surferintheknow' saying, 'You'll never chase anyone in your life like Luster.' He was bragging about himself in the third person. He also was making it clear he knew I was chasing him by making the surfer and Hawaii connection.

# CHAPTER FORTY-THREE

# Wheeling and Dealing

Martin Sheen once predicted I would someday have my own television show. At the time, my focus was on public speaking, working with Tony Robbins, and bounty hunting. I had no delusion about what my true calling was in life, although I had always dreamed that I would become famous. I even practised my autograph when I was a young boy.

Vin Di Bona, creator of *America's Funniest Home Videos*, as well as many other hugely successful television shows and made-for-TV movies, was the first producer to really understand me. He is the nicest, sweetest, most generous man on the planet. He tried to sell a show based on bounty hunting but Hollywood wasn't ready. At the time, I still didn't have that one big capture to make me a household name. Studios and networks were sceptical, unsure that my brand and style would connect with mainstream audiences.

Shortly after the *Los Angeles Times* did an article about me, I got a phone call from Mark Burnett, creator of *Survivor* and *The Apprentice*. He is the most successful reality television producer in the business. I also received a call from Howard Schultz of Lighthearted Entertainment, who had a hit show, *Extreme Makeover*.

When Beth and I got to L.A., we met with Howard Schultz first. He got our vision from the very start. We told him we wanted our show to be true reality, which meant unscripted and shot exactly the way our bounties go down. The action had to be genuine for the show to work. We told him we were thinking of going after Andrew Luster and offered him the opportunity to follow us with cameras for the duration of the hunt as a quasi-audition. In exchange for giving him those rights, we wanted him to fund the hunt from beginning to end. We knew it would be valuable footage. Schultz is a very smart man. He saw the opportunity too.

'What do you mean by "fund"?' Schultz looked dubious, wondering just how much money we were looking for.

Beth shot back, 'Whatever it takes until we bring that prick to justice.'

I wanted to explain it in my own words. 'Look, Howard, if I have to fund this hunt for six months, I will spend all the money I have, buying plane tickets and chasing leads. I'm not a rich man. I won't be able to feed my children.'

I could see that Howard was trying to process how much this all translated into for him.

Beth jumped in again, saying, 'Howard, one thing you ought to know is that Duane doesn't move unless he's sure. He won't leave his office until he is absolutely positive he's got his guy.'

Howard still didn't seem convinced. He told us he wanted to think about it for a couple of days.

The next night, Beth and I met with Mark Burnett. He invited us to his big, fancy, expensive home in Malibu. I was blown away by how spectacular his house was. *I* wanted to live like this, only I wanted to be on an island three thousand miles due west from the beach where I was standing. I remember Burnett's assistant kept asking him, 'Did you tell them yet? Did you tell them the good news yet?' He was acting like an excited schoolboy. I thought they were going to offer us the use of his house to film the show! I had no idea what all the fuss was about, and Burnett hadn't let us in on anything yet.

When Burnett explained *his* vision for my reality show, it was a mix of scripted dialogue and recreated crime scenes, much like *Cold Case*. He didn't want to capture anything live. His idea of reality was to reenact scenes of me chasing and capturing criminals – like *America's Most Wanted*. That wasn't exactly what I had in mind. In fact, it was totally the opposite.

Burnett continued making his pitch, telling me he was the 'king of reality television' and everything he touched turned to gold. He showed zero interest in the Luster story, so I knew he wouldn't be a potential financial backer. Even though I knew Burnett was successful in the reality genre, he and I just didn't see eye-to-eye. In my gut, I felt his interests would take precedence over both mine and those of the show. I left thinking he wanted me to feel lucky he found us – not the other way around.

Beth and I had a lot of thinking and praying to do. We really weren't sure Schultz was the right guy for us, but we definitely knew Burnett wasn't a good match. We spent the next several days in Los Angeles more focused on whether or not we wanted to pursue Luster than on developing the reality show. What was brewing could change the course for all of us. We decided to take our time, so we could assess our options before committing to anyone.

We had already been down this road years ago when I sold rights to my life story for movies that never panned out. I did not want to make the same mistake in television.

# CHAPTER FORTY-FOUR

# The Thai Trail

We had got a number of leads in the first few months of searching for Luster. Most of them were a complete bust. We had received a couple of emails from people claiming to see Luster in Thailand, but we didn't think much of it when they came in. One of the emails said he went to a club called the Mona Lisa. Beth checked the place out on the Web to see if such a spot even existed. Sure enough, it was in Bangkok. Our general rule is never to follow up on a lead unless there are two or more people to corroborate the story.

Then one day, Beth called me in Denver to say she'd received a phone call that sounded pretty legit. 'This British guy named Mike just called and swears he saw Andrew Luster in a brothel in Thailand called the Winchester Club, where men can get young girls for thirty bucks an hour.'

Beth checked out their website, which was filled with page after page of teenage girls. It was like looking at someone's high school yearbook. If he had gone to Bangkok, he was essentially free to do whatever he pleased. He would have been right in his element. Thailand made a lot of sense. It was one of four places we had suspected Luster ran to. Other possibilities were Bali, France, and Mexico. I didn't want to get my hopes up, but it appeared I finally had my first real lead.

Mike also emailed us photos of Luster's Gems, a jewellery store owned by some Americans. It was a believable lead, although it didn't turn up any connection to Andrew Luster. Despite that, we felt positive about having two separate stories that connected Luster to Thailand. I told Beth I wanted to go.

Between hunting Luster and trying to keep my businesses afloat in Kona, Honolulu and Denver, I had my hands pretty full. Beth and I split our time between each location. We rarely saw each other. The hunt for

Luster was taking a huge toll, both financial and emotional. I had to keep hunting other bounties to make enough money to keep up the chase and take care of my family.

I flew back to Hawaii a few days later and followed up with Mike myself. He sounded completely normal. I was feeling good that he wasn't some kind of kook. He told me about his trip to Thailand and about the Winchester Club. He described the place as more of a nightclub than a whorehouse. Mike and his buddy, Dave, spotted a guy at the bar who resembled Luster, only he was heavier than he looked on the news.

Hearing Mike's description of a bulkier Luster made me think back to a conversation I had with some of his friends who said he had built up a lot of muscle before he fled. They said he'd got really ripped. I had even heard he had got pec implants. I asked Mike how certain he was that the man they spotted in Thailand was Luster.

'Eighty per cent. We saw him a couple of times. I'm fairly certain it was him.'

I've never been the type of guy who moves on 80 per cent hunches. Tell me you're 100 per cent sure or not sure at all. There is no in between. I needed more proof, more signs this was the place Luster disappeared to.

I asked Mike, 'Any chance you spoke to the guy?'

'Yes. As a matter of fact I did. He was definitely American. He was nice but seemed a bit depressed. He was checking out a lady friend who was with us.'

To determine if the guy Mike and Dave saw was really Luster, we asked Mike if he would consider going back to Thailand. The plan was to find the man, get a waitress at the Winchester Club to serve him a drink from a brand-new clean glass, and then fly the glass back to a crime lab to determine if the fingerprints were a match. I would even pay for an armoured car to pull up and transport the glass. If it came back positive, then Tim, Leland, Boris and I would fly to Thailand to grab Luster. On 23 May, my FBI contact, Eric Jensen, said I had to get a provisional arrest warrant to be ready. If we succeeded, we'd have some of the most thrilling footage ever shot for reality television, and I would finally prove to the world that I am the greatest bounty hunter who ever lived. If it turned out to be a dead end, no harm, no foul.

That weekend was the first time Beth and I had been together in weeks. I missed her and the kids. We needed some quality time together. As I had done many times that winter, Beth and I took the kids to a beach near our home to spend the day enjoying the sea and sand. Sometimes I drove out there by myself to pray and ask the Lord for His guidance. Today was about being with my family. I was unloading the car when I noticed familiar footprints in the sand. Once again, I felt my mother's presence. I knew in my gut that the footprints were hers. I almost passed out from the rush of emotion.

I turned my head up to the sky and said, 'Lord, I know my mom is with you.'

And then I heard, 'No, Duane, she walks with you. Look straight out, my son. You will find what you are looking for.' I cocked my head and stared straight out into the vast blue sea, wondering, hoping, praying that the Lord was sending me a message about my mother. At the time, I had no way of knowing He was pointing me towards Luster.

We weren't able to work out the details of Mike's trip until the end of May. By the time we set everything up, he had some worries about going through with it. He was engaged to be married. A single mistake could be deadly. His fiancée didn't think it was worth the risk. Dave stepped up and said he would go.

When Dave arrived in Thailand, however, he discovered that the United States Army was conducting a training manoeuvre in the region called Operation Cobra Gold. One thousand U.S. soldiers were all over Bangkok. If Luster had been in Thailand, there wasn't a chance he was hanging around during those exercises. Our plan was spoiled. Dave came back empty-handed. The Thai trail had grown ice-cold.

# CHAPTER FORTY-FIVE

# One Last Warning

Despite not knowing if Thailand would be where I caught Luster, I kept getting a gut feeling that I was getting closer. Your gut never lies. When you learn to tune into your inner voice, you will have the answers to all of life's problems. The Lord gives you all the information you need. Something told me it was time to reach out to Luster's mother. I wanted Liz Luster to know I was closing in on her son. Every chance I got, I put the word out.

Liz was agitated by the mere sound of my voice. I thought, *Good*.

'You have no legal right to call and harass me.' She was growing angrier by the second.

'You're right. I'm not calling you to harass you. I just wanted to give you a courtesy call to let you know I will be getting your son soon. I can do it my way, or you can help by bringing Andrew to me.'

'You don't have the guts to go where my son is hiding.' She was as smug as her kid. The apple doesn't fall far from the tree. Towards the end of the call, Liz gave me her own warning.

'If I were you, I'd start thinking about your own safety instead of spending all of this time searching for my son.'

I read into that threat. What she was really saying was that her son was someplace where money could buy his freedom. That pretty much ruled out most of Europe, but it left Mexico, Latin America and Asia wide open.

Before we hung up, I tried to appeal to the parent in Liz. I told her I have twelve kids of my own. I know what it feels like to have one of them in trouble. Two of my kids have done hard time. I thought I could tap into her sensitive maternal side.

Her response was cruel and very much unexpected. 'You should have been neutered.'

I didn't want to extend the conversation beyond that. But I needed to let Liz Luster know I was not her enemy. I told her I thought Andrew caught a bad break. I thought his legal defence team did a horrible job. I suggested how he might seek restitution once he was back in custody. She wasn't much interested in my advice about the legal system, although she did loosen up a bit. She wasn't unlike any mother who has watched her child suffer. She had to believe her son was innocent, even if she knew in her gut he was not.

Time was running out. Luster's million-dollar bail would be forfeited by mid-July. It was time to turn up the heat.

On 9 June, Rita Cosby called and asked if she could have me on her show to talk about Luster.

She only asked me one question: 'Are you getting close?'

'Close enough.' I had to make her believe I was hot on Luster's trail. I agreed to be on the show that night.

At the end of the interview, Rita asked me if I had anything I wanted to say to Luster. I did.

'Fe, fi, fo, fum. Look out Luster, here I come!' I didn't plan on saying this, it just flew out of my mouth.

She laughed and asked one last question. 'How long until you get him, Dog?'

'One week. I'll have him in a week, Rita.' Why did I just say that?

I think she was caught as much off guard hearing that as I was saying it. Rita, obviously a little taken aback, said, 'Well, good, then. We all look forward to seeing you here again next week!'

Beth was waiting for me off camera. She had a strange look on her face. She looked like a deer in headlights. 'Wow! Why did you say that? You promised Rita a week, Duane. Are you crazy? The entire world is watching you, and you proclaim you'll have Luster in seven days? You better get him, because if you don't your reputation will be ruined and no one will ever believe a word you say.'

'I don't know why I blurted out "a week". The Lord just told me to.'

Beth replied, 'Well, I hope you and the Lord have a plan, because they're counting the days and your career is riding on it.' My mouth has got me into trouble plenty of times in my life, but this time, my words had put my life and livelihood on the line. I went home that night and prayed. I prayed as hard as I ever have.

'Lord, please show me where Luster is. I need to know. I hope You can hear me, Lord. I'm out on a limb. I need You now more than ever.'

# CHAPTER FORTY-SIX

# The Dog Cometh

Immediately following the Rita Cosby interview, Beth flew to Denver to check on business while I flew back to Hawaii to be with the kids. I rarely answer my phone, especially when I don't recognise the number. A few days after getting back to Hawaii, for whatever reason, I answered a call that changed everything.

'Is this Dog the Bounty Hunter?' I could hear a trembling young man's voice on the other end.

'Who's this?' I wasn't sure if it was a fan, a client, or someone just looking to talk to the Dog.

'I think I saw the guy you're looking for in Mexico. My girlfriend and I saw him at a resort near Puerto Vallarta. He told me his name was David Carrera, but I'm positive it was Andrew Luster.'

I'd heard this so many times, I almost hung up.

'We even got a couple of pictures of him.' He said he saw me on Rita Cosby and noticed that the picture of Luster looked just like the guy he met in Mexico.

OK, now this kid had my attention. He had pictures. That was the first time someone was stepping forward with potentially hard evidence that they'd seen Luster.

'They're not great pictures. Carrera didn't want me to take them. Every time I tried, he spun his body away. I only got him from the back and the side of his head.' I asked him to email his photos so we could examine them up close.

I asked my source about his background. He said he was a college student and he and his girlfriend were in Mexico to surf. He had no reason to mess with me. My gut told me this kid was for real. We continued to talk for quite a while. He stayed at a tiny resort an hour and a half north of Puerto Vallarta called Costa Custodio. It was owned by two

Americans named Min and Mona. One afternoon, they met another American by the pool who told them his name was David Carrera. They talked about surfing and real estate. Carrera said he was in Mexico looking for investment opportunities. They talked and partied for several hours. When they woke up the next day, Carrera was gone. His mention of partying got me wondering.

So I asked this kid, 'What did you guys party with? Were there drugs?'

He hesitated. 'Yeah. Carrera had some pot, coke, and some other stuff.'

I knew it was him. Everything in my gut said it was Luster.

'What do you mean by other stuff?'

'It was a liquid. I think it was GHB.'

Blam! My heart started pounding. I felt like I was a holding a lottery ticket with all the winning numbers!

My new-found friend gave me Min and Mona's number. I thanked him for his call. 'You did the right thing.'

'My girlfriend loves you, Dog. Good luck. I hope you find him.' Before we hung up, I asked him to call Beth. I wanted to see if her insight and gut reaction matched my own.

If what he said was true, Carrera and Luster were the same guy.

Not long after, I received a phone call from Min and Mona. One minute into the conversation, they too had me convinced Carrera was Luster. They told me the kid who called me and his friends partied with Luster, but they knew Luster a lot better than he did. Min told me Carrera stayed at his resort twice. He wanted me to know he was in charge of anything that went down at Costa Custodio. He thought something wasn't right; Carrera's behaviour was suspicious. After our conversation, Min realised there was a reward, so he called the FBI to report Carrera on a hunch he might be Andrew Luster.

After Beth spoke to my new best friend with the photo, she agreed the lead sounded real, so she called Boris to get him on to Schultz to finance the trip to Mexico. For whatever reason, Boris didn't get ahold of Schultz before Beth did. She told Howard that we had a big break in the Luster case. She explained that the kid sent us pictures we enlarged that showed a guy with a goatee who looked a lot like Luster, wearing baggy cargo shorts and a Hawaiian-style shirt. His face was shielded in every shot. None of the photos were clear enough to positively identify the man as Luster, but there was enough similarity to feel it might be him.

After careful scrutiny, Beth and I noticed the shorts in the pictures he sent. They were the same shorts Luster was wearing on the beach in another photo I had of him.

Although Beth and I were certain it was him, Howard still needed some convincing. 'How sure are you? I'm staking my career on you. You better be right.' He didn't want to buy my tickets to Mexico, but Beth insisted.

She handed the phone to Boris and said, 'He's got a minute to decide.'

'I'm in.' Howard agreed to back the hunt.

Beth still had concerns about Min and Mona being sincere in their desire to help. She sensed they were only after the reward money. It's true, they were very quick to cut the kid and his friends out of the picture. They insisted they knew everything we needed to capture Luster. Beth also wanted to make sure Howard understood that the hunt was on his dime. At the time, she was still trying to get Mark Burnett and Howard Schultz into a bidding war over the rights. But the Lord kept pointing us towards Howard. Beth called Howard up and said, 'You know that all expenses paid means you pay for *everything* from this moment forward, right?'

'Yeah. Sure. I got it, Beth. No problem. I'm in.' Once he decided, he appeared to be committed.

Just to be certain I was doing the right thing, I called Min one last time before pulling the trigger.

'Brother, how sure are you it's Luster?'

He said, 'Ninety per cent.' That was closer to the answer I always look for, but not quite certain. Even so, it was worth a shot.

Beth had to fly back to Hawaii to be with the kids so I could leave for Mexico. Leland, Tim, and Boris were set to come with me. Tim took a little convincing. He and I were scrapping over a couple of bonds. I didn't want to take him, but I couldn't cut him out of something this big and important. If I caught Luster, he'd never again be a real member of the team if he wasn't there when the bust went down. Beth convinced me to include my buddy, so I swallowed my pride. When I made the call, he was in.

Howard agreed to join us with a film crew to shoot the entire hunt in Mexico. His team consisted of his assistant, Jeff, the cameraman, Richie, and a soundman, Fernando. Seven of us would fly down. Although Min and Mona suggested we stay at Costa Custodio, they weren't giving us the rooms for free. With the airfare, rooms, rental cars, and cell phones, our expenses were enormous. To offset some of his costs, Howard was trying to sell rights to the footage to various news programmes, but so far, only 48 *Hours* showed interest. If Howard decided to pull out for any reason, we'd be stuck paying our own expenses. I was running out of money. If this bust didn't happen, I wasn't sure I could keep hunting for Luster. In fact, I wasn't sure I could keep my house, my business, or anything else I had worked so hard to build back up over the last few years. Once again, I was on the brink of bankruptcy. I didn't tell anyone. Only Beth and I knew how crucial this capture was for our future.

Beth got home a few hours before I had to leave. We spent most of that time arguing. She was unhappy that I had asked her to leave Denver, because two of her bonds skipped. If someone didn't bring them in, we'd be out fifty-five grand. I felt it was more important for Beth to be home before I left.

Usually Beth sits with me before I go on a hunt and asks for a full rundown of my plan. She wants to make sure I've thought everything through. Her job is to arrange all of the details. Mine is to hunt. I was entering what I deemed the World Series of bounty hunting. If I captured Luster, I won the title. If not, I would lose everything.

There was a plan, but I wasn't sure how viable it was. Min said he could get Luster to come back to Costa Custodio to talk about investing in a hotel property. They had already discussed his getting in on the ground floor, so Min thought it would be easy to get him to come back to explore it further. When he showed up, I'd nab him.

Beth drove us to the airport. We barely spoke a word before I got out of the car. I stood on the curb wanting to grab her, hold her, hug and kiss her, and tell her I loved her. Tears welled up in our eyes.

'Duane, what are you going to do?'

I pulled Beth close to me and sang a song I remembered from church.

'This little light of mine . . . I'm gonna let it shine . . . ' I kissed her goodbye. I had an uneasy feeling that this farewell was different from any other.

# CHAPTER FORTY-SEVEN

# You Can Run

On the night of 11 June, I caught the red-eye to L.A. to meet with Howard and Mona. Howard wanted to be sure Mona was on the up-and-up before he flew our team down to Mexico. Mona looked to be in her mid-fifties. She might have been attractive when she was younger, but it was hard to tell. It looked like she'd gained a lot of weight as she got older. She was very earthy, not a fancy woman.

Much to my surprise, Mona backed away from her previous assertion that David Carrera was Andrew Luster. She talked nonstop. She couldn't hold a thought or finish a sentence. She never made eye contact, either. Something wasn't right, but I ignored my gut. I so desperately wanted to believe her that I chose to ignore my feeling that something was wrong.

During that same meeting, Howard got word that another production company was willing to foot the bill for the entire hunt, whether we caught Luster or not. It was a win-win for everyone. There was no financial risk to Howard or to us. The next day, we all hopped a flight to Puerto Vallarta via Guadalajara and headed by car to the tiny town of Tepic, where Min and Mona's villa was located.

We arrived at Costa Custodio. It was beautiful. We passed through the guarded entry gate, where a policeman checked our car before letting us pass through. We drove down a cobblestone driveway with four-foot stone walls on either side. The property was surrounded by lush jungle but still had great views of the ocean. Min met us in the driveway with a tray of tequila drinks on ice. He was in his early sixties, with a full head of silvery white hair. He was thin, with a good build. He wore a Hawaiian shirt, khaki pants, and flip-flops.

The villa was aesthetically breathtaking. On closer examination, however, everything was like a movie set. I turned on a faucet in the bathroom, and no water came out. It all looked real, but it was fake. Min and Mona advertised the villa on the Internet and rented it for lots of money. When guests arrived, they soon discovered that what appeared to be paradise was really a hellhole.

Before we dispersed to our separate villas, I asked Min if he had heard from Luster. I was anxious to get down to business.

'Oh, yes. He is coming by this afternoon.' He was too nonchalant for me to believe it was true.

I spent the rest of the day trying to work Min and Mona for as much insight into Carrera as I could get. Mona told me how they partied with Carrera when he was staying at their house. She spoke of him with great affection. Something about the tone of her voice felt very *off*. The entire exchange was extremely unsettling, but I couldn't put my finger on what was wrong.

When I spoke with Min, he asked me how much Carrera would be worth if he was really Luster.

'Ten, maybe twenty grand.' I could see the smile widen on his face at the thought of making an easy score.

Leland and Tim later told me they thought Mona liked her margaritas a lot. Now it made sense – her inability to focus. I found her as fast as I could.

'Honey, why don't you have another drink and come talk to me.' I knew it would lower her guard enough for me to pump her for information. While I was waiting for Mona to come sit with me, I noticed Min walking around the property with a video camera. He was taping us. Son of a bitch!

'Howard, look. He's got a camera.' If he had footage, the other production company would be pissed. They had optioned exclusive rights of our trip. If they found out someone else had footage, they might pull our funding. Howard convinced Min to stop taping by telling him we would write up a contract to split any reward money received when and if we captured Luster on this trip. Once the contract was signed, Min handed over all of his footage – or so we thought. I didn't know it at the time, but he held back a few tapes.

By the end of the day, Luster was a no-show. I coaxed Mona to call him. She was supposed to act very casual, like it was no big deal he didn't come. I could hear his voice. Sure as hell, it was him. They made plans for Luster to stop by the house tomorrow.

The following day, Friday, Min approached me again to ask how much the capture of Andrew Luster was worth. He said, 'I heard it was as much as $200,000.'

He was clearly trying to figure out how to cut us out of the equation to collect the bounty on his own. I ignored his question and diverted his attention by asking who the guard was at the gate.

'He's a policeman. He works for me when he's off duty. His name is Filiberto.'

I walked up to the gate and introduced myself. Filiberto gave me a Mexican policeman's handshake; it's a three-step shake. First you shake, then you cup hands, and finally you touch thumbs. I showed him a picture of Luster.

'You've seen this guy?'

'*Sí, señor.* He's here a lot.'

I said, 'If you find this guy, I'll give you ten thousand American dollars.' I thought, *That ought to last him until Christmas!* I handed him a hundred-dollar bill just to show this was no joke. I shoved it into his pocket and just smiled.

'*Gracias, señor.*'

That should have been a big flashing red light. What legitimate cop would accept money from a gringo like me? And yet, I had heard that giving Mexican cops money was pretty standard procedure. Either way, he was definitely a cop. Filiberto said he could be a liaison between the Mexican police and our team. I thought he was sincere. I believed he was in law enforcement, that he wanted to get the bad guy as much as we did. I also knew I needed a Mexican cop with me if the bust went down. Without one, taking Luster would be illegal.

Howard was in constant contact with the FBI. Retired agents were calling and faxing him for updates. The CIA was also watching our every move. Howard received email detailing how they could land a plane on the road outside Costa Custodio if we needed them. I'm not surprised that both law enforcement agencies were gung ho in offering their help to make the grab. Experience told me they'd take Luster and then rob me of the bounty and credit for the capture. I was not interested in that scenario.

Once I was in Mexico, I realised Andrew Luster was such a huge fish, he was slipping out of my hands. Howard was working with the FBI and CIA, Min and Mona were working with local officials, which meant my team was the redheaded stepchild.

I called Beth to talk it over. I assured her I believed Carrera was

Luster. Beth told me she believed her email account had been hacked into for information too. She thought it might have been other bounty hunters looking for Luster, until John Walsh and *America's Most Wanted* showed up in Puerto Vallarta. There was no way they could have known where to look for Luster unless they were privy to the same information we had. I felt we were losing control over the hunt.

Another day went by, and still, no sign of Luster.

Despite the promise that Costa Custodio would be well-stocked with food, there was barely anything to eat. Our bodies were weakening from hunger. We were in the middle of a huge waiting game, with nothing to do but hope Luster showed. I decided to take in some sun. I don't know how long I was sleeping, but I awoke to the touch of Mona's hand on my arm. I opened my eyes and saw she was holding a needle.

'My God, honey. What the hell are you doing?' I had no idea what was in the syringe.

'I want to give you a shot of Vitamin B12. You look so tired. This will help you stay strong.' Anyone holding a syringe is unnerving, even your doctor. It made me really uncomfortable to see Mona with one. Mona liked her drinks so I'm not sure she knew what she was doing. Tim was sitting outside with me too. Jokingly, I told him I'd take the shot if he did. Needless to say, we wouldn't let her near us with her needle.

By the end of the day, it was obvious Luster wasn't coming. I wanted Mona to call again, but we had to be careful not to scare him away. This time I asked Howard if he could record the call on camera. He loved the idea. In fact, he had a device that could capture sound from both sides of the conversation. He set it up. Mona made the call.

'*Hola*, David. It's Mona.'

'Mona! Hi!' David sounded pleasantly surprised to hear her voice. Howard just about wet himself because he knew we were getting this all on tape.

'I am so sorry for not coming today. I had some business in Guadalajara.' To convince Luster he needed to come, Mona told him someone else was looking at the property.

'That's too bad,' she said. 'We wanted to see you. Min has some other properties to show you. Is there another day you'd like to come by?'

'How about Sunday?' Mona said that would be fine.

Two more days of waiting. I was growing frustrated by the lack of progress. I also knew the clock was ticking down on my promise to deliver Luster in seven days.

After the call, Howard wanted to check the voice we recorded against footage we had of Luster speaking in court. Fernando, our soundman, set up the tape so we could play clips back to back. He played the conversation over and over, comparing it to the film footage. After several minutes, Fernando looked up.

'It's a match. It's definitely him.' For the first time since we arrived in Mexico, I really believed we weren't on some wild goose chase. Howard was ecstatic. The guys and I needed this positive reinforcement to keep our spirits up. Doubt had been slowly seeping in.

The next morning, I asked Mona about the big river that ran into the ocean behind the house. She told me it was an incredible five-mile hike down the mountain, through the jungle, and into the valley.

'Once you get there, it's paradise. We keep a couple of kayaks down there. Min and I use them all the time.' I thought it might be fun to get out and do something with the guys. Later that day, Mona insisted I take Boris, Leland, and Tim down the trail. She was practically badgering us to go.

What the hell. It sounded like fun and it was definitely a good way to fill the time waiting for Luster. We made the hike and found a couple of two-man kayaks at the bottom of the trail. The water was shallow, though, too shallow to get very far. Boris stuck his paddle in the sand to see if it was firm enough to walk on. It sank.

'Quicksand!' he yelled.

We paddled like hell to get out of there. I never worked so hard in my life. All of a sudden, I noticed the current begin to change. Boris shouted to turn back. The water was so deep, it turned black. I couldn't see the bottom. I thought Boris and Tim were going to get washed away because their kayak was spinning out of control. I turned to Leland and said, 'If we don't make it up this stream, we're going to die, son. Row your brains out!'

We finally reached the water's edge. We jumped out and stood safely on the shore. Just as Boris stepped out of his kayak, a scorpion stung him on his ankle. He started screaming and running. I didn't see him until the next day. Boris wasn't cut out for this kind of adventure.

We struggled with those kayaks. Unusually so. I couldn't figure out what went wrong. Tim kept saying the kayaks were too heavy.

That night, Howard decided to throw in the towel. He felt Luster was on to us and would never show. In fact, he thought he might even be playing with us. I didn't want to admit it, but I sort of agreed. Howard said he felt like he was in Vegas, gambling away his life savings on a bad hand of poker. It was time to walk away from the table. Howard pulled everyone out, but Jeff, our cameraman, stayed.

Jeff came to me to see how certain I was about catching Luster. He explained that his wife was pregnant. If he stayed, he was on his own dime. I told him I was as sure as I am that bears crap in the woods. That guy let his balls hang on his own dime to film the bust.

The next morning, Tim and I went back down the trail to check those kayaks. We turned them over and discovered six little holes had been drilled into the bottom. Those sons of bitches were filled with water! Tim was beyond mad. His blood was boiling at the thought that someone was trying to harm us. It took an hour to calm him. Luster was supposed to come later that day. We were too close to fuck it up now.

When we got back up to the house, Mona was her crazy self. She was mumbling something about how much she hated cooking for ten men. I was guessing she had started partying before everyone else. We all calmed her down. She had to be brought back to earth. I needed her to call Luster one last time.

'Honey, please call him to see if he's coming.'

Mona got him on the phone, but she couldn't stay focused. She asked him when he was coming.

'I'm in Puerto Vallarta. Why do you need to know?' Luster was obviously suspicious.

Mona got very flustered. She began to fumble her words.

I whispered, 'Ask him if he can bring rolling papers when he comes.'

She turned to me and said, 'What?'

'Hang up. Damn it, Mona!' I couldn't believe she showed our hand. There was no way Luster didn't hear her talking to me.

She began to cry. She blew it. Luster would never come to Costa Custodio now. I tried to calm her down, but she couldn't stop crying. I finally went to bed, hoping tomorrow would bring better results.

# CHAPTER FORTY-EIGHT

# You Can't Hide

The next morning, I got up at seven o'clock, much earlier than usual. Mona was nowhere to be found. When I confronted Min, he said she bought a wig and had gone to Puerto Vallarta to hunt Luster down herself. I just about shit.

That double-crossing bitch.

'Tim! Leland! Wake up! We've gotta go, *now*!' I told the boys what was happening. Just then, Filiberto walked into the house. I asked him if he was officially on duty. He said he was. I asked him to go with Tim and Leland. They needed to get to Puerto Vallarta, find Mona, and get her off the streets.

I sent the others ahead. Boris and I didn't go. The hunter stayed put. I didn't want to get caught bounty hunting Mona in Mexico. Luster was a fugitive, wanted by the United States government. Mona was just a crazy, wild woman trying to double-cross me. It was better to let the Mexican cop go after her.

Boris and I went out for a couple of beers while we waited to hear from the boys. They were supposed to call when they made contact with Mona. We sat in the bar for hours. At one point, a couple of Mexicans walked in, stink-eyeing Boris and me. They were two mean-looking Vatos. One guy was shorter than the other, with a bushy moustache. The taller guy was as big as he was tall. His belly hung over his giant scorpion belt buckle.

The fat guy turned to me and said, 'You gonna buy me a beer, gringo?'

I stood up, looked him square in the eye, and said, 'Say what?'

'I said, you gonna buy me a beer?'

I puffed up my chest and said, 'You're gonna shit and fall back into it, José.'

'My name is not José.'

'I don't give a rat's ass what your name is, Esse. I ain't no gringo, I'm an Indian.'

Boris was shaking, thinking we were about to get our asses kicked.

'Boris, relax. They ain't gonna do nothing. They think I can whoop their ass. Just shut up and act cool.'

The fat guy ordered double tacos and burritos and sent them over to us.

'Courtesy of the man down the bar, Perro.' Food is always a good way to get in good with the locals. I drank two Coronas, trying to make the best of our wait.

And then I got a call that would change the course of my life for ever.

'Perro. It's Filiberto. I seen him. Luster.'

I couldn't believe what I was hearing.

'Sí. Min showed up and found Mona. Mona was cruising with her stepdaughter, Gina.' Gina lived in Puerto Vallarta. She knew the bar scene. They were out looking for Luster when the boys caught up with them.

I looked at Boris and said, 'We've got to go.' We jumped in our rented black SUV and made the two-hour drive in less than sixty minutes. Boris was literally on the floorboard lying in foetal position and screaming the entire drive.

I called Leland to ask if he thought it was Luster they saw.

'One hundred and ten per cent, Dad.' My heart was racing as fast as we were driving. When Leland said that, I knew we had him.

By the time I got to Puerto Vallarta, the team had spotted and lost Luster a couple of times. When I connected with Leland and Tim, they pointed to a bar across the street.

'He's in that bar, right there.' Leland pointed with his forefinger. I sent Tim inside to see if it was Luster. He came back and told me he looked like a troll under a bridge as he walked around looking in women's drinks to see if he could find another potential victim.

Just then, Leland spotted him walking out of the bar and on to the crowded street. I focused in on three or four large guys with bandanas around their heads surrounding a very tall American.

It couldn't see his face. Tim and Leland caught a glimpse, though. They knew it was Luster. He was flanked by his bodyguards and had apparently changed his shirt from the one he was wearing when Leland saw him go into the bar. He must have sensed we were getting close.

Much to my surprise, Luster stepped out of his protective circle. I needed to distract the bodyguards so I could keep Luster alone. I saw a couple of pretty hookers standing on the corner next to me.

'Come here, baby.' I motioned them over. 'I'll give you twenty bucks if you take your shirts off and walk by those guys over there.' Apparently, the girls didn't quite get what I asked them to do. Instead of walking past the goons, they walked right up to them, stopped, and started talking to them. Dumb-ass hos! It didn't work. The guys talked to them for a few minutes, and then they moved along.

Leland noticed Luster was walking to his car by himself. We all ducked down behind the SUV. I was the only person in the group Luster could have recognised. Leland and Tim weren't well-known faces yet, like they are today.

When Luster got into his car, we followed close behind, staying back just far enough so he couldn't see us.

'Dad, pull over. He's stopping at a taco stand.' Luster stood on the street eating a taco without a care in the world. He had no idea I was on his ass.

That was the first time I saw Luster with my own two eyes. I recognised every inch of him. 'Oh, my God. It's him.' I was frozen. Stuck in the moment. Fear and pure exhilaration flowed through my veins.

'I'm going first. Tim, you come right behind me. Leland, when I attack, you go.' I looked over at Filiberto to get his signal that it was a 'go'. He nodded his head.

When I popped up, I scared the crap out of that boy. He tried to bolt, but Tim wrapped his arms around Luster's neck. I tackled him at the waist while Leland grabbed him in the leg. We all went down.

I heard a thunderous noise, like a stampede of wild horses. It was the sound of Luster's bodyguards trying to get close. It was too late. I cuffed him, stood up, and said, 'You are under arrest in the name of the United States government and Mexico!'

After I wrestled Luster to the ground, I was surprised to see Mona run up and scream at him. 'You raped me, you son of a bitch.'

The boys and I looked at one another in utter disbelief. I always knew Mona had done more with Luster than party. I could tell by the way she spoke to him on the phone that the relationship had been intimate. But I never thought Luster raped her. Frankly, she didn't fit the stereotype, so it never occurred to me.

While Luster was on the ground, I said, 'Give me your cell phone.' I started looking at the numbers. When I asked him about the first number I saw, he said, 'It's my mommy's.' That woman lied to me every time we spoke, telling me she never talked to her son. I threw his phone in the bushes. He didn't deserve to have the option of making phone calls.

When I put him in the car, Filiberto was on one side, I was on the other. There was a police station one block away. Leland ran ahead and knocked on the door, but it was closed! While we waited for Leland, Min opened the door, and grabbed Luster by the hair. He pulled his head back and tried to force water down his throat from a bottle.

'Min, what the hell are you doing?'

'I'm going to GHB the son of a bitch just like he did my wife!'

He slapped my arm in an attempt to get me to let go of my strong-hold on Luster. I looked at Tim and said, 'This prick just slapped me.' Tim opened the car door. I reached over the prisoner with my booted foot and kicked Min out of the car on to the ground. I watched him run towards a policeman. That's the last I saw of him.

Filiberto said he knew where there was another police station. 'It's only a couple of miles away, but it is open twenty-four hours.' I could see flashing lights ahead.

I called Beth. I wanted her to be the first to know the good news.

Normally I say to her, 'Who's the greatest bounty hunter in the world?'

She always responds, 'You are, Big Daddy.'

For whatever reason, this time all I could muster were the words, 'We got him, honey. I got Luster.' She was screaming and crying and carry-ing on with pure joy.

I put the phone up to Luster's mouth. 'Say hello to my wife.'

'No.' Luster was in no mood to comply with my requests.

'That's not very nice, you prick.'

Tim was driving the SUV down the narrow Mexican streets as Filiberto guided him towards the police station. We kept sideswiping cars, setting off alarms.

'Drive towards the lights, Tim.' I was still on the phone with Beth.

I said, 'You can have that new house, honey. You can have it.' Beth was yelling, 'I've got my house, I've got my house. Woo hoo!' She was overjoyed. We had seen a house we loved in Hawaii, but it was too much money. I promised Beth, *when* I caught Luster, she could buy that house. We used to drive by every weekend, dreaming of someday living in our island paradise. Now that I'd caught him, we'd have the money to fulfil that dream.

I could see a roadblock in the distance. Tim pulled over. I noticed they let Filiberto pass through, so I thought it couldn't be for us. Next thing I knew, there were Mexican policemen holding machine guns all around us.

'Freeze, motherfuckers. Get out of the car.'

I didn't want to move.

I tried to explain that I was Dog Chapman and that I had Andrew Stuart Luster in the car. I agreed to send Leland and Boris out, but I was staying put with Luster. I was never letting him go. Surely the police would understand.

Nope. The officer ordered me to get out. I finally agreed.

'What's your name?'

'Dog Chapman.'

The officer looked at Luster. 'What's your name?'

'David Carrera.' He said it with the straightest face, as if that were really his name!

'That's bull!' I tried to explain the situation to the officer, but Luster began speaking Spanish, really fast, so fast I only caught every third word. The cop looked at me and shook his head in affirmation of what Luster was saying.

Luster said, 'Those guys have been following me around for days plotting to kidnap me. I'm a very rich man!' His face was turning red from pleading to the cops that *he* was the victim.

This couldn't be good. They started to uncuff him.

'Wait! Stop! He's a criminal wanted by the United States government for rape. Look in my car. All the information is there.' I pleaded with the cops to hear me out. They took my binder of material on Luster out of the car. They said they had to verify the story. They told me they wanted to be certain the man I had in custody was Andrew Luster.

'Come to the station. We're not arresting you. We just want to check out your story.'

I turned to Filiberto. 'Are you going to come with us?' Despite the cop's denial, I assumed we were going to jail. Filiberto said he would be right behind us.

# CHAPTER FORTY-NINE

# Mexican Prison

I had walked out of the Texas State Penitentiary almost a quarter of a century ago. I promised God I would never go back to jail. From the moment I left Huntsville, I dedicated myself to living a good clean life. No more crimes. My number-one purpose as a bounty hunter has been to serve truth and justice. I swore I would never hear the sound of the steel door slam shut and lock behind me again. Now, here I was, sitting in a Mexican prison, with thin steel bars between me and freedom. The smell was all too familiar. I looked around, trying to assess my situation. I was stunned by the chipping green paint that half-covered the stone walls. It was the same green paint as in Huntsville. My heart ached from the thought of being back in hell. And I was scared, too. I wasn't afraid of being in prison. No. This time I was afraid of the ramifications.

I looked at my son, my friends. These guys didn't belong here. They're good men. Righteous men. Hell, Boris and Jeff weren't even bounty hunters. They were just along for the ride. I feared that I had lost everything. My family, my business, and now, it appeared, my freedom was at risk too.

For whatever reason, the Mexican cops seemed to be tougher on Leland than they were on the rest of us that night. Perhaps it was because he is my son. Or maybe it was because he was the smallest guy in the group. I watched helplessly as Leland got punched and kicked by the cops who brought us in. He's a tough kid, but no good father wants to see his son hurt – not ever, and most definitely not in a Mexican prison.

Tim, Leland, Boris, Jeff, and I were packed into the same tiny cell. For a moment, we all smiled and relished the victory of capturing Luster. It wasn't just me who poured blood, sweat, and tears into the chase. All of these men put their lives on the line. I don't remember who said it first, but one of the guys let out a shout. 'We did it! We got that bastard!' And we had it all on tape too.

We watched as the Mexican police paraded Luster past our cell. He was going down. He would definitely be sent back to the United States to serve out his hefty sentence. We might be in prison, but each of us knew we would eventually get out. Luster was going to jail for the rest of his life. That alone made us all feel good about what we had done.

The boys and I recounted the week's events as we waited to be set free. Of course, I wasn't sure that was going to happen, but I hoped it would. Filiberto was there to verify our story. Truth and justice always prevails.

Well, not always. And, as I would soon discover, *definitely* not in Mexico.

Not long after we arrived, Filiberto came to the jail like he promised. He was in the room when the police were running Luster's warrant. The cop blurted out that Luster's bond was ten million dollars. It's true, when Luster first went to jail, his bond was ten million, but the judge later reduced it to one million.

'Filiberto. Wait. You don't understand. That was in the beginning. That number isn't right.' I pleaded with him. He thought I was trying to rip him off by telling him the bond was only a million.

'Fuck you. I want more money.'

'Wait . . . ' He wouldn't listen.

Filiberto turned to leave. He stopped, looked back, and said, 'Let's see how you feel about this in the morning', and then walked away. He left us sitting in a Mexican prison. Just like that, Filiberto, my alibi, my compadre, my safety net – in a second, he was gone.

A couple of hours later, the cop came to tell us he was able to verify our story and that the man we caught was in fact, Andrew Stuart Luster.

Duh. Big surprise.

And then they began to book us.

When the cops came to the cell, I was hoping they were there to let us out. They were not.

'Wait, what are you doing?' I had no idea why I was being booked.

'We want to make sure you get to see the judge.'

Judge? This wasn't part of the plan. Why did I need to see a judge? I started to hear some rumblings about kidnapping charges. I didn't get confirmation of that until the next day when a woman from the American consulate paid us a visit.

'I'm in a big hurry, so I don't have a lot of time to talk. Here's the deal. You're being charged with kidnapping. You should know better than to come down to Mexico and grab someone.' Her attitude to me was snippy.

'Wait a minute. I had a Mexican cop with me,' I said.

'You shouldn't have done that. Now I can't help you. Look, you need to get a lawyer who can advise you. Until you speak with him, I wouldn't say another word. Kidnapping is a twenty-year sentence in Mexico, Mr Chapman.'

I was nauseous at the thought that we all could go down for twenty years for capturing a rapist. I had to stop myself from getting physically sick. I didn't want to frighten the others. A group is only as strong as their leader. I had to be tough so no one else fell apart. It wasn't out of the question for Boris or Jeff to cut a deal and throw us to the wolves. We needed to stay united.

By noon the following day, several Mexican cops and what appeared to be FBI agents were filing past our cell, paying Luster numerous visits. By now, word had spread that Andrew Luster had been caught. I wasn't sure what the American news was reporting, but I could see that media people were beginning to arrive in droves.

Later that afternoon, a Mexican cop came to our cell with a photographer. He opened the cell door.

'We need to get a picture, gringo.'

I said, 'No way. No pictures, hombre.'

'*Señor Perro*, you don't understand. Didn't you hear the good news? You're going home. We just need one picture of all of you.'

Did he say we're going home? We were ecstatic at the thought, so the boys and I huddled together, hugging and smiling for the camera because we were relieved and overcome with joy. We were happy as hell to be leaving that pigsty.

Click.

One hour later, the photo was released to the media. The headlines screamed:

'DOG IS DEFIANT!'

Those sons of bitches. They set us up. We were not going home.

Lawyers began swarming to the jail like flies on a turd. Each one came to tell us we had big problems.

'Beth sent me,' one of them said.

'Oh yeah? What's the password?' Beth and I have a secret password we use for situations like this. To confirm the validity of the person sitting in front of me, I asked him again.

'Tell me the password, and I'll believe anything you say.'

'Jesus.'

Wrong answer. I dismissed him with the back of my hand. I knew Beth didn't send this punk.

Every lawyer who came in made the same mistake. Some insisted Beth already sent money to them, others just tried to extort money from me on the spot. They were all a bunch of crooked liars who were on the take. I would soon discover that was true of all Mexican lawyers, even the 'good guys'.

Later that day, the boys and I did the perp walk in cuffs and shackles, from the jail to the court to see the judge. I couldn't believe how many people were camped outside. Mostly it was media, but there were also a lot of good citizens out there holding up signs wishing us well and offering their support. One guy jumped out of the line and whispered in my ear, 'Beth sent me.' Now, this was the fourth guy in two hours giving me the same line.

'Oh, yeah? What's the password?'

'Big Daddy.' I stopped cold in my tracks.

Oh, my God. He knew the password. 'Come here, brother. What's your name?'

'Jorge.' He spoke English. I almost fell to my knees to thank Jesus until he told me he was from Texas. No way would Beth hire a lawyer from Texas.

'You're not my lawyer, you asshole.' I turned to walk away.

Jorge said, 'OK, Big Daddy.'

Something in the way he said those three words made me turn around again. I walked back to Jorge and said, 'Did she really send you?' He nodded. The news footage shot from that day clearly shows this exchange. It was amazing. As I continued towards the courthouse, it suddenly occurred to me we were in the deepest pile of you know what.

The most important thing to know about Mexican jail is they don't care about you at all. The conditions were disgusting. Mexico is a very poor country. Their government doesn't have the money to feed lowly prisoners. You must have family or friends bring you food, or you will starve. They did offer minimal food, mostly tortillas or beans, but guards usually pissed on it before giving it to prisoners. I warned the boys, no matter what, they were not to eat or drink anything the guards offered. I was thankful that Gina, Min and Mona's stepdaughter, and Anthony Galloway, a producer from *Dateline* whom Beth called, brought us food. Over the course of our first three days in jail, we only ate twice.

The cell consisted of three concrete slabs set into the wall as makeshift beds. There were no mattresses or blankets. There was one toilet that looked as if it hadn't been flushed for years. The debris from the overflow was all over the concrete floor. The smell was unbearable. All of us were on the verge of puking from a combination of stress, hunger, and the unthinkable environment.

One by one, the cops kept bringing tough Mexican criminals into the cell. These guys were nasty lowlifes. One of the cops was having a difficult time wrangling his convict, so I reached through the bars, grabbed him from behind, and put him into a headlock. I could have ripped the guy's head right off his neck. The Mexican cop began to beat the crap out of the guy while I held him still. Finally, he went limp. I spun him around so the cop could cuff him.

'*Perro*, why did you do that?'

I said, 'Look, brah, I'm sort of a cop too. I'm not going to let a convict treat you like that. He was disrespecting you.'

'How did you get him in that choke hold?' The cops are always curious about my moves.

'Let me out of here and I will show you.'

'No way. You'll run.'

'I won't run. You badasses will kill me!' I nicknamed the cop Roberto Duran Stonehands, because he fought every night. The rapport began.

'*Sí, Perro*. We will shoot you dead.'

The cop actually let me out. As convicts came through the jail, I showed him how I would take them down – Dog style.

'Hit the wall. Spread your legs. Put your thumbs together.' I turned to the cop, and said, 'Now you try it.'

He loved it. At the very least, it helped pass the time.

The second night in jail, one of the cops came to me and said he needed me to sign a statement swearing I was indeed Duane Chapman and my purpose for being in Mexico was to apprehend Andrew Luster. I looked at the cop and said, 'OK. I'm ready to confess.'

The boys were in shock. Leland said, 'No, Dad. What are you doing?'

I turned to the guys and said, 'I'm sorry, you guys, I have to do this. I'll take all of the blame.' The cops led me from my cell to a table where I sat surrounded by more Mexican cops. One guy lit a cigarette for me, another handed me a Coke. To be honest, I had no intention of confessing. I did it to get out of the stench of my cell for a few minutes. And since I hadn't eaten for a couple of days, the soda tasted really good.

After a few minutes, I turned to the cop who came to get my statement and said, 'You know what? You're making me nervous. There's too many of you. I'm not ready to make my statement. Take me back to my cell.' I did this three more times until they finally figured out I was never giving them a statement. I wanted to meet the guys in charge. I wanted to know who I was up against.

Later that night, the cops put a loud, obviously very drunk man in the cell next to mine. He was a big monster son of a bitch. It took three cops on each arm to get him locked up. When he walked past our cell, he growled at us.

'Fuck you, pigs.' He was speaking a combination of English and Spanish. I saw one of the cops carry a ten foot chain into his cell. They wrapped it around his arms and waist and bolted him down to a hook in the concrete floor.

The boys and I exchanged a look. He sounded like a nasty dude.

A little later, I was startled by the sound of jingling keys outside my cell. All I could think was 'Now what?'

'*Perro*. Come with me.' The guard walked me six feet to the left and put me in the cell with the drunken Mexican. As the guard shoved me into the cell, he pointed at me and said, 'He no like Mexicans.'

I sat down on the bench next to this poor bastard. As far as I could tell, the guards were hoping one of us would kill the other. If they got lucky, we both would die.

I broke the ice by saying, 'I used to think I was Mexican until I was fifteen.' Thank God the guy laughed.

'You know what these pigs are doing, right, brother?'

'I'll kill you.' The guy could barely speak, and his breath . . . well, let's just say he could have used a Tic Tac.

'Yeah, I know you'll kill me. And they're going to laugh at you while watching you do it. It's what they want.'

'I know, *Perro*.' He began to cry like a giant 250-pound baby. I have found it helps to let a criminal cry. But you can't let them cry too much, or they will get mad at you for seeing them in such a vulnerable state.

'It's OK. You just need to relax for a while. Lay down. Take a nap.' He was out cold before I hit the word 'nap'.

I walked to the front of the cell. When the cop saw me, he opened the door, and let me go back to my cell. I think he was in shock that I was still standing.

The next morning, Jorge came to the jail bearing bad news. He held up the newspaper, with a headline that screamed the governor had ordered the judge on our case to charge us all with kidnapping. I asked Jorge to read me the Mexican statute on kidnapping. He described it as a case that involved the exchange of money, crossing a border, and making calls for ransom. That definitely didn't mesh with what went down in our case. We were innocent. We hadn't done any of those things.

Jorge seemed sympathetic. He said he believed that we didn't commit a felony crime of kidnapping, but he thought the judge was going to insist on pressing charges for holding that scumbag Luster against his will. Jorge explained that that charge is a misdemeanour. It's called deprivation of liberty. He thought we had a very good chance to beat the kidnapping rap.

And then Jorge began to tell me he was having a hard time getting enough money from Beth to fight the case. He needed a lot more than the ten grand she had already wired. He was worried he wouldn't be able to get the charges dropped unless he had enough money to 'work the system'. I'd later discover that the Mexican courts run like Enron. Everyone is on the take. You buy your freedom in Mexico. The bottom line is – no money, no chance.

I told Jorge I had a $5,000-money order in my wallet. Miraculously the cops missed it when they were going through my personal effects while I was being booked. Five thousand dollars was more money than Beth and I had ever saved. We pretty much lived hand-to-mouth. We were so proud to have that extra cash for a rainy day. Our intention was to use it on something special. I kept that money order in my wallet for months. Beth and I had no idea the special occasion would be bailing my ass out of a Mexican prison. I told Jorge to take the money, which he did. Even so, I wasn't sure that would be enough to get us out.

# CHAPTER FIFTY

# Posting Bail

On the morning of our fourth day in prison, we were transferred to the jail in downtown Puerto Vallarta. We were told our hearing was going to be in the next day or two. The media frenzy was becoming unmanageable for the Mexican authorities. They thought moving us would help them keep it under control.

I was aware the media had been covering the case, but until we were transferred, I had no clue as to the extent. When we walked from the jail to the van, I was approached by a producer from a major network news show. He was yelling at me.

'Duane, it's me, from the morning show. Beth sent me to get supplies for you. I've got Excedrin and Vaseline, just like you wanted!'

Hold up.

I had to stop. Who was this jerk shouting he got me Vaseline as I'm being transferred from one jail to another? I went after him too, but my hands were cuffed. As it turned out, Beth had sent him, and the Vaseline was for my burns.

The van that transferred all of us had to inch its way through hundreds of reporters, all wanting a statement. There were photographers and camera crews everywhere we looked. It was a blessing and a curse. I knew the Mexican police couldn't do anything horrible to us with the eyes of the world watching them. On the other hand, I didn't want them to get so pissed off from all of the hoo-ha that they didn't give us a fair trial.

When we got to the new jail, it was something of a pleasant surprise. It was like a holding facility with much more humane conditions. I never thought I'd be so overjoyed at the sight of a semiclean toilet.

At this point, Boris and Jeff had one attorney, and Leland, Tim, and I had another. It was in their best interest to separate their cases from ours. My only concern was that their lawyer would attempt to throw us under the bus in exchange for his clients' freedom. It was a risk I could do nothing about.

Six Mexican detectives came to see me. I didn't know what to expect when they all showed up at my cell.

'We have something you might want.'

'Oh yeah? What's that?' They handed me my Colorado Fugitive Apprehension Badge. I was flabbergasted.

'We can't let you keep it. But we thought you might like to see how shiny we made it.' These guys weren't messing with me. They asked me to sign autographs for their wives and kids. They were rooting for this Dog.

My worst day in jail was the day my lawyer came to talk to us about the proceedings. He let me use his cell phone to call Beth. I hadn't spoken to her once since the call I made after catching Luster.

'Honey, are we going to be OK?' I couldn't stop myself from crying.

'I'm not sure, Duane.' I had never heard Beth say that to me. She always tells me things are going to be fine. Hearing her uncertainty scared the crap out of me because Beth never wavers.

'You think they're going to make the kidnapping charges stick?'

'Maybe.' Again, there was doubt. Where was my strong Beth? What the hell was happening?

I've said it before and I'll say it again. Beth is the realist in our family. She speaks the truth, whether I want to hear it or not. I was quickly losing faith that the Lord was going to get me out. I got what I wanted. I was the most famous bounty hunter in the world. Would the Lord play such a horrible joke on me by giving me that title and making me pay for it by spending twenty years in a Mexican prison? *No way*. This was the work of the devil. I've met the devil. More than once he has said to me, 'I know you, boy, and you know me.' Hell, yeah. This was his work.

I began to pray. I kept thinking about a documentary I once saw about sea turtles. They go back to the same spot once every year with a single grain of sand in their gullet. Scientists say it is a remarkable feat. At that moment, I felt like one of those turtles. I had the faith of a grain of sand. What I needed was the faith of a mustard seed. I prayed to the Lord, 'All I have is the faith of a single grain of sand, Lord. Is that enough to get me through this?'

I heard the Lord say, 'Turn around, Duane. There are four more grains of sand behind you. Together, each of your grains of sand measures up to the strength and faith of a mustard seed.'

The Lord, in all of His great and infinite wisdom, was right. I pulled us all together until we formed a circle. Together, we gave praise. 'Right now, in Jesus' name, thank you, Lord, for what You did when You led us to Luster. But now, this is the second step. Show us that You're watching over us, Lord. Show us You love us. In Jesus' name, amen.'

My lawyer walked into the cell as we prayed.

'Duane, I have good news and bad news.'

Being the man I am, I told him to give me the bad news first.

'They've added a charge of association. Essentially what that means is that you all conspired to commit this crime. If you can prove you're blood-related, they will drop that charge.' I excitedly pointed out that Leland is my son. Jorge thought that might be enough to get the charges dropped, but he couldn't be sure until he went to court.

Boris turned and asked, 'So, what's the good news?'

'They've dropped the kidnapping charges. They are only going to charge you with holding Luster against his will, deprivation of liberty. It's a petty crime.'

We all went completely nuts. I shouted, *'Viva la Mexico!'* I just dodged the biggest, scariest bullet ever shot my way. I hadn't felt this happy since I was given parole from Huntsville. Right then, I realised the cops loved me, because they unlocked my cell so I could dance with joy. I hugged every cop in the joint.

'Is there bail?' You can take the bondsman out of America but you can't take the bondsman out of the Dog.

'Yes. Fifteen thousand pesos each.'

I added up the total. Damn. We didn't have seventy-five grand in the bank to get us out. Then it occurred to me the lawyer said *pesos*.

'How much is that in American dollars?'

'About fifteen hundred each.'

I knew I had friends who would help get us out for that kind of money, including Tony Robbins, Chris McQuarrie, Martin Sheen, Vin Di Bona. They all helped.

As I celebrated, I heard the Lord say, 'Do you want to stay here?' I most certainly did not.

I turned to the guys and said, 'We're out of here.'

The next morning we were charged with the misdemeanour. Procedure was to transfer us to the Jalisco State Penitentiary, where we had to wait to be set free. This place made Huntsville look like a

Hawaiian paradise. It's the worst of the Mexican prisons. We all knew we'd be out in a matter of hours, but I felt like I was checking in for life.

We were all placed in separate cells. As the day passed slowly, painfully by, I kept hearing one of the prisoners from another cell sing 'Who Let the Dogs Out.' He was singing it in Spanish, but I recognised the tune.

I yelled, 'You hear that? We're getting out, boys. You know we're leaving here, right?' I needed to make sure no one cracked under the pressure. One wrong move and the decision to drop the kidnapping charges could turn into a 'mistake'. I didn't want to rock the boat.

'Dog, you made bail. You're out. C'mon. Let's go.' The guards came and told us one by one we had posted bail. We were free to go, one at a time.

Something didn't seem right, though. Why did I have this nagging sense I was being set up? I got dressed, walked outside, and heard:

'Freeze! *La Migra*.'

Son of a bitch. It was Immigration. Six guys surrounded me, guns drawn and cocked. All I could think of was 'This is what we do to them in our country. It's about right I'm being screwed with in Mexico.' I had posted bond so many times for illegal Mexicans, only to see them get out and face American immigration. I was all too familiar with this scene.

Immigration took us back to the first hellhole jail. I never saw Tim look so sad. The emotional roller coaster was taking a toll on all of us, but Tim seemed to be taking it the worst. Those bastards painted a fresh coat of sugar water on the floor before we arrived, so the flies were plentiful.

Early the next morning, I was told we could talk to the immigration officer. My lawyer had arranged a Sunday morning meeting. He said the immigration bail wouldn't be much money, perhaps a total of another fifteen hundred dollars.

The immigration officer was a pretty friendly guy. He was curious about our documents when we entered the country. He wanted to know how we filled out the form that asked the purpose of our trip. Was it business or pleasure?

When I came through customs, I told the officer I was here to look for a fugitive and for a vacation. The boys and I never handed in our immigration cards. We still had them with us. I had never travelled outside of the United States before this trip. I was under the impression these cards were supposed to get handed in on departure, not arrival. No one ever asked for the papers. I handed the officer my form. It confirmed everything I said.

When I came out of the office, my lawyer's face was white as a fresh layer of snow on a Colorado mountain-top.

'What's the matter?'

'That was the judge.'

I had no idea. I thought I had been talking to an officer who would report my story to the judge.

Just then, the immigration judge came out of his office. He turned to my attorney and said, 'It's Sunday. I will trust this man until his money can be wired in tomorrow. I'm going to let him go. But I want an armed guard on him until he posts bail.'

Fair enough. We were allowed to check into the Westin Hotel until the rest of this god-awful mess could be cleared up and our nightmare would finally be over.

My lawyer told each of us the hotel rooms would most definitely be bugged. He said the Mexican government likes to record everything. He warned us not to say or do anything that might set us back from finally going home. Guards followed our every move. I didn't care. It had been a living hell. The Westin Hotel was a slice of heaven.

The boys and I walked into one of the restaurants in the hotel to get our first decent meal in weeks. Thirty Americans stood up and cheered for us. The ex-wife of one of Def Leppard's band members came over to introduce herself.

'Way to go. Anything you want, it's on me.'

I told her I had a girlfriend back home. She started to laugh.

'No, not that. You need drinks? Food? Whatever, it's on my bill.'

We didn't know we had become hometown heroes. The warm welcome we received from our fellow Americans was downright heartwarming. I was never more proud to be a citizen of the United States.

# CHAPTER FIFTY-ONE

# America the Beautiful

A day after we checked into the Westin, my lawyer came to see us. He said he'd heard rumours that a few guys connected to Andrew Luster were in Puerto Vallarta looking for me. He heard the guys were flashing around a lot of money to influence certain people in the Mexican legal system to reinstate the kidnapping charges. Worst of all, Jorge said he also heard someone talking about taking me out – lights out, for good.

'You and the boys have to go.' He was legally advising me to flee. I wasn't comfortable with the idea of running. I was under house arrest. If I ran, I would be a Mexican fugitive for the rest of my life and I didn't want that hanging over my head. Besides, by now you all know, 'This blood don't run.'

I *chased* fugitives, I wasn't one. Plus, I promised the immigration judge I wouldn't run. I told him he could trust me. A man is as good as his word, and I am a man of my word. I told the lawyer I wouldn't go. The alternative was to stay in Puerto Vallarta until my case went to trial. It could be six weeks, six months, or six years. No one knew for sure.

The Westin Hotel bill was upwards of nine or ten thousand dollars. We decided it made more sense financially to rent a house until our trial. We found a place through Min and Mona's stepdaughter, Gina. She knew a woman named Silver who used to be married to an American bounty hunter. She was living in Puerto Vallarta in a gorgeous home with vast ocean views. I wanted to go live there until everything settled down. It was peaceful serenity after everything we had been through. Another factor was that the hotel became a magnet for American tourists and the international press who wanted a glimpse of me. Hotel management told me they had never seen anything like it. It was good for business, but under the circumstances, it was hard for me to take people in my face 24/7. Also, I didn't feel safe there, especially after what the lawyer told me. Beth wired me three thousand dollars so I could pay for the house a month in advance. She planned to visit with the kids first chance they got.

While I was in Puerto Vallarta, it occurred to me that my home in Hawaii was a straight shot across the Pacific. I thought back to that day on the beach when the Lord pointed me straight ahead. Until that moment, I didn't realise He was telling me to go to Mexico. I was over-whelmed by the connection.

In retrospect, it was in the Mexican government's best interest to get me out of the country. It made me less accessible to their system, but it took the microscope off of them too. Luster was already gone. He was sent back to California almost immediately. The United States govern-ment had a provisional warrant to deport Luster because he entered Mexico illegally.

The rub here is that Luster got deported while I sat in a Mexican prison.

I thought long and hard about what Jorge was saying. He told me I was as good as dead. Jorge told me he couldn't control what happened in Mexico, nor could he guarantee my safety. By court order, I had to check in every day with the immigration judge. After my last visit with him, I realised it was time to leave Mexico. Tim kept telling me he felt the Mexicans wanted us gone. Although it meant I would break my word to the judge, I came to the same conclusion. I finally told Jorge I would leave on the condition he came with us. I wanted my lawyer pres-ent just in case anything unexpected happened. He reluctantly agreed.

I drove to Western Union to pick up the money Beth sent. I got back to the hotel room where Leland and Tim were anxiously waiting.

I called Beth. Knowing our conversation was being recorded I simply said two words, 'Le Parc'.

She said, 'When?'

'Now.'

Jorge, the boys, and I packed up our stuff, loaded the rented van, and acted as if we were headed to Silver's. The highway on-ramp towards Guadalajara was a short distance from the house. Leland and Tim kept a close watch to make sure no one was following us. 'It's clear, Dad.' Leland gave me the signal to get on the highway.

Jorge told me that we would be safe outside Puerto Vallarta. Even so, I wanted him to go with us. We went through four separate checkpoints. We let Jorge do the talking at each one. We tried to act cool, but deep down, I was scared to death. We made it to Guadalajara without a hitch. Our plan was to check into a hotel until we could catch a flight the next morning to Tijuana. We had to lie low. No one could know we'd left Puerto Vallarta. I wasn't exactly unrecognisable. My face had been plastered all over the news for weeks. A couple of American kids spotted us at a fast food restaurant.

'Aren't you Dog the Bounty Hunter?'

I gave them a blank, cold, death-inducing stare. '*Mi llamo es Martinez.*'

We headed to the airport the following morning. The date was 1 July 2003. Jorge paid cash for our tickets. He didn't want any trace or trail that we were on the move. I was certain we were screwed if the authorities figured out we left Puerto Vallarta. We went through airport security.

'Passport, please.' The security guard demanded I hand over my passport. I was nervous as hell. I barely gave him a second to read before grabbing it and walking on through. Tim did the same thing. Leland was worried about something happening at the airport all morning, because he hid every article written about us in the bottom of his suitcase. If they checked his suitcase, they'd know exactly who we were. In preparation that something might go terribly wrong, he took a pair of his shorts and doused them with water. He laid the wet shorts on top of the things in his suitcase. If someone opened it, the first thing they'd find would be a pair of wet, soiled boxer shorts. Sure enough, Leland got picked out of the line for a full security search. When the guard opened his suitcase, he was disgusted by the wet shorts. He zipped the case back up as he motioned Leland to go on through. That's my boy!

We made the short flight to Tijuana. Jorge had arranged a van to meet us curbside. We piled in as fast as we could. A few minutes into the trip, the driver told Jorge he didn't have any identification. I thought this had to be a set-up.

'Jorge! What the hell? What's going on?' We had made it through two airports and four checkpoints. We were a couple of miles from the American border. We'd never get through border patrol without the driver presenting ID. We couldn't go back. Not now. We were so close. But going forward would mean going back. We were stumped.

'What are we going to do?' I looked at Jorge with puppy dog eyes.

Leland was seated in the back of the van. While Jorge and I tried to figure out a plan, Leland noticed a Mexican checkpoint soldier chasing us, waving with one hand and pointing his rifle at the car with the other.

'Gun it!' I yelled at the driver to crash the gate and get us to American soil.

Just as we approached the American checkpoint, the driver pulled down the visor above his head. 'Here it is! I have my papers!' I wanted to scream at him, but I was too eager to get to the other side of that gate.

I could see the Mexican soldier in the distance behind us, still waving. Right in front of us was a large official-looking white man in a uniform instructing the van to pull over.

The officer opened the van's side door, pointed directly at me, and said, 'You. Come with me.' I couldn't believe this. We were so close. This time I would fight to the end. I wasn't going back to jail. No way. I couldn't shoot the guy – I didn't have a gun – but I could beat his ass to death. I took two steps forward.

'Dog Chapman?'

I didn't want to answer.

'Welcome home. We've been waiting for you. I'm with Homeland Security. You are safe. You're free.'

I fell to my knees. I didn't realise we had crossed the border. I looked up and saw the largest, most beautiful American flag waving above me. I cannot put words to how I felt in that moment. Free, blessed, safe, loved, relieved, lucky. None of those words combined or alone accurately describe that feeling. I kissed the ground.

'Oh, my God. Sweet Jesus. I'm home. Thank you, Lord.' We all wept tears of joy.

The driver took us to a nearby Budget Rental Car at the San Diego airport.

The woman behind the counter immediately recognised me.

'Dog?' I thought I knew her from Tony Robbins.

'You're in *People* magazine, sweetie.'

I couldn't believe it. She gave me the nicest, newest car on the lot.

The journey had taken a toll on all of us, but Jorge seemed especially drained from the pressure. He just wanted to go home. Tim, Leland, and I got into the car and raced up the 15 freeway towards L.A., where our loved ones were waiting for us. We were doing at least a hundred miles an hour to make the two-hour trip as fast as we could. Somewhere in Orange County, about halfway there, I saw flashing red lights in my rearview mirror. I didn't want to stop. All I could think of was getting to Beth. The cop pulled up alongside the car and motioned for me to pull over.

I pulled off the highway on to the median. The cop was pissed. I could tell by the way he approached the car he didn't appreciate our short-lived chase. I opened the car door and got out. I was wearing a suede poncho someone gave me on the beach in Puerto Vallarta, my dark glasses, jeans, boots, and a leather cowboy hat. I looked like a mix of Zorro and Pancho Villa!

'Stop right there. Fucking freeze! First, you're smoking. Second-hand smoke is known to kill, so now, you've already tried to kill me.' The cop took a minute to look me over. The he squinted and said, 'Dog?' He hugged me on the spot. The boys got out of the car and he hugged them, too. He was so excited to see us. The reaction we were getting from people was startling. We had no idea how big a story this had become.

'Do you want an escort?' By now, two other California Highway Patrolmen had pulled up. I thought an escort would bring too much attention to the fact we were home. I wanted the chance to see Beth before the media got ahold of us.

'Thanks guys, but if it's all the same, I think we'll take a pass on the escort.'

The cop radioed ahead to be on the lookout for our car. 'Under no circumstances are you to pull this man over.'

Roger that.

I pulled up in front of the Le Parc Hotel in West Hollywood. Beth and I had used that hotel as our headquarters for most of the hunt for Luster. I knew she'd know to meet me there when I called. The entire hotel staff stood with Beth and Tim's wife, Davina, waiting to welcome us home. Leland's wife, Maui, stayed in Hawaii. Beth, my honey, came running towards the car in her high heels. I remember drinking her in, smelling her perfume, feeling her heart beat next to mine. It was the strongest love I've ever known. It was pure joy. We held one another for more than ten minutes before letting go.

While I was in Mexico, Beth, my Rock of Gibraltar, had shown signs of cracking. When she told me she wasn't sure I was going to make it this time, I wept at the thought of never holding, kissing, and being with her again. I worried she felt helpless. I was sure she was in a lot of pain. I can't imagine how she must have felt while I was incarcerated. Seeing her now, in this moment of pure bliss, was better than I dreamed. It was just me, D-o-g, and Him, G-o-d, down there in Mexico. Now that I was home, I would never be alone again.

# CHAPTER FIFTY-TWO

# Justice Denied

Thirty-six hours after I was reunited with Beth, she and I found our-selves thrust into a media feeding frenzy, the likes of which we had never experienced. We scheduled our first press conference to answer as many questions as we could. Beth was adamant the lawyers do all the talking, but I had a lot to say. I still had a black eye from fighting in jail, so I wore my sunglasses to hide my battered face. I was flanked by two lawyers, one on each side – Les Abell and Jim Blancarte. These are two of the best defence attorneys in the world. Forty cameras pointed directly at me, with a multitude of journalists waiting to hear first hand what happened in Mexico. I began to speak. Twenty minutes later, the press was still mesmerized by my story. My lawyers were so taken by what I was saying, they forgot to stop me from talking!

The media asked some very poignant questions. Some I could answer, others I still wonder about.

'Dog, why did the FBI abandon you?'

I said, 'Did you hear what the FBI was doing the night I got arrested? I'm sure they had bigger fish to fry.' I had no way of knowing what the FBI was doing or not. I had to believe it was something more important than helping me since they left me in Mexico to fend for myself.

'The FBI said they had no idea what you were doing. Is that true?'

I laughed. 'They're the FBI. The have to say that.'

'Would you ever go back to Mexico?'

'Never.'

'Do you feel the government tried to trap you?'

'Yes, I do. I communicated everything I knew. The FBI told me nothing. Despite their claims, I received no help. They were in the loop every step of the way.' At one point, after I was arrested, Beth told me she received a call from a prominent FBI agent saying they had to disassociate themselves from us. They couldn't let it leak that they were always in the know.

The press conference was a huge success. My goal was to let the world know the truth about Andrew Luster, Mexico, and the Dog. Tim hung in there, staying in L.A. to face the press with Beth and me for a week. But Leland was uncomfortable with all of the attention, so after the press conference, he caught the next flight back to Hawaii to be with his family.

There was additional unexpected fallout from capturing Luster. A small group of bounty hunters from New Hampshire began to campaign against me. I have been dealing with these guys repeatedly over the years. The more recognition I received, the more they resented me. Their distaste for my unique, nonconformist, untraditional way of doing business makes them terribly uncomfortable.

They have tried to run me out of the business more times than I can count. In their effort to discredit us, our Mexican mug shots began popping up all over the Internet. 'These men are Wanted.' Suddenly, everywhere I went, there were Wanted posters of Tim, Leland, and myself. As part of their well-organised smear campaign, the four guys from New Hampshire did a television interview – faces hidden, of course – saying we were immoral vigilantes and dangerous, hardened criminals. They claimed I was a bad example, a bounty hunter who did not reflect the rest of the industry in my practices and therefore was damaging their good names and reputations. It was laughable.

One of the guys even threatened me during an interview. He held up an eight-inch metal pipe, looked right into the camera, and said, 'You see this, Doggie? You see this, Chapman? This is going right up your ass when I see you. Oh, yes. You will have my babies!' He was surrounded by what appeared to be six Ku Klux Klan members, who all laughed at the thought of this jerk sodomising me. That threat is a stone-cold felony, but I can't get anyone to take action. In the eyes of the feds, all it would do is bring more attention and publicity my way. That's the last thing they're looking to do. One thing is certain. That footage has never and will never air again.

The New Hampshire bounty hunters have made it their personal mission to get an arrest warrant to send me back to Mexico to stand trial for the charges against me. To be clear, I am not a wanted man in the United States of America. In order for me to stand trial, I would have to somehow end up back in Mexico. There are only two ways that will ever happen. Someone would have to kidnap me and somehow get me over the border into the hands of the Mexican authorities. Or, the United States government would have to extradite me to Mexico. At the time, the idea of either of these scenarios ever happening was beyond comprehension.

Beth did her best to shut down the attack, but the four New Hampshire bounty hunters were attempting to destroy me at a time when I was already quite vulnerable. In fact, to this day, they are still gunning for me.

After the interviews and media attention died down, Beth and I flew back to Hawaii to reunite with our family. We had spent our last dollar chasing Luster and getting me out of jail, and now the harsh reality was sinking in that, once again, we were completely broke. A couple of days later, the electric company shut off our power. We couldn't even scrape together enough money to pay the overdue bill. I checked our family into a hotel until we could financially get back on our feet. We lived off our credit cards, hoping they wouldn't get cut off too. We borrowed money from everyone we knew, expecting to collect the three hundred grand we were owed for the capture of Andrew Luster.

Three hundred thousand dollars is a lot of money for one hunt, but we were legally entitled to 15 per cent of the bond, plus expenses. We worked hard and earned every penny. When we got to court, Judge Brodie was bombarded by people asking for their share of the bond money. The Ventura County Sheriff was there with his hand out. Min and Mona had the nerve to hire a lawyer to try to collect. Everyone expected a slice of the pie. Beth and I were stunned.

The judge was confused by the number of people standing in front of him wanting their cut. He said, 'I can read the newspaper. I don't know why all of you other people are here asking for money. I'm well aware of who caught Andrew Luster.' Beth and I looked at each other with great relief. Finally, someone willing to acknowledge what we did in the name of truth and justice.

The judge looked directly at us. 'Mr Chapman, do you have your bills to substantiate your expenses and fees?'

Beth had our receipts, but Howard Schultz hadn't submitted his expenses to us yet so we could collect the total amount owed. We didn't want Howard to take a bath, but he never gave us his receipts. We tried to protect his investment by including his expenses with our own, but we didn't know how much he had actually spent.

Beth answered the judge: 'Your Honour. We would need some time to figure out an exact number. Why don't we say three hundred grand and call it even?' The judge asked to see everything we had. He adjourned the proceeding while he studied the receipts. Beth and I waited in the corridor until the judge called us back in. I went outside for a smoke. While I was gone, the judge asked us to reassemble. Beth went back to the courtroom by herself. I was two minutes late, because I got trapped outside by some fans asking for my autograph. I never heard my name called by the bailiff.

'Where's the Dog?' the judge asked.

Luster's attorney was now present. He addressed Brodie, saying, 'You realise Mr Chapman is wanted in Mexico, right? He probably ran thinking you were going to arrest him, Your Honour.'

Somehow, the judge wasn't aware of these 'alleged' facts. I walked into the courtroom just as Brodie asked, 'He's wanted in Mexico?'

I sat down next to Beth. She had an 'Oh, crap' expression plastered across her face.

'Mr Chapman. I have given this a lot of consideration. In fact, I have a document here on behalf of twenty-five hundred California bail agents expressing their displeasure with you and your conduct.' Judge Brodie believed the document he was reading was authentic. It was not. An administrative person at the California Bond Agents Association offered up the letter without consent of the members, making it look like the entire association was against me. I had no way of knowing this to be true at the time, but I now know that is what happened.

'Are you a wanted man, Mr Chapman?'

'No sir, I am not.' My attorney was supposed to have paperwork to substantiate my innocence, but he didn't have those documents in court that day.

'Your Honour, of course Mr Chapman can't produce documents proving his innocence. He is guilty. He is a fugitive.' Luster's attorney was practically mocking my lawyer.

The judge asked me one final time, 'Are you a wanted man or not?'

'No, sir. I am not.'

'Mr Chapman, I am not awarding you a dime. I will not condone your vigilante tactics.' The judge continued to chew me out. Somewhere in the middle of his holier-than-thou speech, Beth and I stood up. I grabbed her by the hand as we turned our backs on the judge and walked out. I didn't understand his anger towards me. It made no sense.

I was certain the bailiff was going to arrest me on the spot for contempt of court. Thank the Lord all of the media cameras were on us as we exited the courtroom, or I might have landed my ass in jail.

'Dog, why did the judge do that to you?' reporters shouted left and right.

'Aw, you know. If he'd paid me, it would have opened the door for a flurry of amateur bounty hunters to start arresting their neighbours for parking on their property or whatever.' I acted humble, but I was pissed. The Lord told me to watch my mouth as I left the courtroom. He warned me not to say what was really on my mind. But what I was really thinking, and I couldn't be completely wrong, was that someone had got to the judge. It's no secret that friendships make every business run and let's face it – people don't want to believe that people they know have committed crimes. For her son, Mrs Luster had hired a well-connected defence attorney. Luster's bail went down nine million dollars, and that's a really nice thing to happen if you're Luster. Then I never got paid for capturing her son. If Mexico dropped the charges against me, I would be able to come back to the Ventura County Superior Court to ask for my money. If not, I would be plain out of luck.

We had lost the battle, but not the war. We had to strategically retreat and find another tactic. What bothered me the most about the judge's decision was his dismissive attitude about bringing Luster to justice. He overlooked the importance of my participation to the outcome: the fact that Luster would serve his sentence. He truly sucked the air out of me that day. I am not a vigilante. I am a man of dignity and great pride. I hated someone in law enforcement labelling me an outlaw for capturing one of the most wanted fugitives in the world.

As Beth and I got into the elevator to leave the courthouse that day, Richard Dunbar, one of the New Hampshire Dog-haters, followed us in. 'You see that, Dog? We did this to you.' That motherfucker smiled as he relished his victory.

In the end, the prosecutor was awarded a small amount, as was the Ventura County Sheriff's Office. The worst part of this story came when I found out Andrew Luster got over $200,000 back. Thankfully, all of that money got snatched for victims' compensation. No money could ever heal the damage done to those four women – and Lord only knows how many other nameless, faceless souls Andrew Luster hurt.

On the way to my car, Roger Diamond, Luster's attorney, approached me with a twenty-dollar bill in his hand. 'Here you go, Dog. You won the bet.' I had to laugh. It was the only money I collected for the capture of Andrew Luster.

Beth and I flew back to Hawaii. We had borrowed money from many friends, and I had to get back to work so we could pay everyone back. Their kindness and generosity will never be rewarded enough. By the time we got home, our power had been turned back on, but now our phones were disconnected. We had thirty-one hundred dollars in phone bills from Mexico. I didn't have time to worry about Luster any more. I had a family to care for, a wife who needed me, bills to pay, and a career I needed to get back on track.

When we got back to Hawaii, life began to get back to normal. Now that all of the craziness had died down, I realised I had to renew my driver's licence. I don't have really good vision but I refuse to wear reading glasses. In an effort to prepare for the eye exam I asked Baby Lyssa to find eye charts on the Internet. They all start with the same letters: E-P-S-M. I memorised each of the charts so I knew I would pass.

'Thank you, Lord. I don't want to be bothering You with something like my driver's licence, but I am so grateful for your blessings.' I gave thanks to God as I so often do.

Just then I heard a voice. It said, 'You are on My mission. You are doing My work. If you don't know this, you will die when your mission is done. If you are to live, you must know in your heart that I am with you.'

Now, I have conversations with God all the time. But this was the first time He spoke to me about the importance of my mission. I thought about what God said as I walked to the window to pick up my new driver's licence. As usual, His words came just in time. I was frustrated and disappointed by the judge's decision refusing to pay me for capturing Luster.

The woman behind the glass panel looked confused. 'Would you look at that!' She was staring at my licence, 50911007. The numbers were amazing:

50, five-o, as in *Hawaii Five-O*
911, nine-one-one, as in police emergency
007, double-o-seven, as in Bond, James Bond. Or Bail Bond.

The Lord showed me He walked beside me that day.

A week later I was in the police station booking a prisoner I'd captured. The lieutenant looked at my licence. 'This is a bunch of bull.' He gave me the stink-eye, thinking I was trying to pass off a fake ID. 'What are they doing down there at motor vehicles?'

I looked the lieutenant straight in the eye. 'It was the luck of the draw, brotha.' But I knew it was more than that. I'm on God's mission.

# CHAPTER FIFTY-THREE

# My Wedding Day

One day in early 2006, Gary and Bonnie, my two youngest children and my only children with Beth, came to me and asked, 'Dad, are you married to Mom?'

I'm not the kind of dad who lies to his children, but when the kids asked me if Beth and I were married, I said, 'Yes.' In my mind, I thought of us as married.

Then they asked Beth.

To my surprise, she said, 'No.' She was always quick to point out that Hawaii doesn't honour common-law marriage. Even though she had told lots of people over the years that we were married, and this would be a second wedding for her, Beth wanted the real deal.

Uh oh. Here it comes.

'Dad, you lied to us. You're not married to Mom. All the kids in school want to know why our mom and dad aren't married.'

It didn't take me but a second to realise the kids were at an age when what other kids said had an impact on them. They'd watched our television show and could hear that Beth was only referred to as my 'life partner' or 'Dog's sidekick'. I realised that that description wasn't fair to anyone. In truth, I had asked Beth to marry me before, but I had never really meant it. I proposed to her several times during the course of our relationship, even when I was married to someone else. In my heart, though, I've always known Beth would be my forever wife.

My first real proposal came while we were in Vegas in the fall of 2005. I looked right into her eyes and said, 'All right. Let's do it. Will you marry me?'

Beth just laughed. 'Yeah, right. You're not going to do it.'

But she was wrong. I wanted to get married right there and then – well, sort of.

'Let's go right now,' I said. We had fifteen minutes to get our licence before the courthouse closed for the night. I knew we didn't really stand a chance of making it, but I thought I'd give it the old college try. If time wasn't a factor, I would have married her in a tacky Vegas chapel that night. To this day, Beth still isn't convinced I would have gone through with it. But I would have, because our little Bonnie Jo is the miracle that finally brought us together forever. I was in love with Beth. I loved all of my wives, but I never really fell *in* love with any of them.

I'd been married so many times, I didn't want a big wedding. More important, if things weren't going to work out, I couldn't afford another divorce. I genuinely thought Beth was satisfied with our arrangement. I'd vacillate between calling Beth my girlfriend and referring to her as my fiancée. She didn't like either one of those terms, because in both our minds, we were as good as married. After years of on-again off-again dating, we had finally settled into a real family life together. There were no other women, no distractions. It was just the kids and us.

I had procrastinated for fifteen years. Now that things were going really good, I thought the time was right. I could never think of Beth leaving me or me leaving her. We are so much a part of each other. If it did happen, I wouldn't do anything stupid, but I can say with great certainty that I would never get married again. Beth is my final hope, my last frontier. Our relationship is different than any other I've ever known. No other woman could put up with me. I come with a lot of baggage. And to be honest, any other guy would probably kill Beth!

Since that trip to Vegas, I kept telling Beth to pick a date. I was serious about getting married. When we began filming our third season of *Dog the Bounty Hunter,* the producers heard some discussion of a possible wedding. Beth was overwhelmed by her day-to-day responsibilities as a wife, mother, and reality television star, so her sister Melinda picked up the slack and helped her plan the wedding. Even if I wanted to, there was no way I could back out now!

The date was set for 20 May 2006. We decided to get married on the Big Island at the Hilton Waikoloa, where I was a speaker at a Tony Robbins seminar. That hotel meant a lot to me. Whenever I was going through rough times, I drove out to the Hilton for peace and serenity. I took Beth on many dates there too, so the place had a lot of significance for us. It was the perfect spot to commit ourselves to each other for the rest of our lives.

Beth wanted a traditional wedding, including seeing me in a tuxedo, which was never going to happen. She flew to Los Angeles to have her dress made. As for me? All I wanted to do was bounty hunt. The closer the wedding day got, the more I thought about ways to push it back. I didn't like all the fuss that was being made. I was grateful for Melinda's help, because she is one of the few people in the world who can keep Beth calm. I jokingly sang, 'Here Comes the Dog' to the tune of the wedding march to ease my nerves. It made everyone laugh.

Almost all of our family and friends flew to the Big Island for a weekend of fun and festivities. My eldest daughter, Barbara Katie, didn't come. She was having a hard time, fighting her own personal demons, trying to get straight and sober. I begged her to go into rehab so she could kick her drug habit, but she flat-out refused. She didn't want to be branded as 'Dog's daughter who went to rehab.'

Barbara and I had a very special relationship. When the doctors told me I had a baby girl, I was certain they had made a mistake. I was the type of guy who fathered boys. When she was born, I had just got back custody of Duane Lee and Leland. Zebadiah had died. Wes and J.R. were living in Utah with their mom. I was afraid I wouldn't know what to do with a little girl; all I knew was taking care of baby boys. When the nurses let me hold Barbara for the first time, though, I just melted. She went everywhere with me. She was an excellent student. In fact, she did so well in school that Neil Armstrong wrote her a letter telling her to keep up the good work. That made me very proud, because I was never good in school.

When Barbara was a teenager, I thought it was time to send her to live with her mom. A little girl transitioning into womanhood needs a female role model. I was a single dad who didn't know what to do with a young girl going through changes. Barbara was my first daughter.

I had just ended my marriage to Tawny, who wasn't the kind of inspiration I thought Barbara needed. I called her mother, Lyssa, and we both agreed Barbara would be better off living with her for a while. That's when everything changed. Barbara went from a straight-A student to doing drugs and getting pregnant with my grandson, Travis. Whenever she called for money, I sent whatever I could, but she never used it for things like diapers or food. The money usually went towards buying more drugs.

It broke my heart not to include Barbara in my wedding. What she needed was some tough love. I would have done anything to help her get sober. In fact, Little Travis came to live with Beth and me for a year before the wedding. I thought looking after him might free Barbara up to take care of herself. No such luck. Despite our efforts, she wouldn't straighten out. I decided not to send her a ticket to come share in our big day.

I woke up feeling really happy on the morning of the wedding. I kept saying out loud, 'I'm getting married today.' I said it with pride and love. Everything was great. That is, until I realised I was still asleep. I was dreaming. In my dream, I had a premonition that something happened to one of my kids. I saw paramedics trying to save a child. I couldn't tell which one.

'They're not going to make it. I'm so sorry.'

But then . . . 'Wait! We have a heartbeat. It's OK.'

I woke up feeling panicked and unsure of what just happened. I was so relieved it was all just a dream.

Beth got up hours before me. I hadn't heard a word from her since she crawled out of bed. Usually she snuggles with me. I had an inexplicable, unshakable feeling that my world was about to be rocked – and not because I was getting married.

Beth came into the bedroom terror-stricken.

'Duane. One of the kids has been badly hurt.' I will never forget the look on her face or the tone of her voice.

My mind flashed back to my dream. My first thought was it had to be one of the younger kids. 'Was it Gary?'

Beth was pale and so shaken. 'No. It's Barbara. Duane, she was in a very bad car accident last night.'

Tears were streaming down my cheeks. 'Not my Barbara. No. Please, Lord. Not my little girl.'

'She didn't make it.'

Whoosh. I have never felt such anger and pain wash over my body. I went crazy. I was screaming and yelling, 'They brought her back, Beth. I saw the paramedics. They said she was going to be fine.' Of course, Beth had no idea what I was talking about. 'They brought her back. I saw it with my own two eyes.' I was in total denial.

'Duane, they didn't bring her back. What are you talking about? You're not making any sense, honey. Barbara is gone.'

I wanted to go to Alaska. I was so mad at Barbara's mother for not watching over our daughter. I paced and paced until I finally locked myself in the bathroom and howled like a wolf. I screamed until my voice went hoarse and finally was completely gone. I was in agony. I couldn't handle the heartache. I didn't want anyone around me.

The camera crew from our show was there as usual and kept trying to get shots of me. 'No cameras. Don't you dare!' I wanted to rip the cameras out of their hands and smash them to the floor.

Looking back, I know they were only trying to do their job. Our show is very real, no scripts or second takes. What was happening was painful and private, but the cameras were part of what I signed up for when I agreed to let them follow me around for the sake of creating compelling television. Even so, I warned the guy not to lift the camera off the ground or I'd crush him.

I cried and cried. Saying over and over, 'Why didn't I bring her here? If only I had bought her a ticket, Barbara would still be alive.' I beat myself up for choosing to leave Barbara in Alaska.

Thankfully, our pastor, Tim Story, arrived to console me. He was in Hawaii to officiate at my wedding. And now, he would preside over my daughter's funeral. His infinite wisdom and guidance were the only reason I made it through that day. He reminded me of the importance of family and the Lord's great and mighty plan. Tim and I prayed. I needed to understand God's will – that on this day, of all days, my wedding day, He took my child.

'Lord, I know you have great power to giveth and taketh away. But why, Lord? Why today? Why Barbara? Why?' I kept asking the same questions over and over. It made no sense.

I wasn't convinced we should go through with the wedding. I had so many questions. I needed answers. I was very upset and distraught. And yes, I was angry.

I called my ex-wife Lyssa.

'I left my babies in your care. One was raped and now the other is dead. How did this happen? You're their mother.'

I began grilling Lyssa with questions I so desperately wanted answered: 'What drugs did Barbara die with in her blood? Who was the guy in the car? Do you even know who our daughter was with when she was killed?'

Reluctantly, she said, 'I'd like to say I didn't know.' Which told me she either knew the guy and fully understood he was bad news, or she was so out of it herself that she had no idea where Barbara was going or with whom. Either way, it wasn't good. The longer I spoke to Lyssa that morning, the angrier I became. I was mad at both her and Barbara for making such dumb decisions.

I stayed angry until the day of Barbara's funeral. Lyssa and I locked eyes. The Lord spoke to me and said, 'As bad as you're hurt, her pain is double. She doesn't have your strength. She won't make it if you don't love her.' I realised you can offer love, even when it's kindled by death.

After hearing the news, it took me a couple of hours to calm down. I called a family meeting with Beth and our children to discuss whether or not we should proceed with the wedding. Initially, the older boys expressed their concern about moving forward. I knew that God wouldn't kill one of my babies to keep me from marrying Beth. I often turn to the Old Testament when I am being challenged by God, and now I spoke to some Jewish friends who came to celebrate with us. They said it was in the Old Testament that no matter what happens, you have to go through with the wedding. In my gut, I knew it was God's will to go through with our plans.

I think it was what Barbara would have wanted too. As confirmation that I was right, Baby Lyssa turned to me and said, 'Dad, if Barbara were here, she'd want you to go ahead.' She was right. Barbara was Baby's hero, so she knew what Barbara would have wanted better than anyone. I never knew how deep Baby Lyssa's love for her sister was until that day.

I am the leader of our family. It was up to me to be strong, forge ahead, and set an example. I'm not sure we could have proceeded without all of my loved ones. We had each other to lean on. Tim Story told us there would be time to mourn. I had to put away all of my emotions about losing Barbara and be present in this moment. As hard as it would be for everyone, we would make it through the day.

I decided the wedding would go on as planned.

I got dressed in my white leather vest, a pair of Levi's, and my favourite black-and-white python boots. I wore white armbands and my favourite pair of black sunglasses. Tim Story and I rode up to the resort in a canoe, Elvis Presley-style. The two canoes pulled up on either side of the platform where the ceremony was to be held. There was a huge archway adorned with stargazer lilies and white roses. It took four people to hold it down because it was a terribly windy night.

Beth looked beautiful in her flowing ivory dress. I watched her as she navigated her way down the grand spiral staircase. This was Beth's big day, and I wanted it to be the happiest day of her life. I watched her come closer. She was carefully taking each step one at a time. Her dress was so huge, if the wind caught her just right or if she caught a heel in her train, she was going over the rail. I remember thinking, 'Don't fall!' Just what we needed – a trip to the hospital! I breathed a great big sigh of relief when she finally stood by my side. It had been such an emotional day. We couldn't believe we were actually getting married. I will never forget my wedding day, ever.

# CHAPTER FIFTY-FOUR

# Room for Two More

After Barbara died, Beth and I decided to raise her son Travis as our own. He is, after all, my grandson. From time to time, Barbara spoke to me about the boy's biological father – whose name is also Travis – but according to her, he didn't want anything to do with the baby. I had never met the father, so I had nothing to go on except what Barbara told me. I thought he hadn't taken any responsibility for the boy and had refused to acknowledge him or see him, which is something I simply could not understand.

Not long after Barbara's funeral in Denver, I received a call from Travis. He said he wanted to meet his child. I was pretty surprised to hear from him, because Barbara had painted a slightly different picture than the one he was presenting.

No way was I about to hand over my grandson to a young man I had never met. Beth and I were the legal guardians. We didn't have to allow Travis the opportunity, but he is the baby's daddy. I didn't care that other people warned me not to give him a chance. I'm Duane 'Dog' Chapman. I know first-hand what it feels like for a man to be denied the right to visit his children. I was in Travis's shoes more than once in my life. No one gave me the chance to prove I could be a good dad. LaFonda took Duane Lee and Leland from me. Ann took Wesley and J.R. I prayed it was the right thing to do, but my heart said Big Travis deserved a chance to prove he was worthy to be this boy's father.

I told him if he was serious about raising Travis, he needed to get on a plane and come to Hawaii for a while. I bought him a plane ticket and within days he was here to be with his son.

When I introduced the two of them it was nothing short of miraculous. At first, Big Travis was scared to be around his son. He didn't know how to be a dad. It reminded me of myself when Duane Lee was born. I explained to him that he had the instincts to be a great dad. He would know the right things to do the minute he held his son in his arms. Little Travis never knew he had a father. I brought him into our family room and said, 'Travis, this is your daddy.'

Little Travis looked up at Big Travis, who must have seemed like the jolly green giant to him because he is so tall, and said, 'Hi, my dad.' He reached towards his father. They touched and hugged. I cried tears of joy seeing this young man connect with his boy. It was a feeling I had craved and longed for, so many times in my life. I understood Travis's need for fulfilment.

Big Travis got a job at a local supermarket. He is a good man, trying to do right by his son. It has taken Little Travis some time to get used to the idea that he has a dad other than me. Until Big Travis showed up, I was the primary male figure in his young life, but his father has proved to me he is a stand-up guy who loves his kid very much. He has become part of our family. I consider him my son. There's always room for one more.

Not long ago, Little Travis asked to spend the night at his dad's house. This was the first time he ever asked to sleep away from our home. I jokingly told him I could whoop his daddy. The boy looked up at me and said, 'You might be able to whoop my daddy, but he's taller than you!' I had to laugh. He was right. I knew the time had come to let my grandson go home. There's no replacing the love a child gets from his real dad – not even a grandpa's love.

# CHAPTER FIFTY-FIVE

# Second Chances

Reality television is a tough gig. Our A&E show made its official debut in 2003. I am extremely proud to say it has become the number-one-rated show on the network. Everything you see on *Dog the Bounty Hunter* is pure. It is not staged or acted in any way. There are no scripts or story lines, just real captures of actual fugitives. No one comes up with my lines or gives me a second chance to catch a target on the run. It has been a bit of a transition going from bounty hunter to television entertainer, but my job description is still pretty much the same: get the guy.

If I make a mistake bounty hunting, it can cost me my freedom. I could go to jail for doing the wrong thing – with no Get Out of Jail Free card. Also, I have to try to make sure the people I bond are worthy of my trust. Over the years, I've developed an innate sense of who will or won't run. Still, some do. Lucky for me, my television show is predicated on fugitives.

If I only wrote safe bonds, I'd have no career and definitely no TV show. I am not involved in the day-to-day production of the show, but I do come up with themes based on the bounties I'm hunting. My primary role is to just be Dog and do my thing. I never watch the show, because I already know the outcome. Our show is unique, because it captures both sides of my life. We are a family business, so viewers get to meet my wife and children. They get a rare view inside both lives I lead, Duane and Dog. Duane is the soft, sensitive, God-loving family man. Dog, well, he's the guy who's gonna hunt you down.

When I first started doing other television shows, before I had my own, producers wanted me to do things that weren't natural. They'd ask me to fight with a guy or jump off a roof to tackle someone. They wanted more action, more blood. I know how to taunt someone to engage in a good fight, but the truth is, that's not how I work. I wanted my show to be *real* reality television. I'm like a football player who knows just how hard to hit without really hurting my opponent . . . unless I absolutely have to. At the end of the day, it's the hunt I love. I don't need any of that phony crap.

I'm extremely proud that we include our faith in the show. If people come closer to God as a result, we will have served the Lord. Joel Osteen, one of the most respected television evangelists in the world, doesn't have as big an audience as *Dog the Bounty Hunter.* The Lord doesn't care who spreads His word. He wants to reach everyone, so it makes sense that He would use a guy like me to reach a wider audience. *Dog the Bounty Hunter* is now syndicated in a dozen countries all around the world, including places like Russia, the Netherlands, New Zealand, Australia, and the United Kingdom. I dreamed about someday having my own television series that would reach millions of viewers each week, and now it has finally happened.

The first time I met Tony Robbins, in 1981, he told me to go out there and be the absolute best man I could be. And then he said, be better than you already think you are. Do something better than anyone else in the world and you will succeed. Set new standards and leap forward to break records that can never be challenged by someone else. And when you do that, give it one more final push. Add faith to that equation, and you have a foolproof formula for guaranteed success.

One fun aspect of having my hit show was to be spoofed on *South Park.* You know you've really made it when they include you in their show. I loved Cartman being Dog the Hall Monitor, and if you've seen the episode, you know their depiction of Beth was classic. She was featured as a big cartoon circle, with two huge boobs. All you could see were tiny little eyes sticking out above her cleavage. Our whole family laughed when we saw the show.

On the other hand, due to the popularity of the show, my bail business is down significantly, because people know I'll come for them if they run, and I'll bring my television cameras. It won't be a private event if Dog catches you. In fact, my competitors in the business use that fact as a tactic to keep clients away from us.

Another change for me since *Dog the Bounty Hunter* began to air is that I can't screw girls for information any more. I can't say I really miss that part . . . OK, maybe just a little. But the truth is, it used to an easy way to infiltrate circles of the friends and family of someone I was looking for. With my new-found notoriety, I am forced to be more creative in turning up clues. I have been blessed with the gift of discernment, which means I have the ability to read people pretty accurately. If I'm going to spend more than five minutes with someone, I soak up everything I can about who they are, where they come from, their actions, movements, the way they speak, anything I can use to create a full picture of who that person really is. I can tell if someone is as gentle as a dove or harmless like a wise serpent. I'm rarely wrong.

Fifteen years ago, I met a ninety-eight-year-old man sitting in my dentist's waiting room. I asked him his secret to longevity. He said the reason he lived to be so old was because he spent his entire life honouring his father and mother. He turned and asked me, 'Do you honour your father and mother?' I said I did. And then I proceeded to tell him how my dad used to beat on me when I was a little boy. I told him I used to ride my motorcycle and pray to God that Flash would die. I hated him for years for what he'd done. But after I found out about Flash's abuse, I told the old man, I didn't hold it against him any more. Of course, I spoke of my mom with loving-kindness. As the nurse called me into the dentist's office, the old man turned to me and said, 'Honour your mother and father, Duane, and thou shalt have a long life.' I asked the dentist who the old man was in the waiting room. He said there was no one sitting out there but me.

That experience has led me to help my clients understand that they have to honour their mothers and fathers too. All parents just want what is best for their children. I see it every day when parents come to us because they are tired of their kid being on dope and in and out of jail. They know Beth and I are their last hope, because we talk to them in a way no one else does. We make our clients check in daily and force them to try and clean up their act. We are willing to give anyone a second chance. Without second chances, Beth and I would be two unknown citizens just trying to get by. We understand the value of tough love and forgiveness. That is why we keep doing what we do. We want to effect positive change in the lives of these young kids who have fallen away from their righteous path. So far, we've been doing pretty well.

Sometimes I take chances and they really pay off. Wesley, who works in our Da Kine Bail Bonds office, is one of my great success stories. Several years ago, he was busted for stealing industrial soap from his janitorial job. He'd sell the extra gallons for a few bucks to support a bad gambling habit. His small bets eventually caught up to him. Before he knew it, he was in way over his head, owing more than seven grand to his bookie. The more he owed, the more he stole. He finally got caught and was sent to jail. The court set his bail at five thousand dollars.

Wesley spent a week in jail before I posted his bond. A person arrested for a first offence is usually out in a couple of days, but Wesley's girlfriend refused to post bail. She wanted to teach him a lesson. I don't think she understood what it feels like to have your freedom taken away. Even after Beth and I tried to explain what it means to lose your liberties, she still refused. This made me mad as hell. Wesley didn't belong in jail.

Beth and I decided to help get him out, but I had to go away for a few days. Beth told him we'd post his bail if he could get us some extra business from other guys inside. He hustled up some more bonds for us. A few small ones and one big one – Jack Gibbs, who needed to post a twenty-thousand-dollar bond.

Beth saw this as an opportunity to make a little extra money, so she bailed Gibbs out. At this point, she was eight and a half months pregnant with our son Gary Boy, so she had trouble getting around. Jack told Beth he had the whole twenty grand in cash at his bank. All she had to do was take him down there, and he'd give her the full amount. She didn't understand why he wanted to give her the extra money. Gibbs explained he wanted to post bail for a few friends who were inside, especially Wesley, because he'd been so helpful to him. Beth questioned whether Gibbs had enough money to do an all-cash collateral. He said he did, and sure enough, he handed over twenty thousand dollars to get four or five of his buddies out. The good news was that two of the guys jumped bail. I caught them both and got to keep all the money for the bounty, as well as getting my expenses paid.

To be clear, someone like Jack Gibbs is a one in a million case for me. Unfortunately, he also failed to appear in court, which meant he was once again a wanted man. I didn't want to hunt him down, so I let the cops find him.

The silver lining was that Wesley began helping me around the office. He began running errands for us all the time. He followed Beth around and started to learn our business. There's no better teacher for bail bonds than Beth. The court clerks often see Beth as Cruella De Vil, so Wesley balances her abrasive nature with his soft-spoken, polite ways of getting things done. He can charm anyone for anything we need at the courts. I see a little bit of myself in Wesley. He's someone who was headed down the wrong path and has made great strides towards straightening out his life. It makes me proud to know that giving him that second chance paid off for everyone.

# CHAPTER FIFTY-SIX

# Federal Marshals

The impact of what happened in Mexico was hard on the entire family. But after nearly three years, we had got back to living life as usual.

That is, until the morning of 14 September 2006.

Beth gets up early in the morning to get the younger kids ready for school. Summer vacation was over. The kids were just starting to get back into their regular routine. We had been filming the television show all week. I had made a bust the night before, so I was trying to sleep in. Beth was awake but still lying in bed when she thought she heard a car door close. It was five-thirty in the morning, so she dismissed it, thinking it had to be one of the kids milling around. Then she thought she heard people whispering and rustling about, outside the sliding glass door of our bedroom. We live in a single-story U-shaped house. There's a pool and a large cement patio in the backyard, which is flanked on every side by our home. There are large glass sliding doors from every room leading to the lanai. The sound carries and echoes inside that U. If someone is outside, we can generally hear every word they say.

I could feel Beth move close to me and snuggle up like she does every morning. She kisses me from my shoulders to my ears, nuzzling and holding me close before she gets out of bed. I watched her as she put her robe on, something she hardly ever does. She's usually in a G-string for the first ten or fifteen minutes. I love watching her move in the morning sun that creeps in through our bedroom window. She always looks sexy to me in that light.

Beth slid open the glass doors from our bedroom and stepped outside to take in the gorgeous Hawaiian sunrise. I just drifted off back to sleep.

Baby Lyssa helps get the younger kids ready for school in the mornings. She was up too.

'Beth, Beth! There are men outside! Beth!' Lyssa was hysterically screaming as she came running into the kitchen. 'There are strange men in the house!'

Beth grabbed all of the kids. 'What do you mean there's men in the house, Lyssa? *Inside* the house? What the hell do you mean?' Beth always puts her warrior armour on when she senses we are about to come under attack.

'They're cops, Beth. I swear.'

'They're not cops.' Beth and Lyssa often disagree about things, but this morning was not the time to doubt each other.

*Clunk! Clunk!* Just then, the double front doors were kicked open and a whole pack of SWAT guys invaded our home.

Beth came running out of the kitchen yelling, 'Stop! Stop!' She tried to block the front door to prevent anyone from coming in, but it was too late. I could faintly hear her from the bedroom, but I had no idea what was really happening. I just thought Beth was yelling at one of the kids.

'We're here for . . . ' It wasn't just local cops. They were U.S. Marshals and men from the Sheriff's Department!

'For who? What are you here for?' Beth yelled to Baby Lyssa to get television cameras to the house as fast as she could. Lyssa raced into the kitchen to call our crew from the A&E show to come down and film the whole event. Beth wanted this all documented on tape.

'There will be no cameras!' one of the marshals announced.

'You're not going to tell me there'll be no cameras in my own house! Lyssa! Get the cameras here . . . *now*!'

The crew lived in a production house about twenty minutes away. There was no way they'd make it, but Beth wanted the marshals to believe they were already on their way. The threat of filming the arrest was not something they wanted to deal with. They began to rush the process to get me out of there before the crew showed up.

'Ma'am, we've got a warrant for—'

'For what?'

'For the Mexico case . . . it's a warrant for Duane Chapman for kidnapping.'

'Duane was never charged with kidnapping. This isn't right. They just called us a few days ago and said the warrant was expiring.'

The officers and SWAT team kept pouring into the house. They started breaking off into teams, surrounding every room from inside as well as outside the home.

Now, I'm going to tell you something no one really knows about this old Dog. I'm a pretty vain guy. No one sees me in the morning except my family. I never leave the house without taking a shower and making sure I look just right. I'm a clean-freak. My clothes have to be perfectly pressed and crisp and my hair has to be done. The last time anyone saw this Dog looking less than perfect was three years ago, when I got back to the States from Mexico. Beth knows this about me, so she pleaded with the officers not to bust into the bedroom.

'Please let me wake him up so he doesn't have a heart attack when he sees all you guys.' Beth was genuinely worried about my health. I'm a fifty-three-year-old man who's been through a lot in my life. I was still having horrible nightmares about Mexico, so Beth knew a shock like this might actually give me a heart attack. But, she also knew I would have been humiliated to have anyone see me first thing in the morning, especially my fellow law enforcement people.

The marshals followed Beth into the bedroom, stopping at the door, which they insisted she leave open as she woke me. I heard the door crack open, but still I had no idea what was going on.

Beth stood next to the bed. Quietly she said, 'Duane. Wake up.' I jumped right up. I thought something happened to one of the kids. The last time Beth woke me like that was the morning Barbara died. I had that same feeling when I saw Beth at the side of the bed again. She only wakes me when it's bad news. My heart ached waiting to hear which kid was gone now. I was terrified.

'Duane, honey. Wake up.'

'What's the matter?' I jumped up but was still half-asleep.

'The marshals are here to arrest you for Mexico.'

All I could say was, 'No. No. No . . . ' Even in my disbelief of what was happening, I was relieved none of my children were gone.

Before I could gather my thoughts, the marshals surrounded the bed with their guns drawn. I froze in fear. I could see some of the guys smirking at me. For a second I actually thought I was being *Punk'd*. We had been asked to do the MTV show, but I didn't want to be part of it. I was afraid of coming off dumb or losing my temper in front of the cameras, so Beth and I decided to decline the opportunity. But I kept hearing Beth scream, 'Where are the cameras?' A couple of the guys were smiling just a little too big to be for real. One even apologised. That's when I thought for sure I was being *Punk'd*.

'OK, you all got me. Good one. Great. Nice try. Let's stop this now.' I thought I'd play along, you know, let them see I was in on the joke.

But this wasn't a joke. It was real. Very real. I read the situation all wrong. Two of the marshals looked as confused as I felt.

'This ain't no joke, brother. This is real.'

'This can't be real. It's a damn misdemeanour, man. What are you doing here?' I could now see it in the marshals' eyes. They were taking down the Dog. Yeah. They were happy as hell to be there.

They had a valid warrant for my arrest, but no search warrant. Just the paperwork to take me in. My first inclination was to run. Jump. Go out the back door, down the street towards the beach, and run like the wind. I am innocent. I know not everyone who bolts is guilty. Some are overwhelmed by the system, others are just plain scared. The warrant expired in twenty-six days. I actually believed I could have made it if I tried.

I was worried about Leland and Tim, too, because I knew they were probably going through the same thing that morning.

I was half-dressed, wearing only an old pair of jeans. I have trouble with my stomach in the morning too. It takes me a solid forty-five minutes to get myself together. I can barely move my hands in the morning from all the years of boxing, and now I had handcuffs around my wrists!

'Beth, get my wedding ring. I want my ring, baby.'

One of the sheriffs turned to me and said, 'You ain't gonna need that where you're going, Dog.'

'I need a cigarette, man. Can I have a smoke?'

'This isn't your damn show, man. You ain't gettin' a smoke. You ain't gettin' shit.'

Beth told me she'd rather keep the ring because she worried I might never get it back. I wore a gold band around my thumb the entire time I was hunting Luster in Mexico. Beth had an identical ring with diamonds all the way around it. I liked knowing we both wore our rings while I was gone. It made me feel connected even though I was thousands of miles away. After I was arrested, someone stole that ring. I know who it was and he knows he did it. I hope he reads this and returns it anonymously. Someday I will retrieve it from him.

I thought about the news crew from NBC who had just come to shoot some footage of me a few weeks earlier. One of the guys told me they had gone out with twelve federal marshals to get some footage of them capturing fugitives. They got nothing. Zero captures. He said that the entire time they were on the hunt, all the marshals kept talking about me, like they were jealous, envious. That was the first time I connected jealousy and envy. It's a lethal combination when it comes to judging a guy like me. These marshals looked at me with utter disgust and pure anger. I could feel their hatred, even if I didn't understand it.

They took hold of me by the arms and began dragging me from the bedroom through the house towards the front door. My little son, Gary Boy, stood with his hands over his ears screaming as he watched his daddy being brought around the corner in handcuffs by several scary men with guns.

'Beth. Get Gary Boy. I don't want him to see me like this.' I tried to protect my son, but it was too late. He was already traumatised, and Beth's attention was on watching me go out the door. By now Cecily was awake. She grabbed Gary Boy and tried her best to hug and console him. Bonnie Jo came out just as I left her line of sight. Thank God she never saw me in handcuffs. In their eyes, Daddy's a superhero. Daddy's not a lawbreaker. He's the guy who handcuffs the bad guys; seeing me in handcuffs confused them.

One of the marshals kept asking me if I knew where Leland was at. He was either taunting me or trying to find my son. Either way, I wasn't answering. I'd never give up one of my children to the cops.

Baby Lyssa put a lit cigarette in my mouth as I walked down the driveway. I was able to get three or four drags off of it before one of the cops tossed it in the bushes.

'Where's Leland?'

Beth was screaming, 'Find him yourself.'

Beth was right behind us as they shoved me in the back of the black SUV.

'You'll see your day in court, you motherfucker.' Beth was still yelling as we drove away. She was wild and angry. They had her man. Beth doesn't take too kindly to anyone who wants to hurt me or any member of our family.

She tried to reach Leland and Tim on their cells, but they never answer their phones. Ever. She finally got Tim's wife, Davina, to answer the phone. 'Why don't you answer your damn phone?' Beth was screaming at Davina. 'They're coming, Davina. They're coming for Tim.'

'They just split open our sliding glass doors and came into our house while we were sleeping. I was naked, Beth. It was horrible. They surrounded the bed like we were criminals.' Davina wept as she told Beth what happened. Beth later told me she could hear Tim screaming in the background. He's not one to go down without putting up a solid fight.

Beth sent Tucker up the street on his moped to wake Leland. She wanted to get to him before the cops did. Tucker took off as fast as he could.

Beth finally got Leland on the phone. 'They don't know where you are, Leland.'

He threatened to run. Beth talked him down. The first instinct is always to run but it's not the best way to go.

'Don't run. Don't run. Just stop. Stay where you are. Just don't call anyone. Get off your cell phone right now. Call me from the landline, got it?'

Beth knew from our own experiences bounty hunting that cell phones are easy to trace. It's called *pinging*. The authorities can get a cell phone number a lot faster than they can track a current address. Since the television show and because of the inherent danger in what we do as bounty hunters, all of us are unlisted in the phone book. I'd later find out they got our address from a traffic ticket issued to me a few months earlier. Without that information, they never would have found me. In fact, they went to our old house first. They broke into the wrong house looking for me that morning.

When all of the arrests took place, we were in the middle of our third season of our A&E show. By now the cops knew we didn't carry weapons. We weren't armed and dangerous criminals. We're a family that works together to help defend the law. Who did they think they were arresting? Kidnappers? What a joke.

On the way to jail the marshals told me they knew where Leland was – they said they found his truck. They asked me if I wanted to go there first so I could be with Leland when they picked him up.

Leland is a fighter. I think they thought he'd put up less of a fight if he knew they already had his daddy. They were right. Leland came out without any fuss.

# CHAPTER FIFTY-SEVEN

# From Misdemeanour to Felony

By now, our A&E crew was filming everything they could get to and feeding the footage to the newswires. Beth dove right into her Rolodex and began working the phones to make sure the entire world knew what was happening. She has a pink notebook where she keeps all the names of her contacts at CNN, NBC, ABC, CBS, MSNBC, AP, Fox, *Dateline*, 20/20, and *Larry King Live*. You name the show, and she's got a contact. They all love Dog the Bounty Hunter stories. Beth pulled two phones on to the patio and began making her calls. She had a production assistant from the show dialling as fast as Beth could talk. We have a lot of friends in the media, but one of the kindest has always been Rita Cosby. Within fifteen minutes of hearing from Beth, there was a scroll running along the bottom of MSNBC. Shortly after that, Rita broke the story live with Beth over the phone.

'Hi, Beth. We're live on the air. Tell us what has happened to Dog.' Rita set Beth up for the kill.

'The Dog has been arrested. Armed federal marshals just burst into our house and took him. It was horrible, Rita. Duane's no criminal.'

Twenty minutes after that interview one of the marshals came to my holding cell. I already knew by the look on this poor bastard's face why he was there.

'Get your damn wife on the phone and tell her to stop talking to the media.' It was the exact thing they did to me in Mexico when Beth worked the press.

Note to everyone: you do not want the wrath of my Beth when she's pissed.

I took a deep breath and called Beth, knowing damn well it wouldn't make a difference. 'Honey, I'm in jail. You can't talk to the press. Honey, please promise me you won't do any more interviews.' I pleaded with her, almost convincing myself I meant what I was saying. But I knew Beth understood they forced me to make that call.

'I'm sorry, Duane. I'm sorry, baby. Don't worry, honey. It's gonna be fine. I swear.' Beth told me what the cops wanted to hear. The truth is, I wanted to hear that everything would be all right too. I don't like negativity. I thought this was all behind me. I didn't want to be in jail again. I wanted to be home with my family. Deep down, I know Beth was as scared as me, but this time she never let it show. We both hold on to our faith and believe the Lord will deliver us from whatever situation we're in.

Sometimes I don't have enough faith and Beth might not have enough faith, but together, between the two of us, we've got enough for that mustard seed.

The cop who let me make the call to Beth turned his back for a minute.

I whispered in the phone, 'Blast 'em, honey. Do you hear me? Get me outta here. Blast the news and get me outta here.'

From years of experience, we understood that cops can't behave badly when the media is watching. And all eyes were on the Dog.

The marshals made a lot of mistakes that day, but the biggest one by far was not arresting Beth. If they had taken her out of the picture, she would never have got the national spotlight shining on my arrest the way she did. It was pure genius on her part. I am sure the government was pretty pissed off to hear Beth giving interviews within an hour of the arrest. She had unadulterated, truthful knowledge of the case and was able to spin opinions before anyone else got out there. She worked the press like a pro. If Beth had been taken out of the picture, the government would have been successful in doing their dirty business any way they wanted to.

That's my Bethy. God, I love that woman.

Beth called our lawyers, congressmen, and local lobbyists. Something didn't smell right. How could I have been taken in on kidnapping charges, a felony, when the Mexican government had only charged me with deprivation of liberty, which is a misdemeanour? It wasn't something the United States government would ever extradite a citizen for. It didn't make sense.

At some point that day, Beth called a local bondsman and my number-one competitor, James Lindblant, to tell him I had been taken into custody. We weren't sure if there would be bail or not, but she wanted to be prepared to get me out. Beth told him I was being held in the

Federal Detention Center, in the bottom of the Federal courthouse in Honolulu. The holding cell (also called a shoe) was small, like the size of a closet. It was an outrage. They treated me like Hannibal Lecter, but worse. One of the lieutenants came into the shoe, cuffed me, walked me twenty steps, and told me to get naked. Next, he said, 'Bend over.'

Leland and Tim were by themselves in separate cells somewhere nearby. Because of Beth's outreach to the media, the boys and I had to be treated with respect. They couldn't beat us or put us in cells pretending nothing was happening. Once the public knew what was going on, the uprising began.

Later that day, the same lieutenant came back to talk to me. He sat me down and said, 'I'm sorry this is happening to you, Dog.'

'I appreciate that, brother.' I felt like one of the guys I talk to on my show. This lieutenant was giving me the 'Dog speech'.

'Dog, this is all going to work out. It's politics.' He encouraged me not to do anything stupid, like attempt to run or try to kill myself. He intimated that the warden was afraid of me. That's why the warden ordered the lieutenant to act the way he did. I appreciated his words, but I was still mad as hell because I was treated so inhumanely.

The U.S. Marshals started coming under attack almost immediately after the story broke. The media wanted to know why I was being charged with kidnapping when the charge was deprivation of liberty. Ron Johnson and the federal prosecutor's office also began to feel the heat, as well as the judge who signed the warrant. The concerned public, fans and nonfans alike, began calling radio stations and talk shows to express their outrage. Geraldo Rivera called to see if there was anything he could do to help. Donny Deutsch called to offer his assistance. Sharon Osbourne called from England to tell Beth that Ozzie was issuing a statement to the press in support. I could see the marshals were reeling from the fallout.

The media surrounded our home, the courthouse, everywhere they could to make sure they got the story as it was unfolding. It was like Diamond Head was erupting all over Hawaii.

Duane Lee got to the house later that afternoon. He was devastated by the thought of his dad being in jail again. At twenty-eight years of age, he was watching his father go back to jail for a crime he didn't commit. Duane Lee was five years old when he watched me get hauled off for first-degree murder. He was that little boy with his hands over his ears, the same age then as my Gary Boy now. My two sons will forever have that in common. It breaks my heart to think of any of my children being in pain. A child shouldn't have to witness a parent being carted away in handcuffs like an animal.

One thing I've learned over the years is that when you're in jail in a good ol' boy state, you've gotta call a good ol' boy to get you out. That meant calling my lawyer, Brook Hart.

The law is very specific about setting bail in my situation. The bottom line is, there is no bail for a fugitive wanted on kidnapping charges. The only way I could get out was to prove special circumstances, which is a phenomenally tough job, if you can do it at all. Brook never wavered. He went to the hearing the next day and did the good ol' boy thing with the judge, practically winning him over on the spot. They agreed to process the request, which would set me free while all of this mess got straightened out. Brook came to my cell to give me the good news.

'Dog, it's going to be two to three weeks before we get a hearing, but I think you'll be able to get out after that.'

I grabbed the screen separating Brook and me and said, 'You're fired.'

He looked stunned. I'm guessing he thought he was delivering good news when he said I'd be spending two or three weeks in a federal facility.

'Get me the hell outta here. I'm not waiting a couple of weeks.'

In all fairness, Brook didn't have time to prepare a 'special circumstances' case in the few hours he had before appearing in court the first day. He had no trouble figuring it out for the hearing the following day. Carl Smith was there from the law offices of Carl Smith Ball, because James Blancarte was still flying to Hawaii. I had a powerful legal team assembled within hours. Across the table, fighting on behalf of the government, was Ron Johnson. My team successfully argued that Leland, Tim, and I had no place to go. We couldn't run, we couldn't hide. They argued that as a television personality, I was too high-profile, which meant I wasn't a flight risk. The lawyers did everything they could to get me out. Somehow, they got the judge to agree. After a day and a half, I was out of jail.

As of the writing of this book, my case still hasn't been resolved. This issue looms over my head every single day. I cannot express how disappointing it has been that the United States and Mexican government can't seem to forgive the 'crime' of finding Andrew Luster. Until this case is resolved, I remain unsettled and fearful about my future, not to mention weary of the whole shameful process. I can only hope and pray the Lord has a plan.

# CHAPTER FIFTY-EIGHT

# A Final Thought

After writing this book, I got to thinking about all of the crazy stuff that's happened in my fifty-three years of living. I wondered how my obituary might read if I bit the dust, hit the dirt, keeled over tomorrow. Would I be remembered as badass biker, a convicted felon, or a murderer? Would my good deeds and pursuit of justice and freedom define me? All my life, I have felt like a leader, someone setting new standards, and someone who is not afraid to break traditional rules. Everything that has been taken from me in my life, God has given me back three times over. I cannot dwell on that which is missing, because I have truly been blessed by God in every way.

I don't think everyone I pick up is a bad person or a career criminal. In fact, most of the people I go after these days are just making bad choices in their lives. It's degrading and humiliating to be caught for a crime, so I try to treat these people with dignity if it might help them see their life in a new way. Being kind helps me affect positive change, which is truly my motivation for being out there in the first place. Where mercy is shown, mercy is given.

I am emotionally impacted by every capture. On one hand, the experience is still exhilarating. I still get the same thrill out of a chase that I did the first time I caught a bounty. My adrenaline gets pumping and my heart still races with excitement every single time. The hardest part of my job comes a few hours after I make the bust. Once I calm down, I begin to think about the people I caught. I feel terrible having to put them in jail. I cry for their pain, families, and future because I know first-hand they will be destined for failure if they don't make some life-altering choices when they get out.

Several years ago, I went to a house in Denver to pick up a fugitive. When I met his parents, I could see the pain in their eyes because their son was no longer recognisable to them. He had become an angry and abusive drug addict. As I stood listening to his mother talk about her boy, I was reminded of my own childhood. That was the first time I realised how I must have crushed my parents with the choices I made as a young man.

I looked around the house and noticed there was nothing of value in sight. Anything that could have been hocked was bolted down or hidden behind a large padlocked door. My heart ached for their pain. The boy's mother grabbed my hand, looked into my tear-filled eyes, and said something I'll never forget:

'Please, Dog, go get him. Save him.'

Every criminal leaves behind a path of destruction. Carrying their pain in my heart makes me the Dog. I am the voice of those who fear they cannot change their lives for the better, because you must trust me when I say, you can. It's not the size of the dog in the fight, it's the fight in the dog. I am living proof that with unshakable faith and God's love, anything is possible.

I usually tell people that bounty hunting is what I do best, but the truth is, I am the greatest criminal who ever lived. I took my conviction and turned it into something good by becoming a defender of the law instead of an offender. I am reminded of the old Indian woman who told me I would someday lead millions. At the time, I knew she saw something I couldn't comprehend. But my Indian heritage guided me towards becoming the leader of some kind of tribe. So it makes sense that I have become the President (or Chief) of the Convicts in this world. It hurts me to make such an admission, but the truth is, it's who I really am. I can't walk in their leg irons any more, but I can serve them as their leader, hoping they want to follow in my footprints down the road to redemption. I have to live my life as an example of what one of the 'good guys' really looks, lives, and loves like so that everyone believes they can have a better life.

A lot of people ask me why I am so compassionate when I capture fugitives. The reason is pretty simple. I've been in the system. I know what it feels like to be mistreated and disrespected. I've been that person. I understand how hard it is to get off drugs and to stop living like a crook.

To this very day, even as I continue to fight the law for my rights as a United States citizen, as I look down the barrel of doing four years in a Mexican prison on trumped-up charges that are blatantly false, I haven't lost hope for the American judicial system. The belief that I committed an extraditable crime by capturing Andrew Luster is simply wrong. That September morning I was arrested by federal marshals, I was picked up on a bad warrant. It stated I was wanted for kidnapping, which is totally outrageous. The charge against me in Mexico was deprivation of liberty, a misdemeanour and non-extraditable offence. Why this issue has failed to resolve itself is far beyond my comprehension.

One thing I know for sure.

I am a man on a mission. There will be many more turbulent days in my future. Despite that, I will continue to forge ahead and capture many more people who commit crimes against women and children. I will carry on my mission to defend truth, justice, and the American way. I will maintain my dignity to keep serving the Lord.

Every heartache, every setback, and every moment of truth I have faced, I have done so for you. I want everyone to understand that no matter what your circumstances are, you have the power, the strength, and the courage to persevere. I wrote this book as an inspiration for you to know that if I can turn my life around, so can you. I am the poster child for rehabilitation. Even when people still continue to lie about me, saying I conspired to kidnap someone, I'm still faithful to the end because I know the Lord has put me on this mission – a mission I will remain on until I take my last breath.

May God bless you all.

# Acknowledgments

I have so many people to thank for so many things in my life. However, I'm going to keep it simple by thanking only those who directly helped me write this book, which allowed me to tell the story I've wanted to share for so many years. There will be other opportunities for me to thank all the others in my life to whom I owe so much and who have touched me deeply.

I first must thank my wife, Beth, for her insight and intelligence in seeing that there is better in me than others expect. I'm no angel for sure, but I'm trying my best to help people understand who I am by educating them about my past. We all have a past that affects our present and knowing your brother, your neighbour, your boss, will help you love him or her for who they are. Beth, I love you for all you do to protect me and to help make my dreams come true. You are the yin to my yang and the love of my life and my true soul mate.

I want to thank my manager and literary agent, Alan Nevins, who stepped into my life the day before I was arrested in Hawaii by U.S. Marshals. I don't think he knew what hit him that first morning he awoke to Beth crying on the phone at the crack of dawn. He thought it would be all champagne and flowers that day, and it's been a huge undertaking ever since. He's put enormous energy and hours into this book dealing with every aspect you can imagine, albeit some from a hotel room overlooking Diamond Head in Waikiki. I know he's aware how appreciative Beth and I are for him stepping into our chaotic lives. I've grown to love him and his dry humour, which keeps Beth occupied so I can relax. We wouldn't move three feet without him today. And that goes for his colleagues at The Firm, both Mindy Stone who helped clear photos and Robert Choi, whose days we keep busy by keeping Alan with us.

Laura Morton, one of my new-found friends. The one thing I needed to do if this book was going to get written was not sit on it forever. Laura stepped right in and took control and helped me write a book that made me cry the first time I picked up the pages to read them. She organised my many hours of rambling stories and Beth's notes into a coherent story, and it turned out to be the story I wanted to tell. She worked under pressures no one can imagine, although she had even better views and beaches than Alan, as she lived with us here on our island paradise that I love so much. I will be forever thankful for her patience, her hard work, and her understanding. I also need to thank Laura's colleague, Adam, who helped divide and conquer so we could tell the story twice as fast.

I also want to thank my publisher, Robert Miller, who is obviously a highly intelligent man since he bought my book and I didn't have to chase him. He surrendered immediately. He's been a gentleman in all senses of the word and gave me the words of encouragement that allowed me to tell the story I wanted to tell. He and my wonderfully patient editor, Zareen Jaffery, were hugely helpful in that they understood our needs and allowed me and Beth to vent when appropriate. They listened, they understood, and they gave us the time and room we needed and I am deeply grateful to them both for their help. I know there are many others at Hyperion who I've not met yet at the time I write this but who have also spent countless hours helping me create my book. I thank you all and hope to meet each of you personally, especially the attorneys, who had much work on their hands.

I also want to take the time to thank those people at the production company who work around me and my team on a daily basis, including my team, Jason Hedrich and Phillipino Roy, along with my producer, Lucas Platt. It is their work that allows me the opportunity to reach out into the world and touch people. It's that exposure that gave me the ability to even write a book that someone might want to read.

I specifically want to shout out to David Houts, my executive producer. Despite my trouble with Mexico and the ensuing production problems that have delayed our shoots, they made space in my life, at their cost, so I could write this book. They allowed me days off and travel when I should have been working. They allowed Beth to be sidetracked by research and legal for the book while we were hunting and shooting shows, and they even allowed Laura and Alan to ride along and participate on our hunts – something very few people have been privy to.

There are many people at A&E who need to be thanked for the show but, in regards to the book, I also want to thank Neil Cohen, the executive at the network who oversees our show. They were probably breathing down Neil's neck constantly but had the class never to suggest directly to me that the 'show must go on' and the book could wait. He's our great supporter and we appreciate his every moment fighting for us and my dream to have a television show and a book of my own.

I also want to personally, and in writing, say 'thank you' to Andrew Dunn, who chose us when he had other bounty hunters to choose from. We will always remember what he did for us and how he changed our lives for ever. We are indebted to you, Andrew, and you will have a special place in our hearts until the end.

Mostly, I have to thank the Lord and His love and the wonderful family He has given me. I try to keep all my babies as close to my side as possible, as it's my family that keeps a smile on my face and purpose in my life. I hope my children understand the lessons of the life I have led and that there is good and evil in many forms. I hope they circumvent many of my own experiences by listening to Dad's stories rather than making the mistakes I made. I love each of them desperately and I've given them all I can – my legacy. If I've left you any money, it's a terrible miscalculation on my part. May God be with you and your families long after your daddy is gone.

Duane 'Dog' Chapman
7 August 2007